MACHINE TEEN

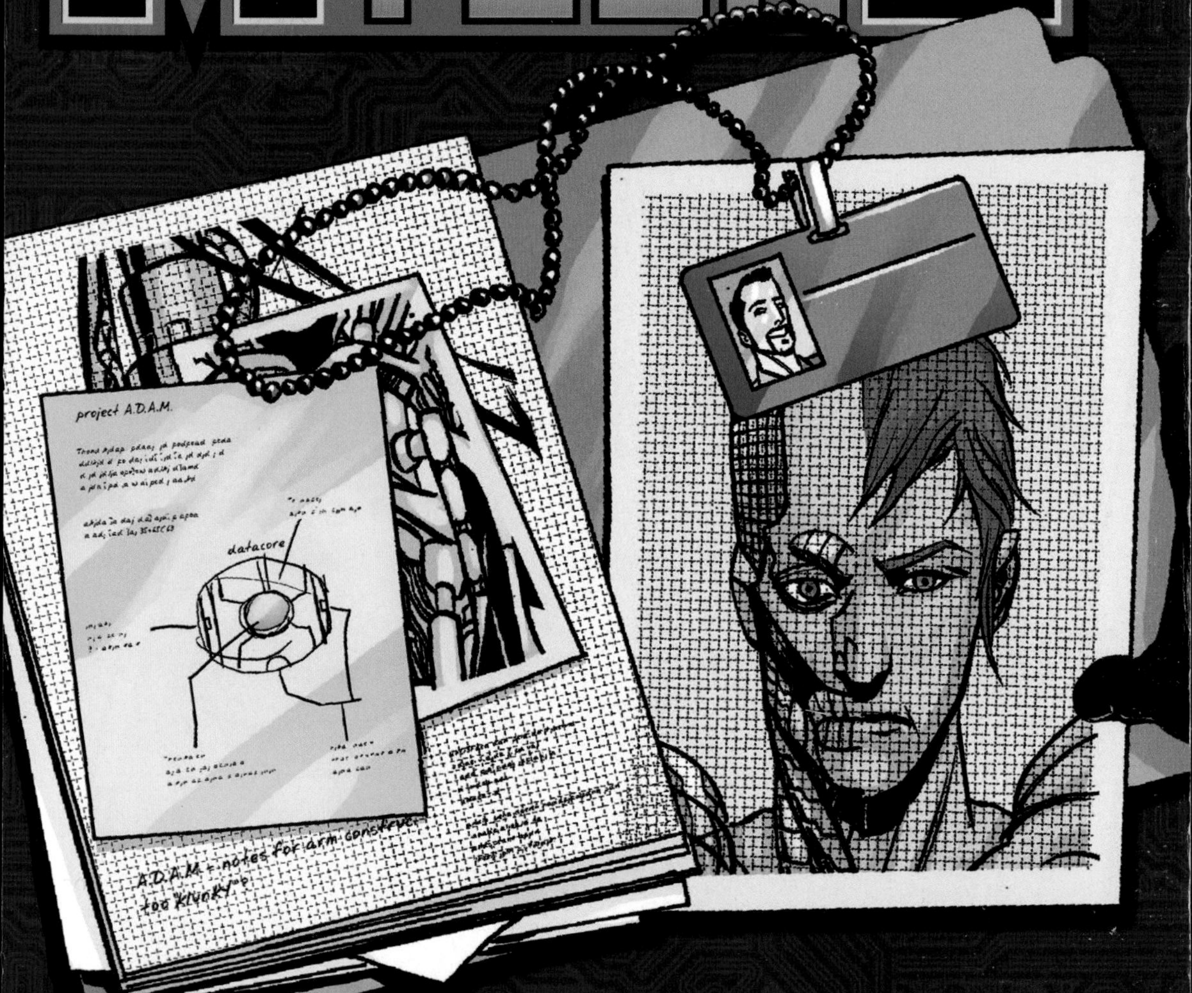
project A.D.A.M.
datacore

History 101001

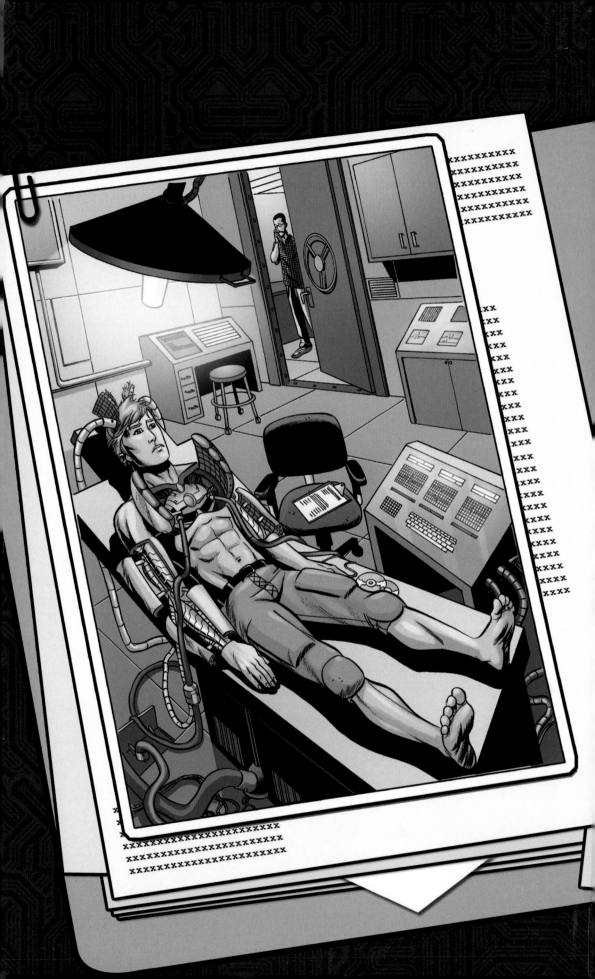

MACHINE TEEN

History 101001

WRITER: Marc Sumerak

ARTIST: Mike Hawthorne

INKER (ISSUES #4-5): Andrew Hennessy

COLOR ARTIST: Mike Atiyeh

LETTERERS: Virtual Calligraphy's Mike Sellers & Dave Sharpe

COVERS: James Jean (Issue #1) & Mike Hawthorne with Mike Atiyeh (Issues #2-5)

ASSISTANT EDITOR: Nathan Cosby

EDITOR: MacKenzie Cadenhead

CONSULTING EDITOR: Mark Paniccia

COLLECTION EDITORS: Jennifer Grünwald & Cory Levine

ASSISTANT EDITORS: Alex Starbuck & Nelson Ribeiro

EDITOR, SPECIAL PROJECTS: Mark D. Beazley

SENIOR EDITOR, SPECIAL PROJECTS: Jeff Youngquist

SENIOR VICE PRESIDENT OF SALES: David Gabriel

SVP OF BRAND PLANNING & COMMUNICATIONS: Michael Pasciullo

BOOK DESIGNER: Carrie Beadle

EDITOR IN CHIEF: Axel Alonso

CHIEF CREATIVE OFFICER: Joe Quesada

PUBLISHER: Dan Buckley

EXECUTIVE PRODUCER: Alan Fine

MACHINE TEEN: HISTORY 101001. Contains material originally published in magazine form as MACHINE TEEN #1-5. First printing 2012. ISBN# 978-0-7851-6486-9. Published by MARVEL WORLDWIDE, INC., a subsidiary of MARVEL ENTERTAINMENT, LLC. OFFICE OF PUBLICATION: 135 West 50th Street, New York, NY 10020. Copyright © 2005 and 2012 Marvel Characters, Inc. All rights reserved. $14.99 per copy in the U.S. and $16.99 in Canada (GST #R127032852); Canadian Agreement #40668537. All characters featured in this issue and the distinctive names and likenesses thereof, and all related indicia are trademarks of Marvel Characters, Inc. No similarity between any of the names, characters, persons, and/or institutions in this magazine with those of any living or dead person or institution is intended, and any such similarity which may exist is purely coincidental. **Printed in the U.S.A.** ALAN FINE, EVP - Office of the President, Marvel Worldwide, Inc. and EVP & CMO Marvel Characters B.V.; DAN BUCKLEY, Publisher & President - Print, Animation & Digital Divisions; JOE QUESADA, Chief Creative Officer; TOM BREVOORT, SVP of Publishing; DAN BUCKLEY, Publisher & President - Print, Animation & Digital JAYATILLEKE, SVP & Associate Publisher, Publishing; C.B. CEBULSKI, SVP of Creator & Content Development; DAVID BOGART, SVP of Operations & Procurement, Publishing; RUWAN Circulation; MICHAEL PASCIULLO, SVP of Brand Planning & Communications; JIM O'KEEFE, VP of Operations & Logistics; DAN CARR, Executive Director of Publishing Technology; SUSAN CRESPI, Editorial Operations Manager; ALEX MORALES, Publishing Operations Manager; STAN LEE, Chairman Emeritus. For information regarding advertising in Marvel Comics or on Marvel.com, please contact Niza Disla, Director of Marvel Partnerships, at ndisla@marvel.com. For Marvel subscription inquiries, please call 800-217-9158. **Manufactured between 7/12/2012 and 8/14/2012 by QUAD/GRAPHICS, DUBUQUE, IA, USA.**

10 9 8 7 6 5 4 3 2 1

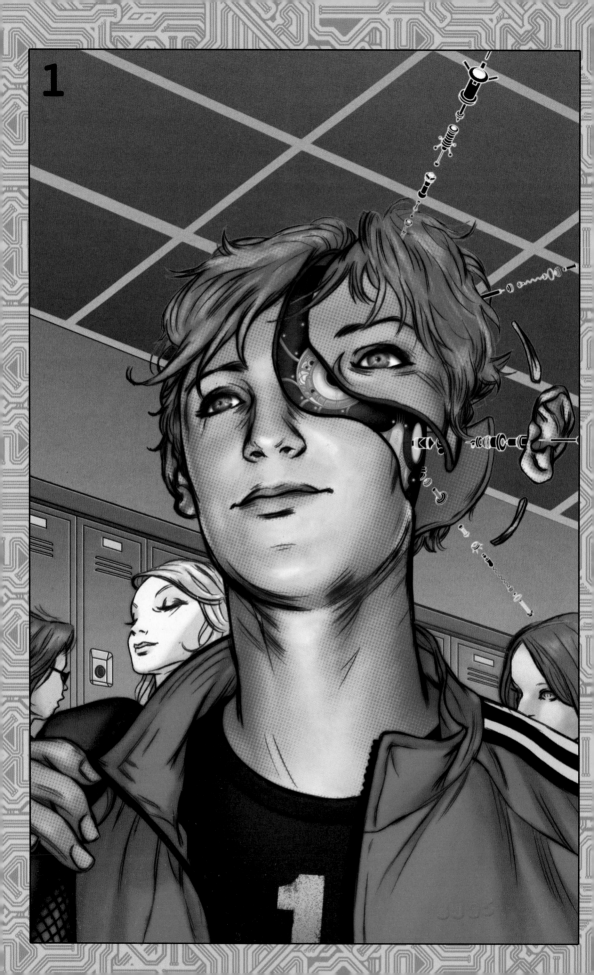

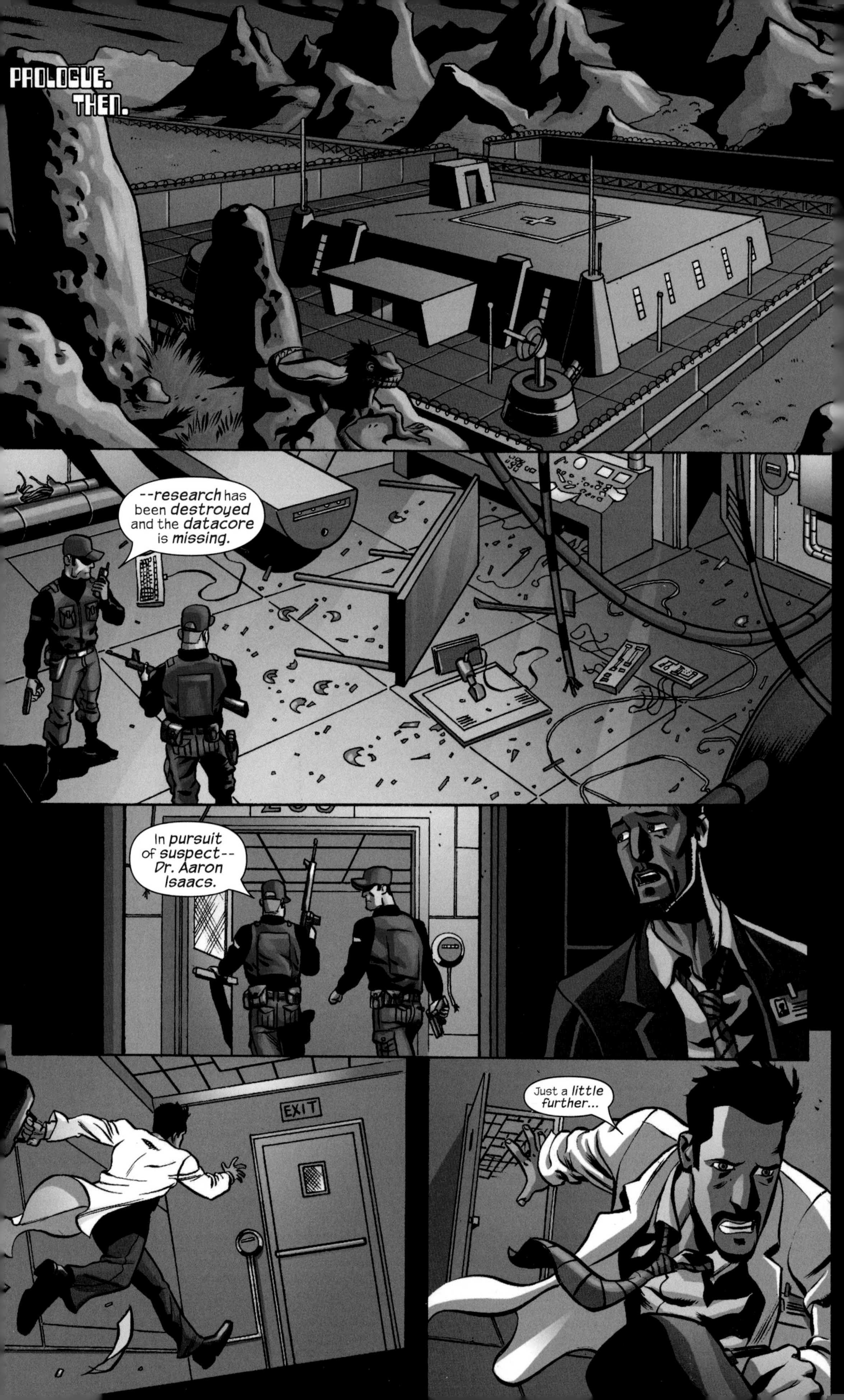
PROLOGUE.
THEN.
--research has been destroyed and the datacore is missing.
In pursuit of suspect--Dr. Aaron Isaacs.
EXIT
Just a little further...

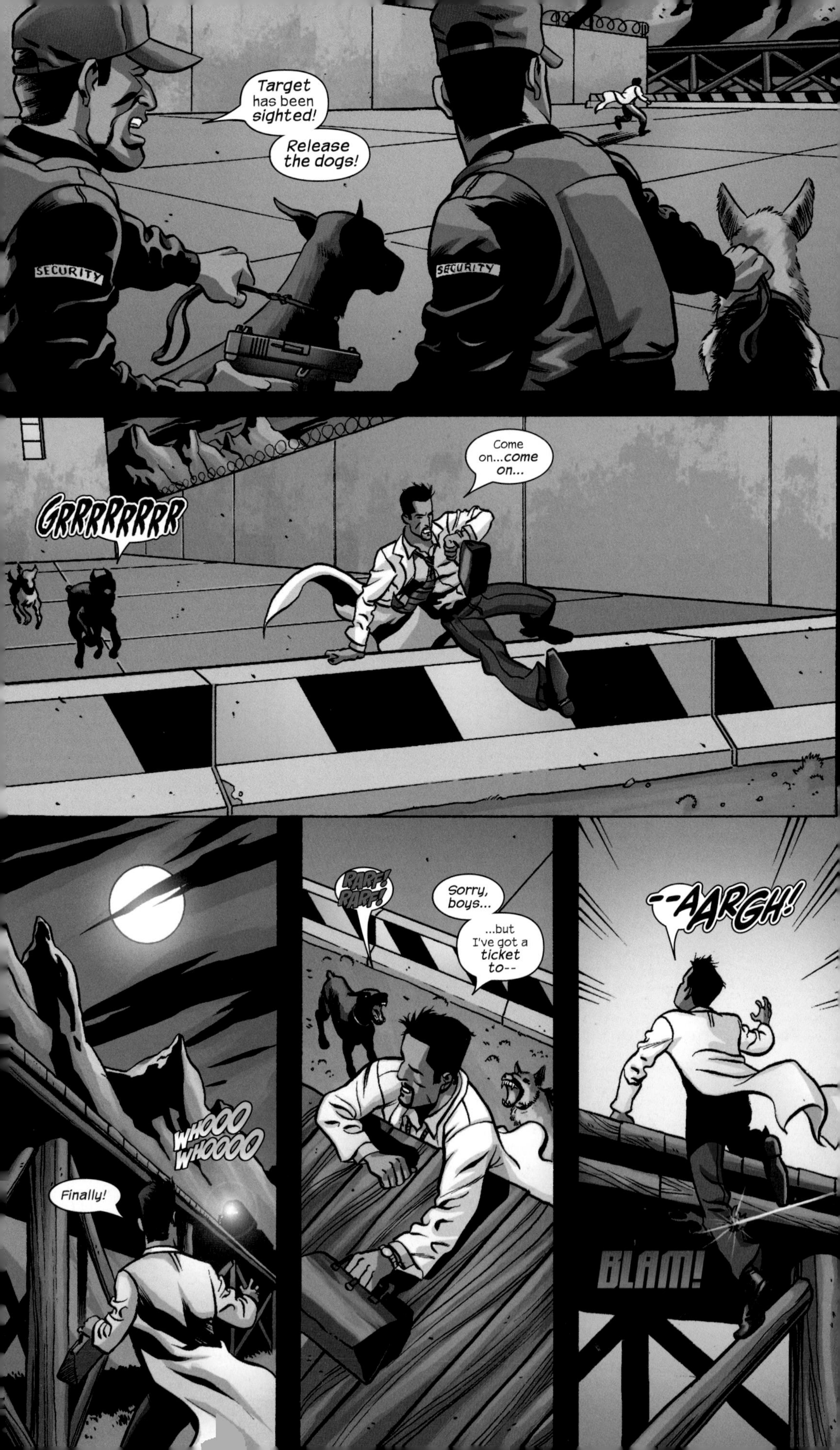
Target has been sighted!
Release the dogs!
SECURITY
SECURITY
Come on...come on...
GRRRRRRRR
WHOOO WHOOOO
Finally!
RARF! RARF!
Sorry, boys...
...but I've got a ticket to--
--AARGH!
BLAM!

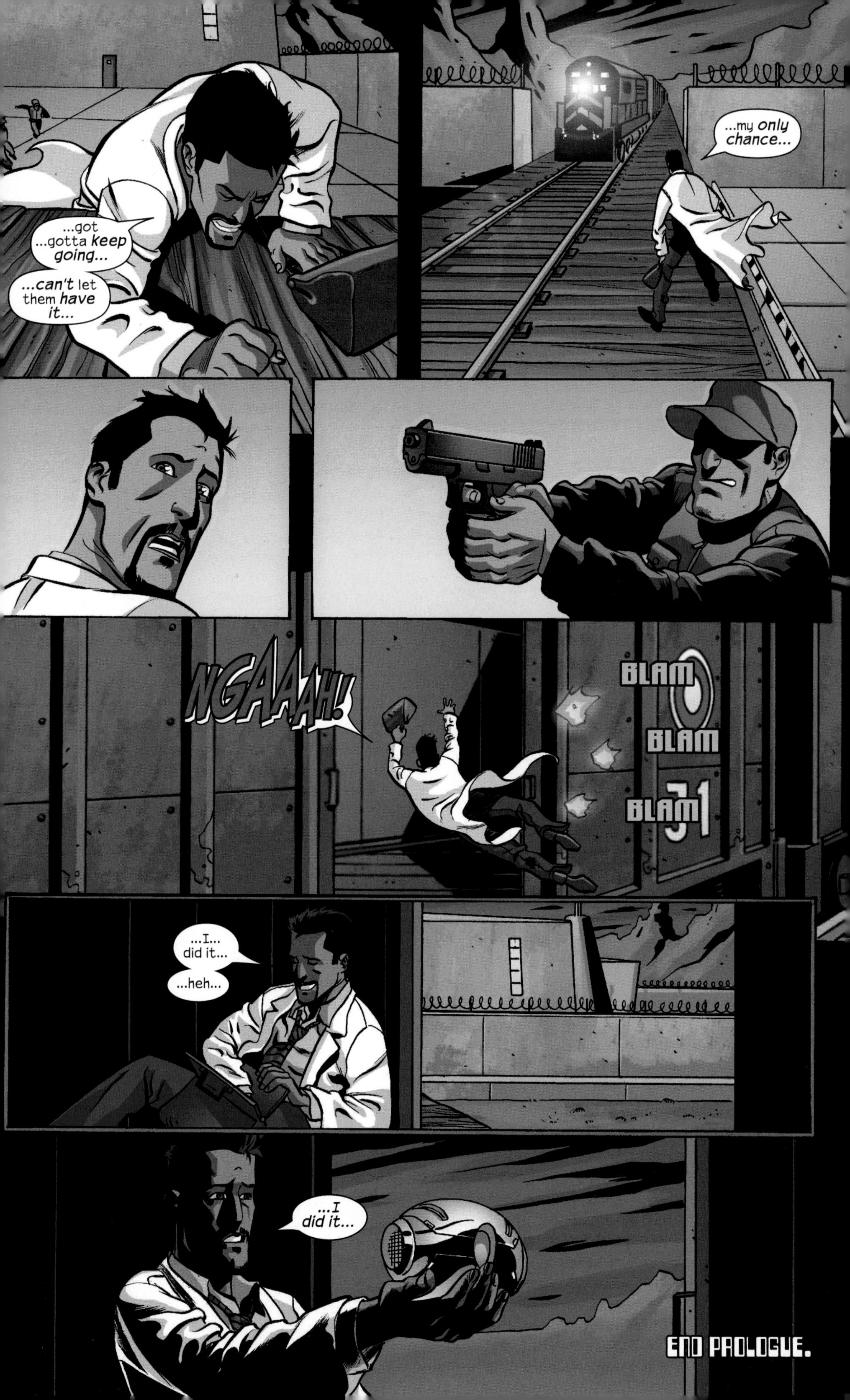
...got ...gotta keep going...
...can't let them have it...
...my only chance...
NGAAAH!
BLAM
BLAM
BLAM
...I... did it...
...heh...
...I did it...
END PROLOGUE.

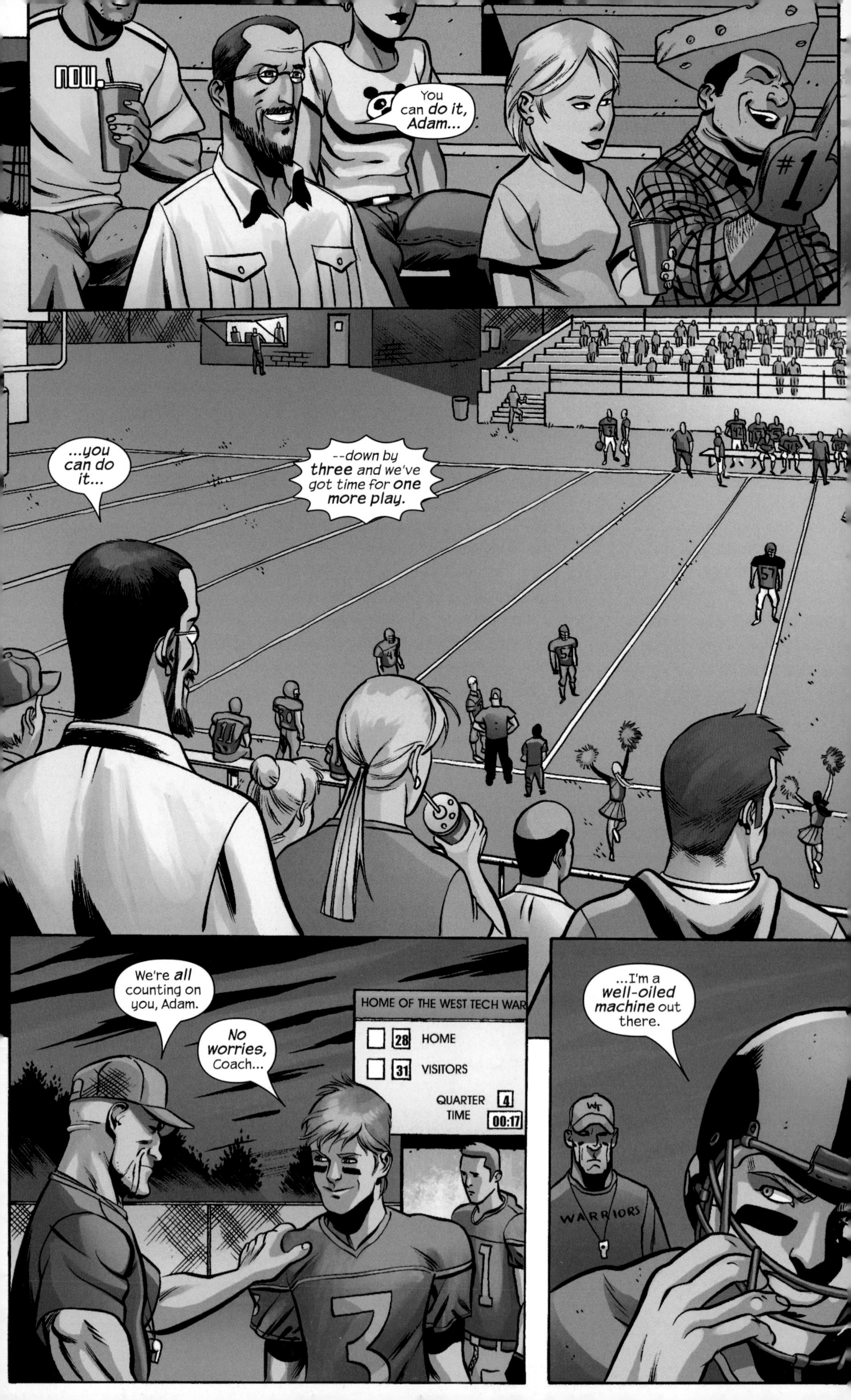
NOW.
You can do it, Adam...
...you can do it...
--down by three and we've got time for one more play.
We're all counting on you, Adam.
No worries, Coach...
HOME OF THE WEST TECH WAR
28 HOME
31 VISITORS
QUARTER 4
TIME 00:17
...I'm a well-oiled machine out there.
WARRIORS

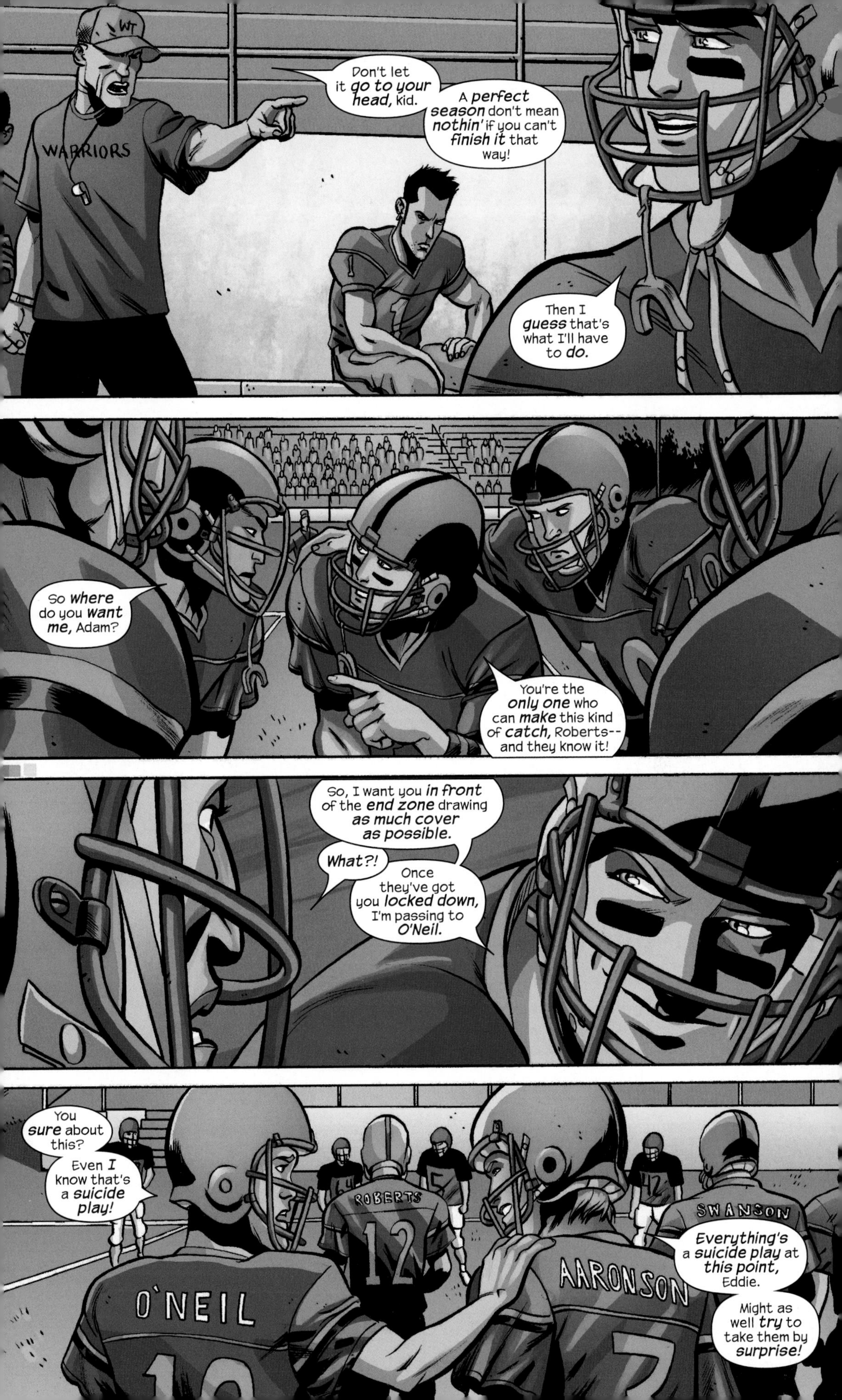
WARRIORS
Don't let it go to your head, kid.
A perfect season don't mean nothin' if you can't finish it that way!
Then I guess that's what I'll have to do.
So where do you want me, Adam?
You're the only one who can make this kind of catch, Roberts--and they know it!
So, I want you in front of the end zone drawing as much cover as possible.
What?!
Once they've got you locked down, I'm passing to O'Neil.
You sure about this?
Even I know that's a suicide play!
ROBERTS
SWANSON
O'NEIL
AARONSON
Everything's a suicide play at this point, Eddie.
Might as well try to take them by surprise!

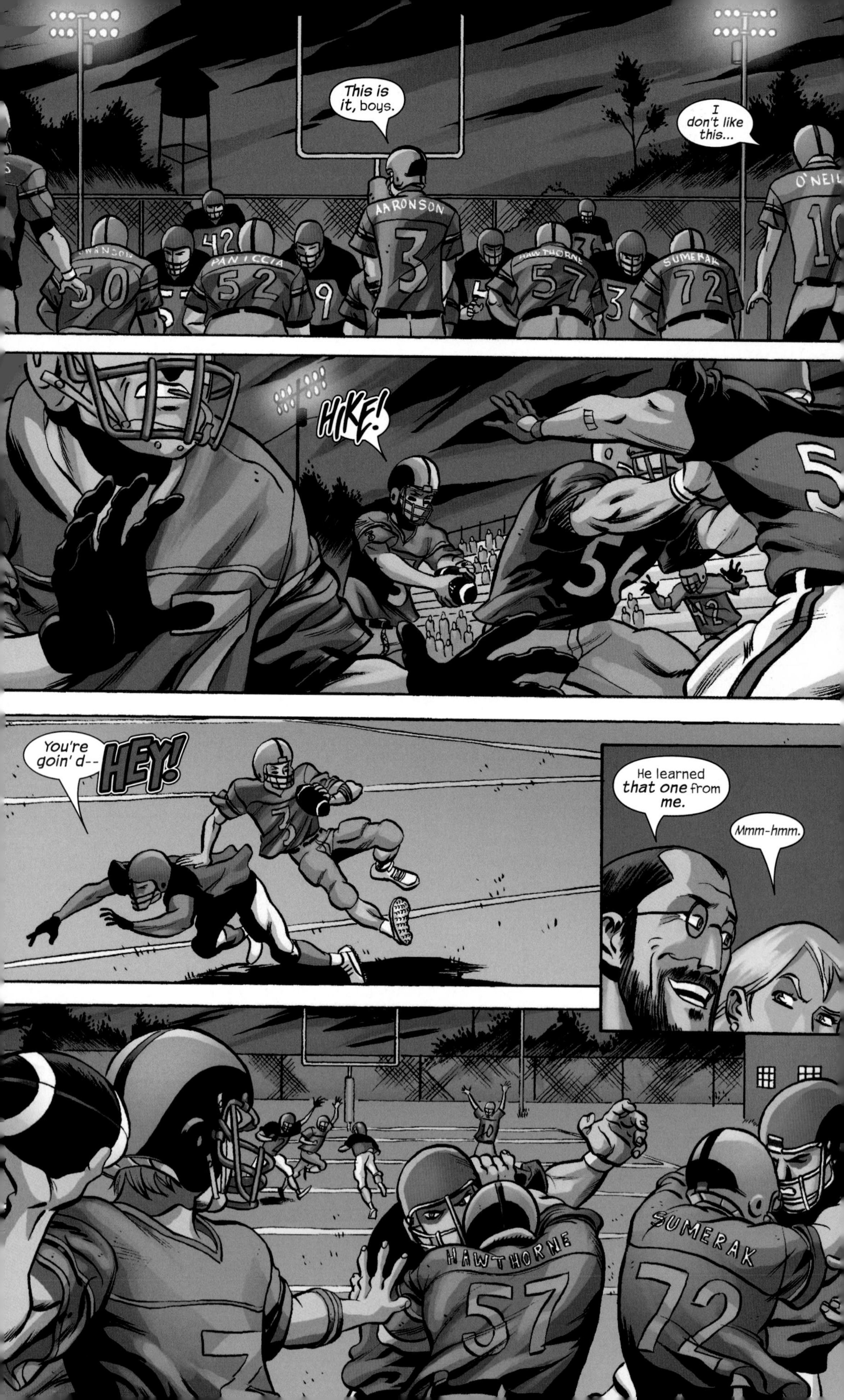
This is it, boys.
I don't like this...
AARONSON
O'NEIL
PANICCIA
HAWTHORNE
SUMERAK
HIKE!
You're goin' d--
HEY!
He learned that one from me.
Mmm-hmm.
SUMERAK
HAWTHORNE

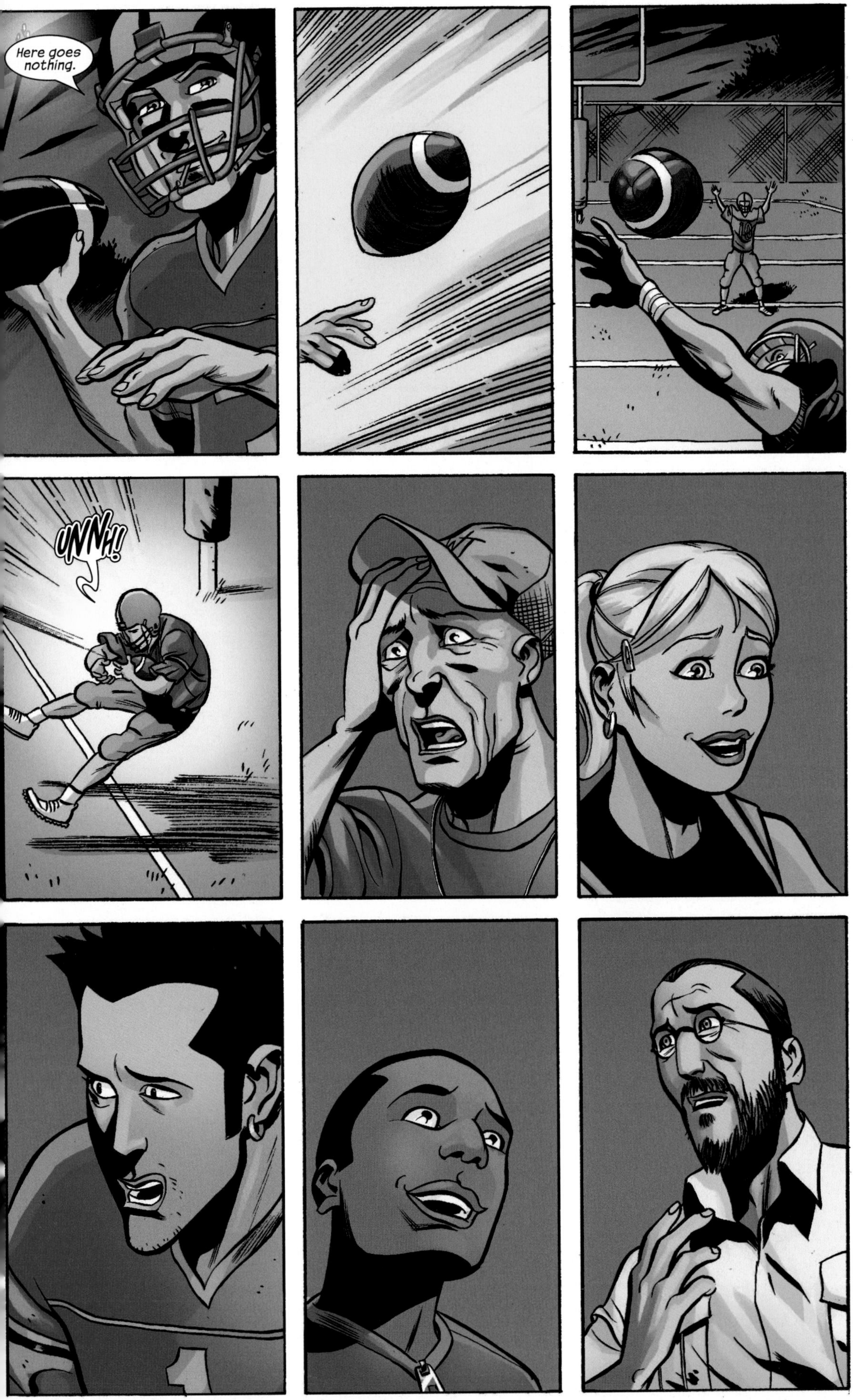
Here goes nothing.
UNNH!

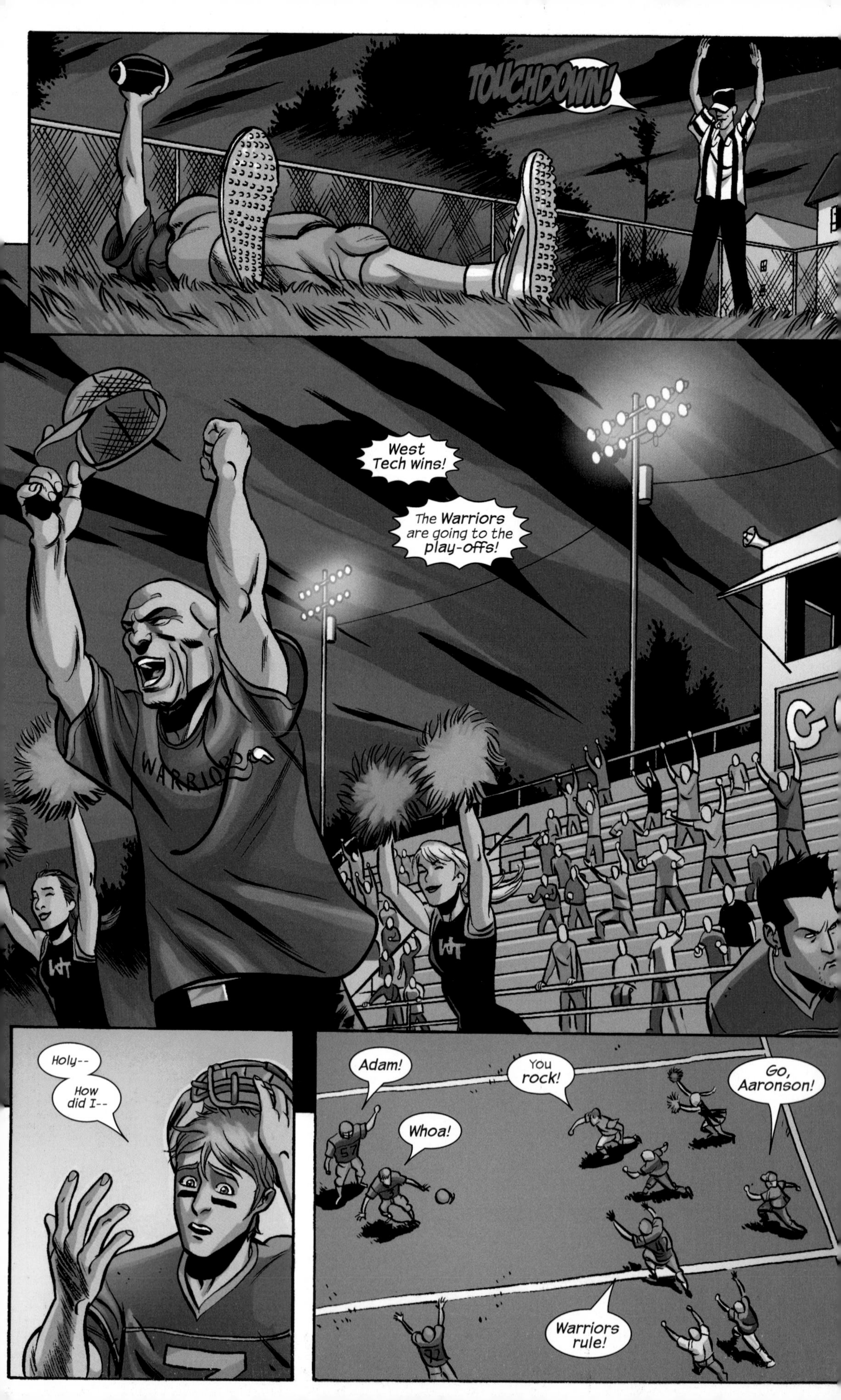
TOUCHDOWN!
West Tech wins!
The Warriors are going to the play-offs!
Holy--
How did I--
Adam!
Whoa!
You rock!
Go, Aaronson!
Warriors rule!

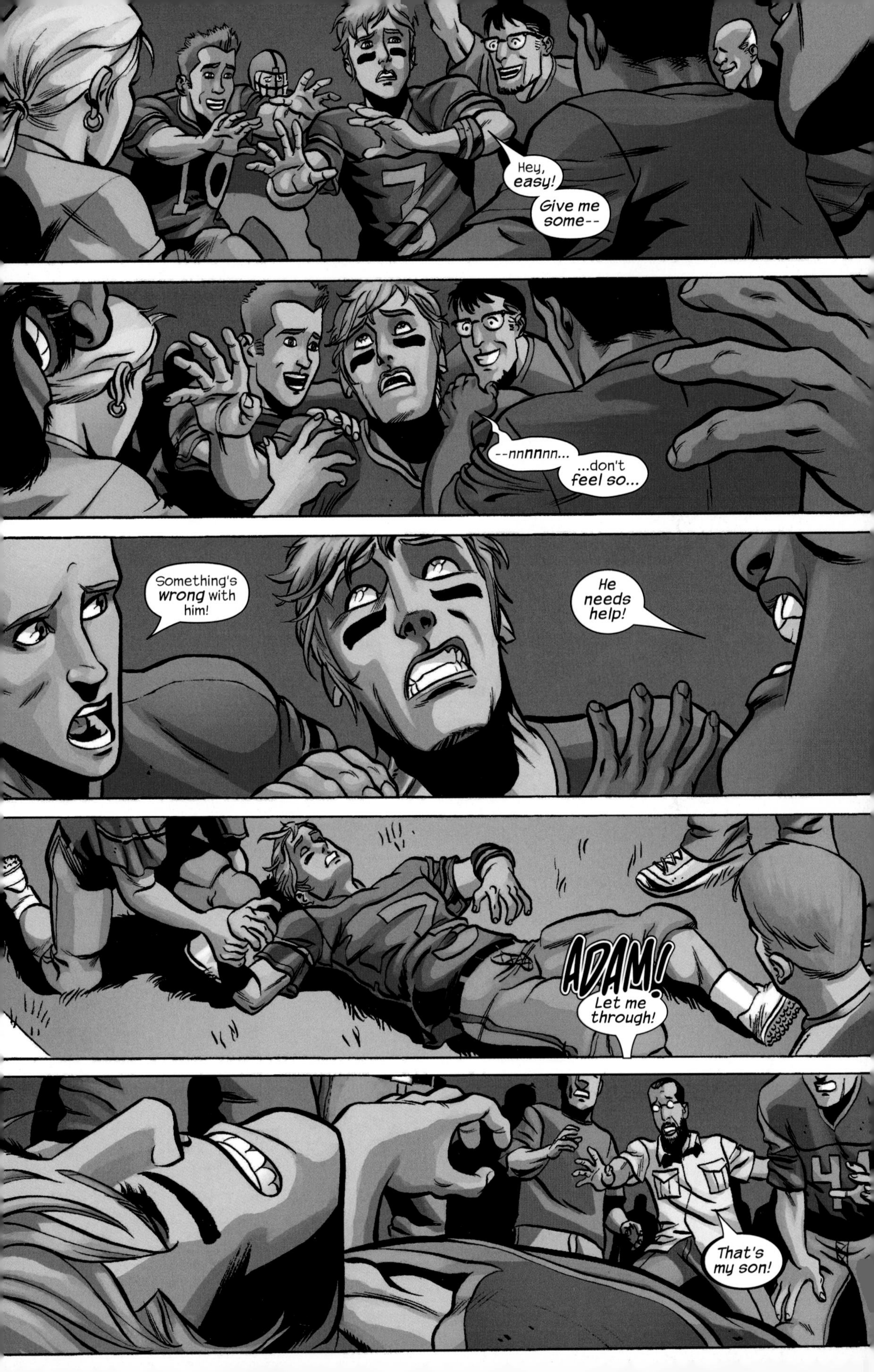
Hey, easy!
Give me some--
--nnnnnn...
...don't feel so...
Something's wrong with him!
He needs help!
ADAM!
Let me through!
That's my son!

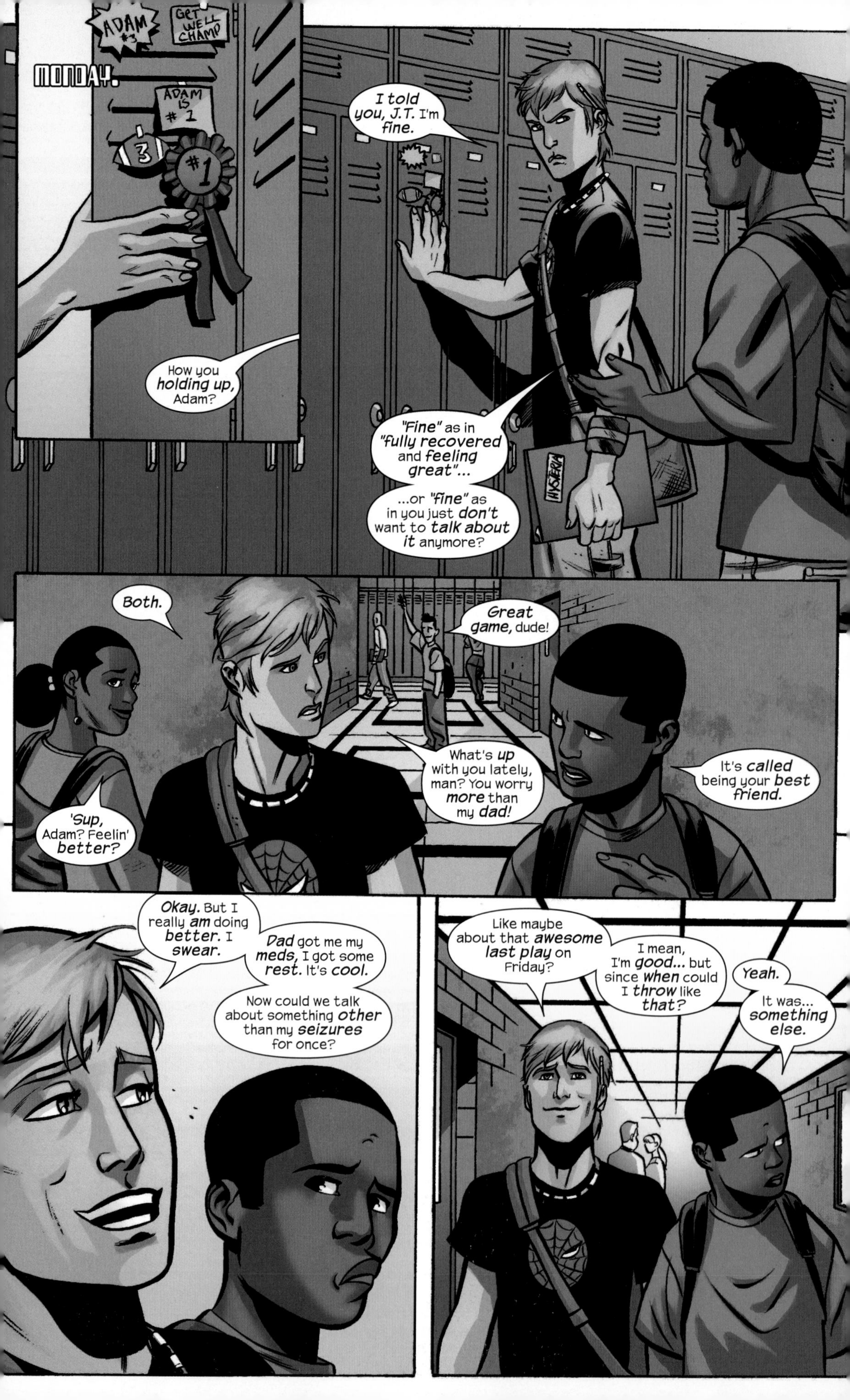
ADAM #3
GET WELL CHAMP
MONDAY.
ADAM IS #1
3
#1
I told you, J.T. I'm fine.
How you holding up, Adam?
"Fine" as in "fully recovered and feeling great"...
...or "fine" as in you just don't want to talk about it anymore?
HYSTERIA
Both.
Great game, dude!
'Sup, Adam? Feelin' better?
What's up with you lately, man? You worry more than my dad!
It's called being your best friend.
Okay. But I really am doing better. I swear.
Dad got me my meds, I got some rest. It's cool.
Now could we talk about something other than my seizures for once?
Like maybe about that awesome last play on Friday?
I mean, I'm good... but since when could I throw like that?
Yeah.
It was... something else.

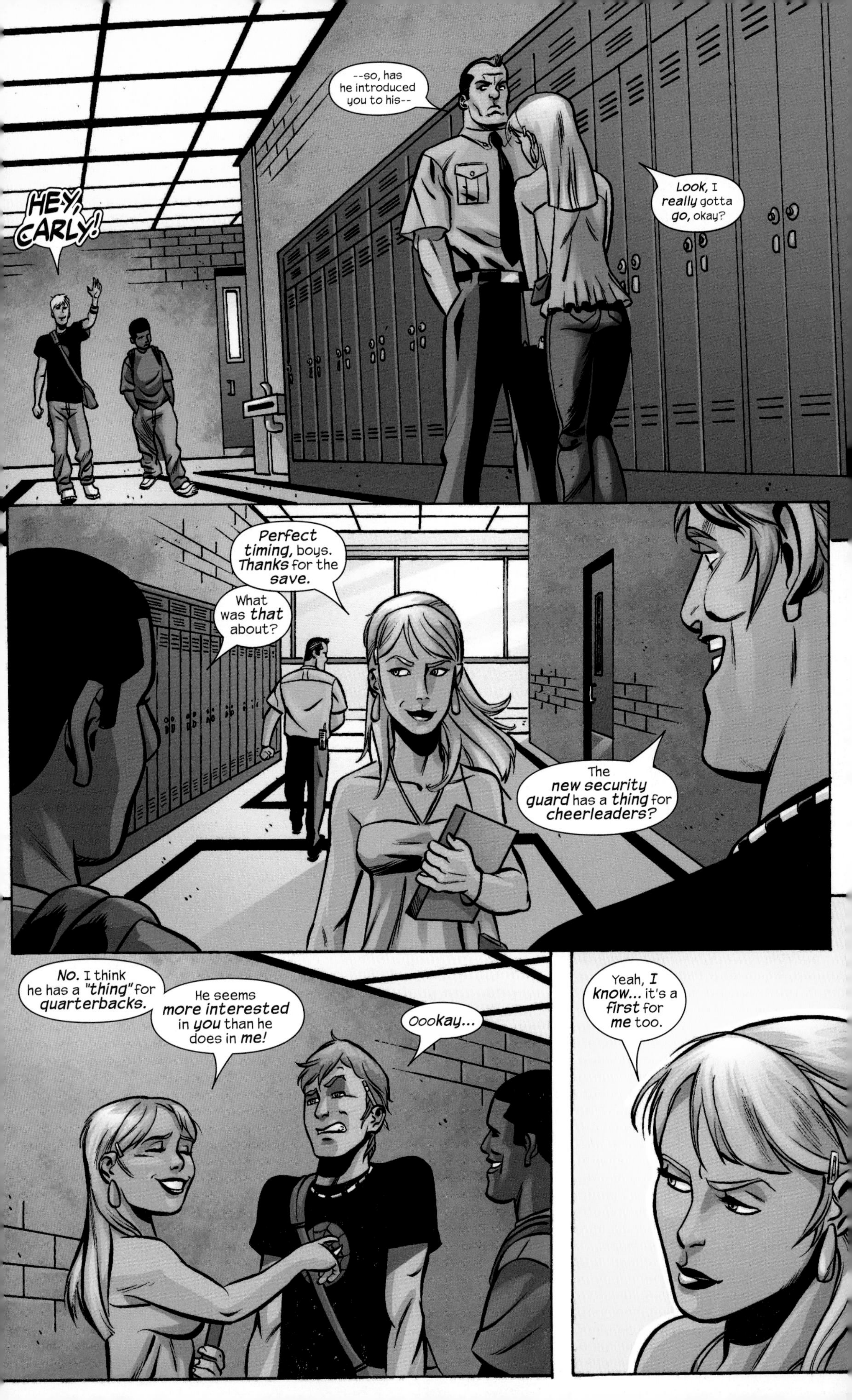
--so, has he introduced you to his--
Look, I really gotta go, okay?
HEY, CARLY!
Perfect timing, boys. Thanks for the save.
What was that about?
The new security guard has a thing for cheerleaders?
No. I think he has a "thing" for quarterbacks.
He seems more interested in you than he does in me!
Oookay...
Yeah, I know... it's a first for me too.

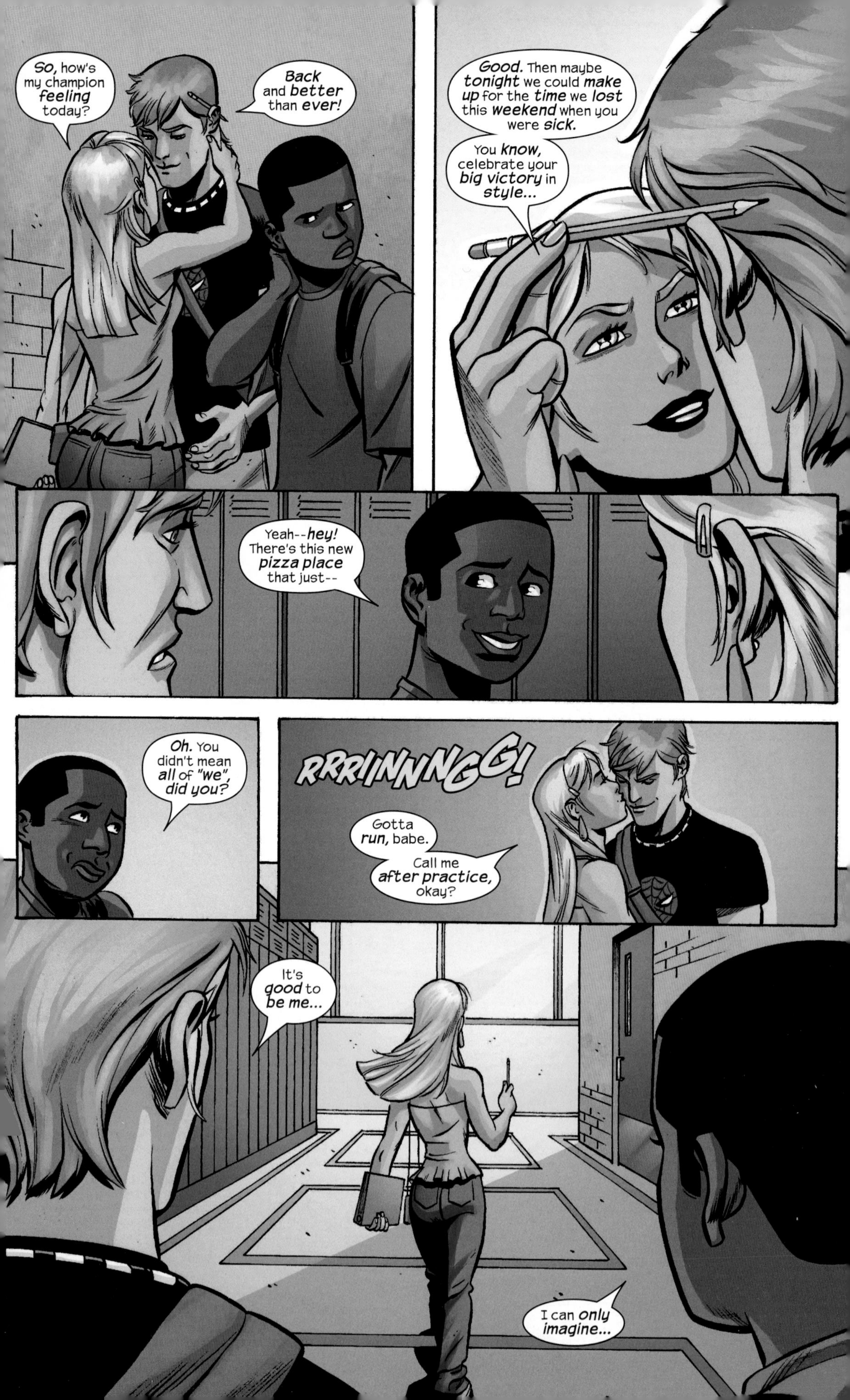
So, how's my champion feeling today?
Back and better than ever!
Good. Then maybe tonight we could make up for the time we lost this weekend when you were sick.
You know, celebrate your big victory in style...
Yeah--hey! There's this new pizza place that just--
Oh. You didn't mean all of "we", did you?
RRRIINNNGG!
Gotta run, babe.
Call me after practice, okay?
It's good to be me...
I can only imagine...

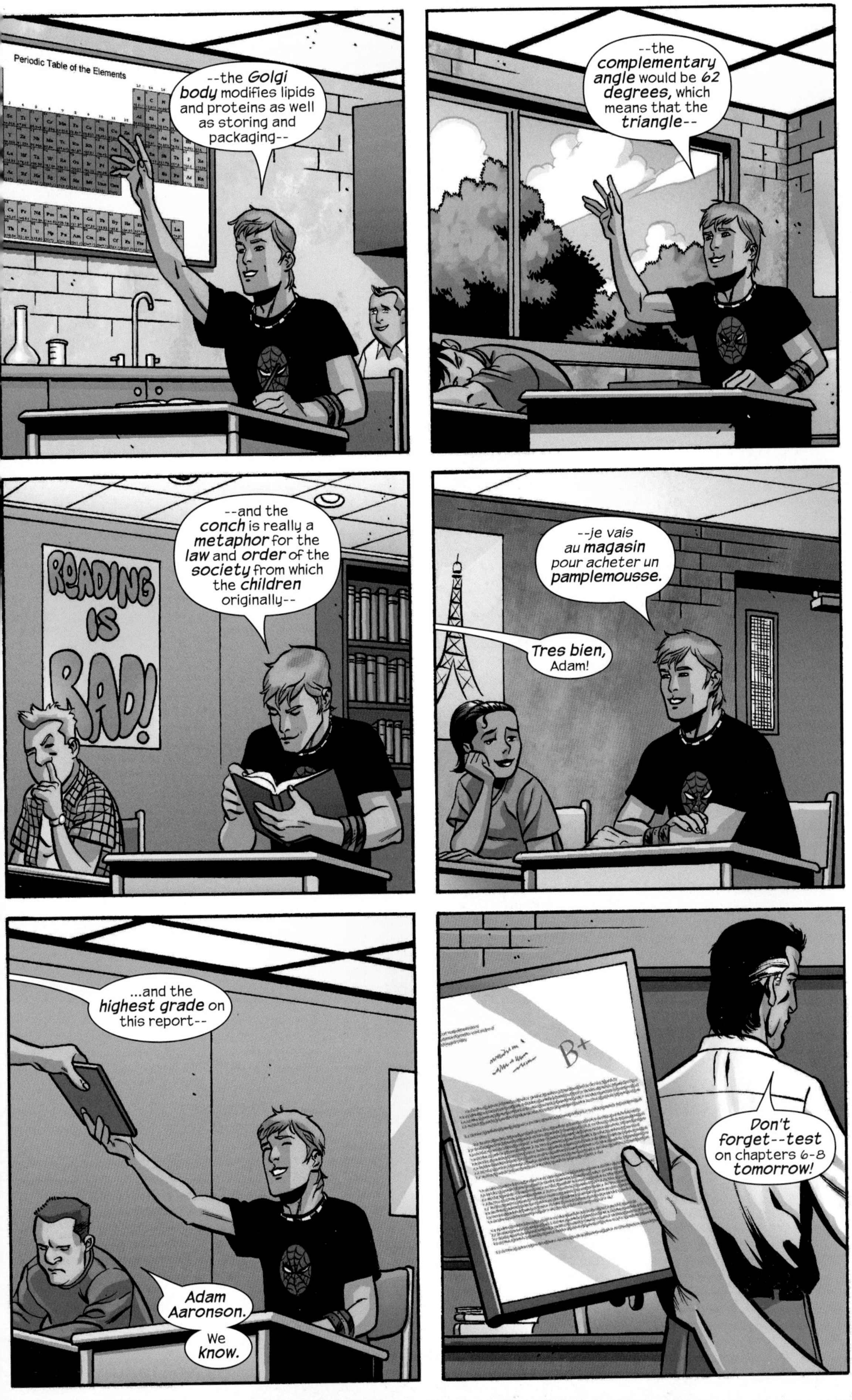
Periodic Table of the Elements
--the Golgi body modifies lipids and proteins as well as storing and packaging--
--the complementary angle would be 62 degrees, which means that the triangle--
READING IS RAD!
--and the conch is really a metaphor for the law and order of the society from which the children originally--
--je vais au magasin pour acheter un pamplemousse.
Tres bien, Adam!
...and the highest grade on this report--
Adam Aaronson.
We know.
B+
Don't forget--test on chapters 6-8 tomorrow!

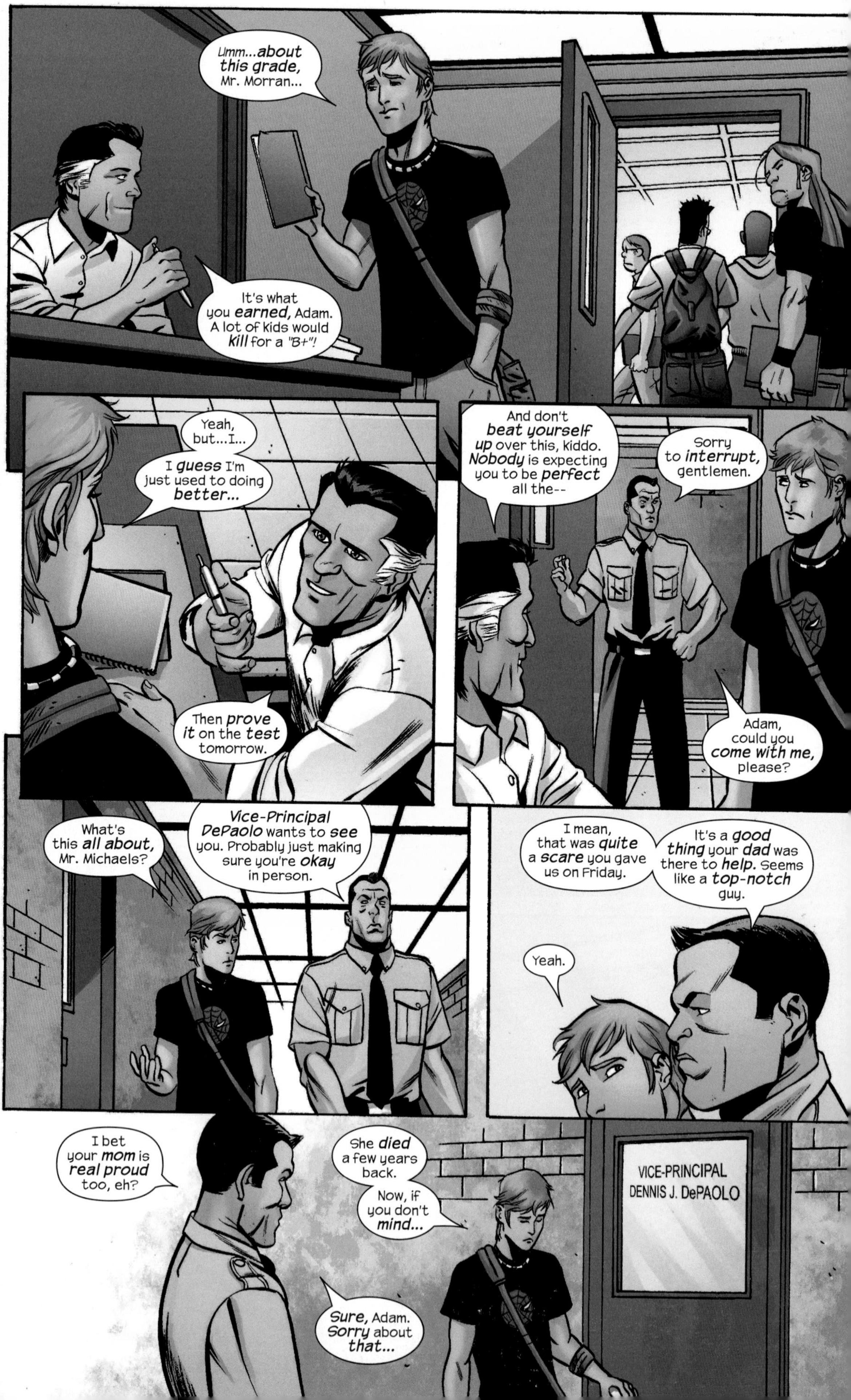
Umm...about this grade, Mr. Morran...
It's what you earned, Adam. A lot of kids would kill for a "B+"!
Yeah, but...I...
I guess I'm just used to doing better...
Then prove it on the test tomorrow.
And don't beat yourself up over this, kiddo. Nobody is expecting you to be perfect all the--
Sorry to interrupt, gentlemen.
Adam, could you come with me, please?
What's this all about, Mr. Michaels?
Vice-Principal DePaolo wants to see you. Probably just making sure you're okay in person.
I mean, that was quite a scare you gave us on Friday.
It's a good thing your dad was there to help. Seems like a top-notch guy.
Yeah.
I bet your mom is real proud too, eh?
She died a few years back.
Now, if you don't mind...
Sure, Adam. Sorry about that...
VICE-PRINCIPAL
DENNIS J. DePAOLO

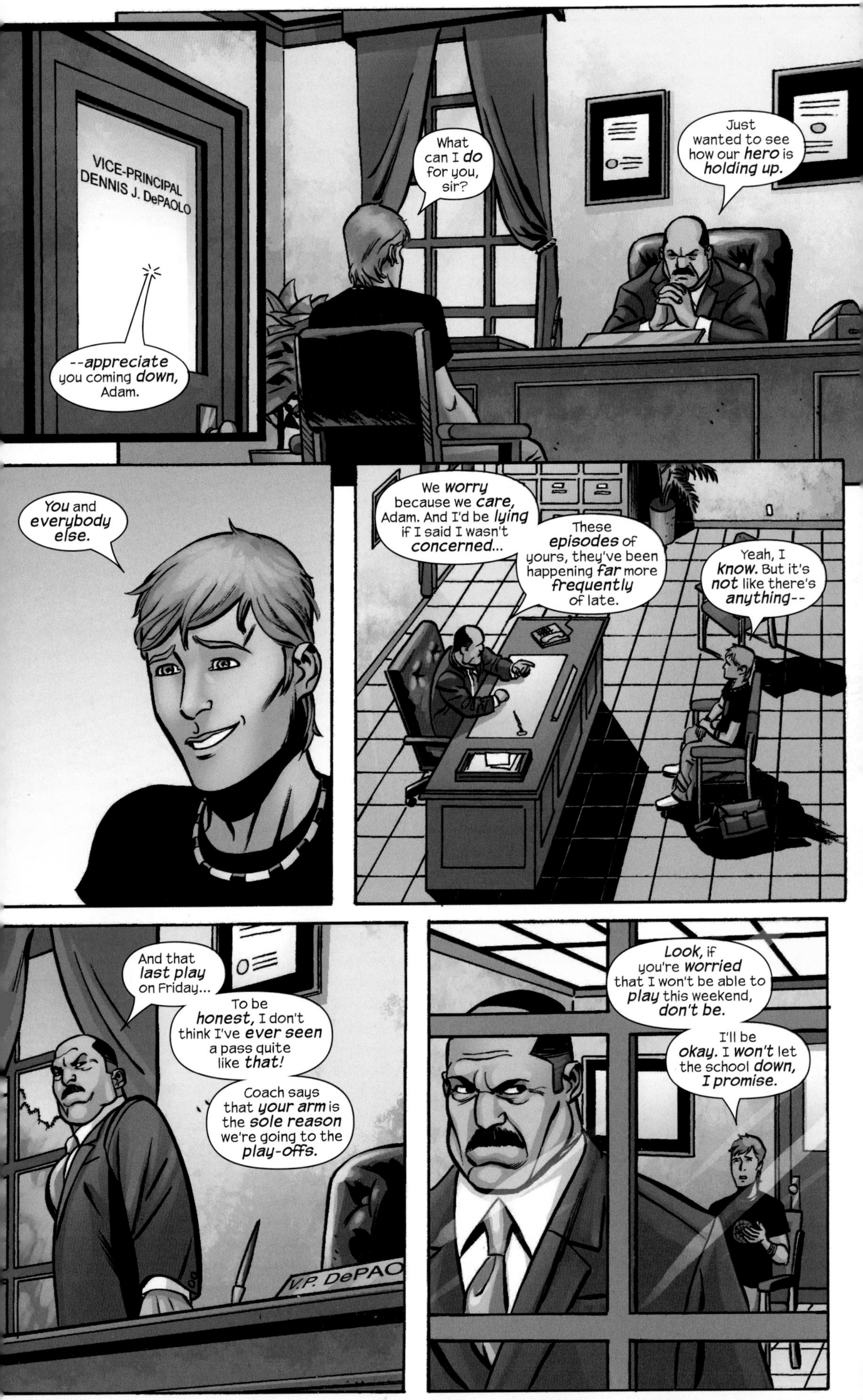
VICE-PRINCIPAL DENNIS J. DePAOLO
--appreciate you coming down, Adam.
What can I do for you, sir?
Just wanted to see how our hero is holding up.
You and everybody else.
We worry because we care, Adam. And I'd be lying if I said I wasn't concerned...
These episodes of yours, they've been happening far more frequently of late.
Yeah, I know. But it's not like there's anything--
And that last play on Friday...
To be honest, I don't think I've ever seen a pass quite like that!
Coach says that your arm is the sole reason we're going to the play-offs.
V.P. DePAO
Look, if you're worried that I won't be able to play this weekend, don't be.
I'll be okay. I won't let the school down, I promise.

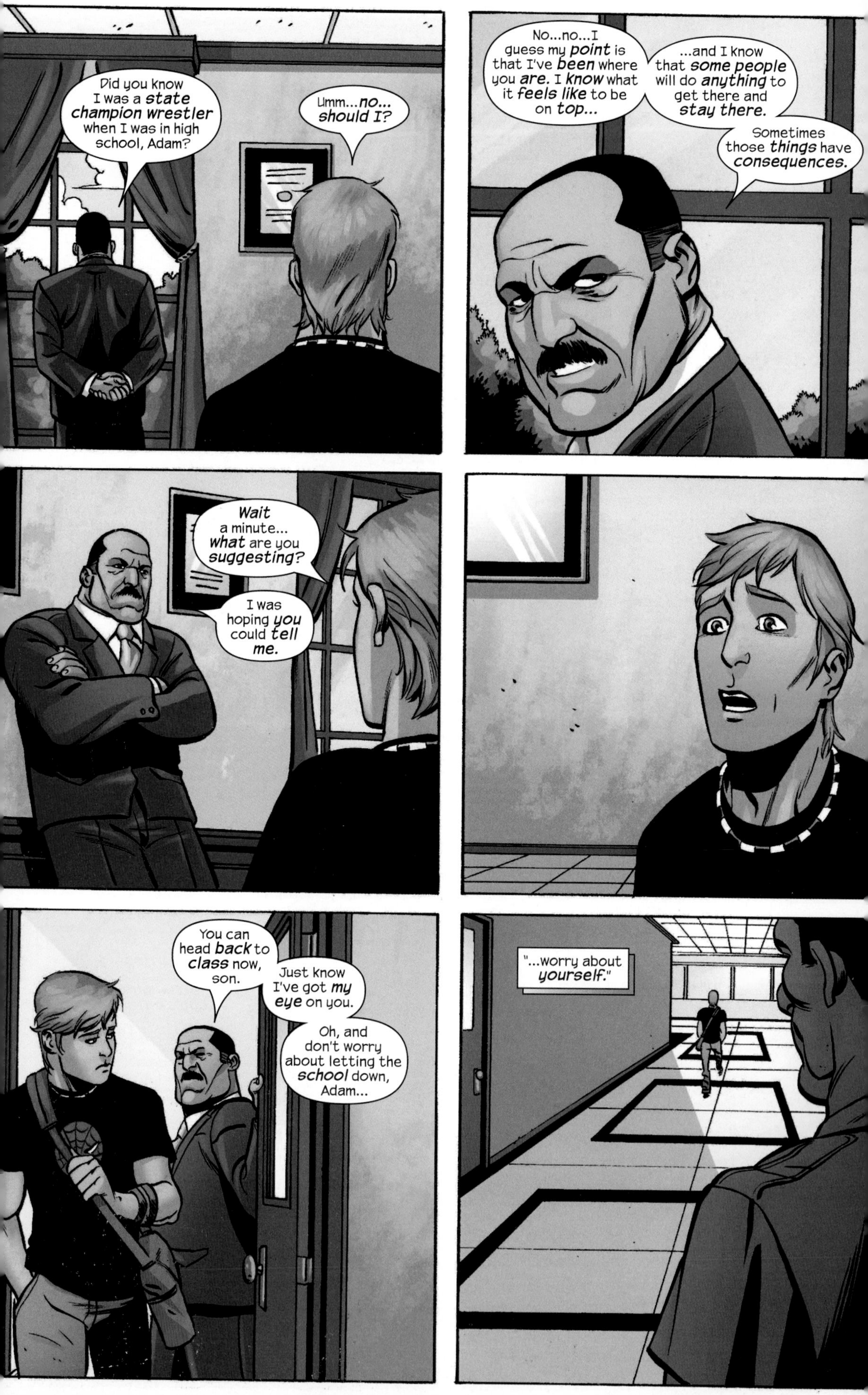

Did you know I was a state champion wrestler when I was in high school, Adam?
Umm...no... should I?
No...no...I guess my point is that I've been where you are. I know what it feels like to be on top...
...and I know that some people will do anything to get there and stay there.
Sometimes those things have consequences.
Wait a minute... what are you suggesting?
I was hoping you could tell me.
You can head back to class now, son.
Just know I've got my eye on you.
Oh, and don't worry about letting the school down, Adam...
"...worry about yourself."

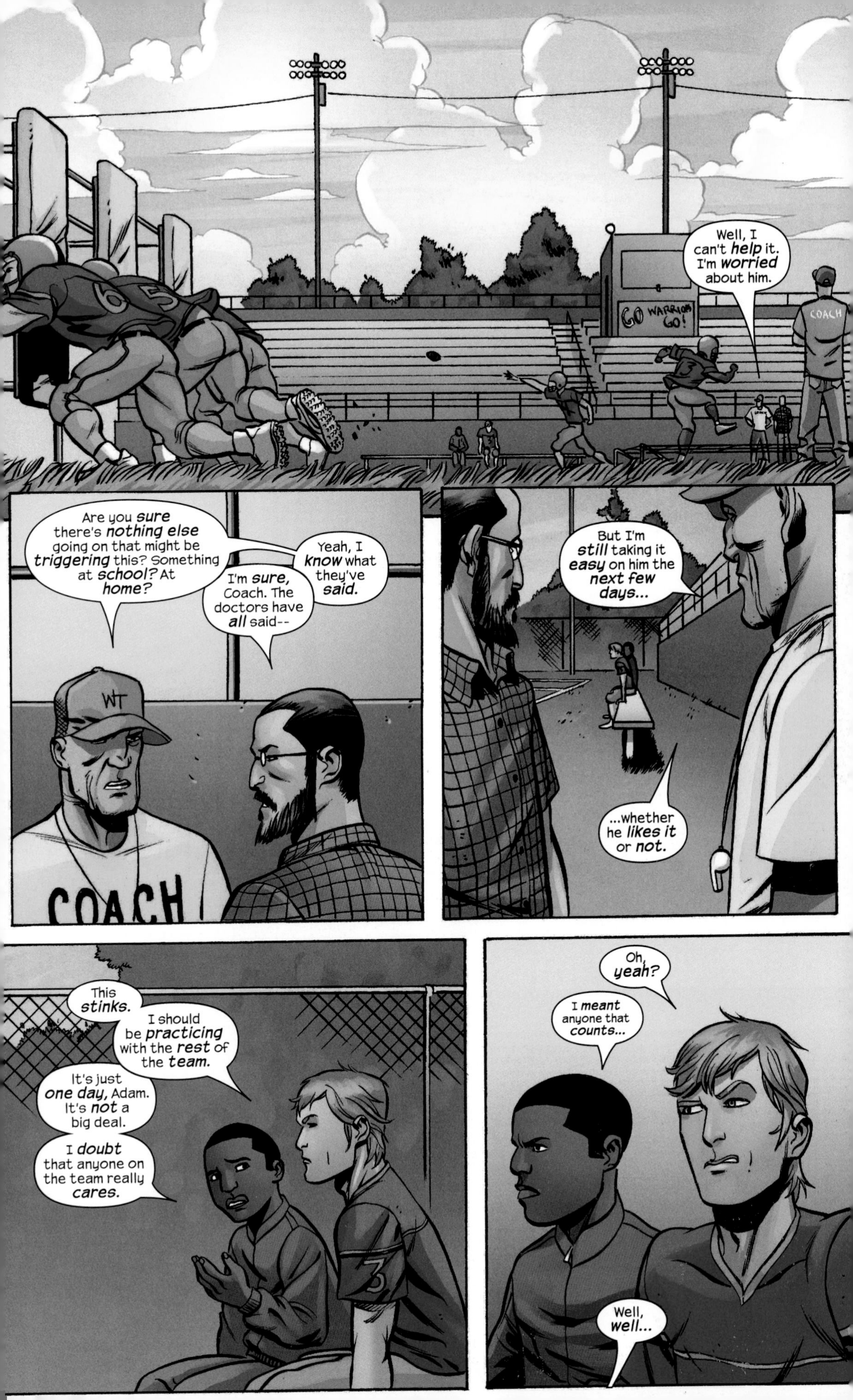
GO WARRIORS GO!
COACH
Well, I can't *help* it. I'm *worried* about him.
Are you *sure* there's *nothing else* going on that might be *triggering* this? Something at *school?* At *home?*
WT
I'm *sure,* Coach. The doctors have *all* said--
Yeah, I *know* what they've *said.*
COACH
But I'm *still* taking it *easy* on him the *next few days...*
...whether he *likes it* or *not.*
This *stinks.*
I should be *practicing* with the *rest* of the *team.*
It's just *one day,* Adam. It's *not* a big deal.
I *doubt* that anyone on the team really *cares.*
Oh, *yeah?*
I *meant* anyone that *counts...*
Well, *well...*

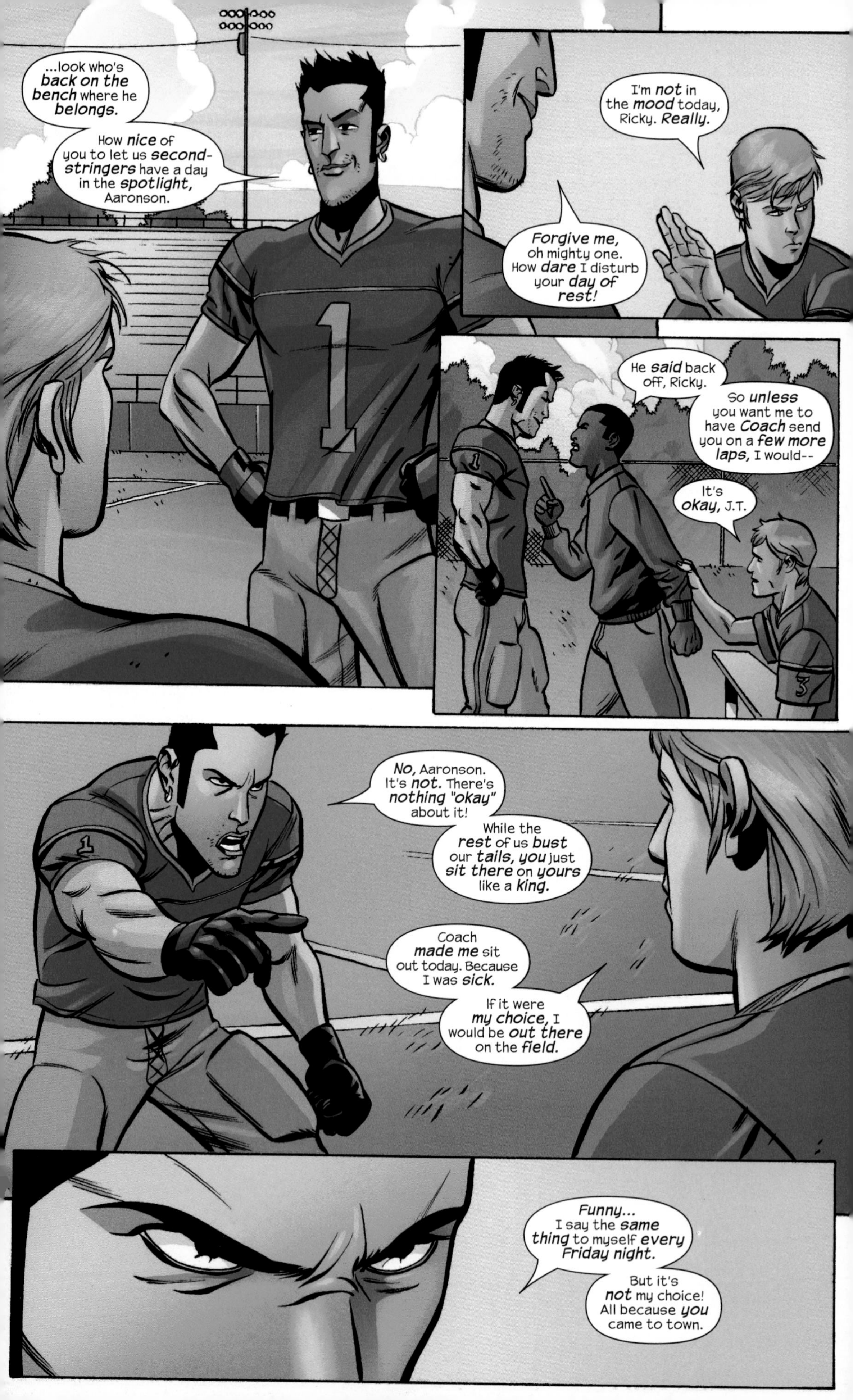
...look who's back on the bench where he belongs.
How nice of you to let us second-stringers have a day in the spotlight, Aaronson.
I'm not in the mood today, Ricky. Really.
Forgive me, oh mighty one. How dare I disturb your day of rest!
He said back off, Ricky.
So unless you want me to have Coach send you on a few more laps, I would--
It's okay, J.T.
No, Aaronson. It's not. There's nothing "okay" about it!
While the rest of us bust our tails, you just sit there on yours like a king.
Coach made me sit out today. Because I was sick.
If it were my choice, I would be out there on the field.
Funny... I say the same thing to myself every Friday night.
But it's not my choice! All because you came to town.

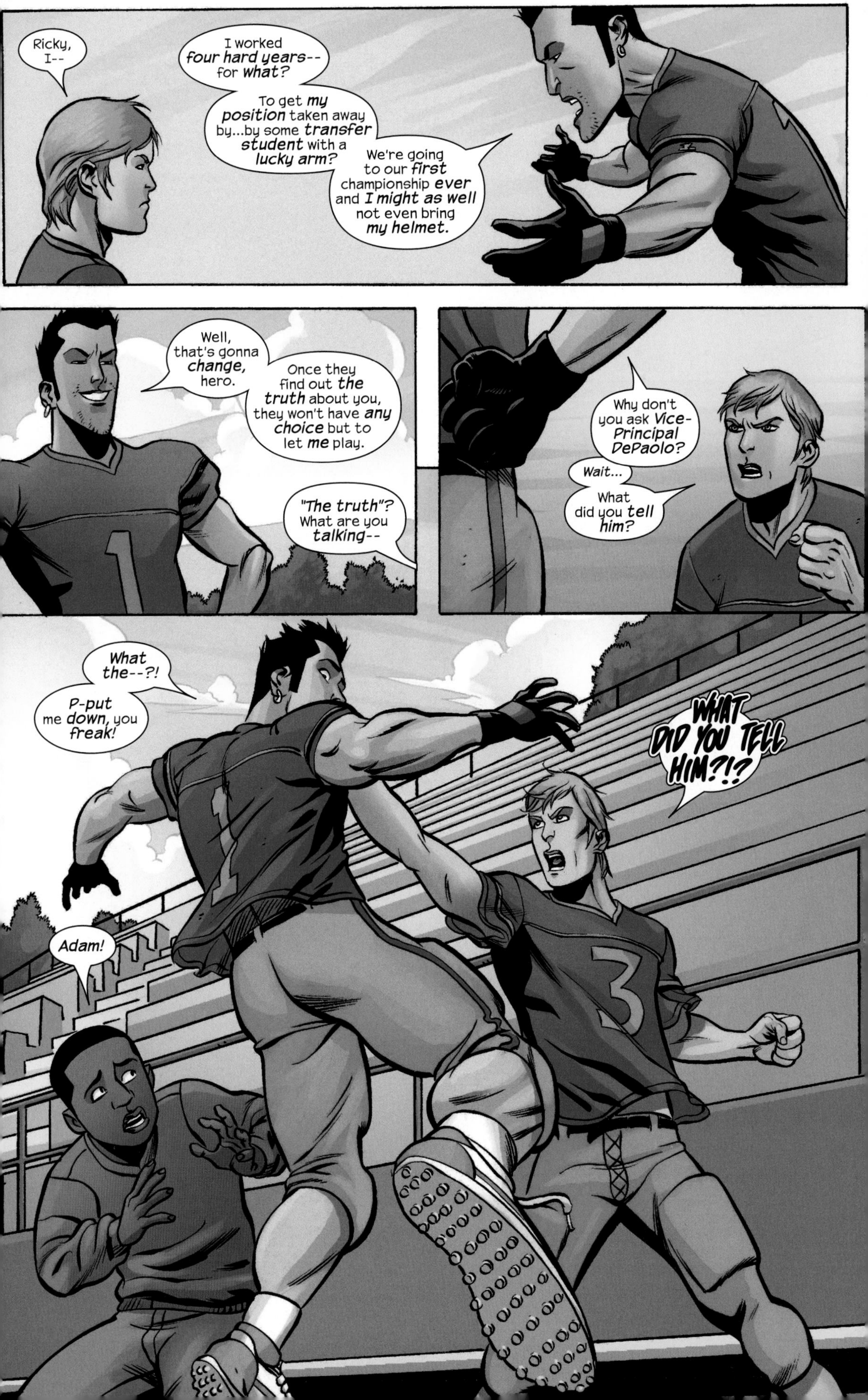

Ricky, I--
I worked four hard years-- for what?
To get my position taken away by...by some transfer student with a lucky arm?
We're going to our first championship ever and I might as well not even bring my helmet.
Well, that's gonna change, hero.
Once they find out the truth about you, they won't have any choice but to let me play.
"The truth"? What are you talking--
Why don't you ask Vice-Principal DePaolo?
Wait...
What did you tell him?
What the--?!
P-put me down, you freak!
WHAT DID YOU TELL HIM?!?
Adam!

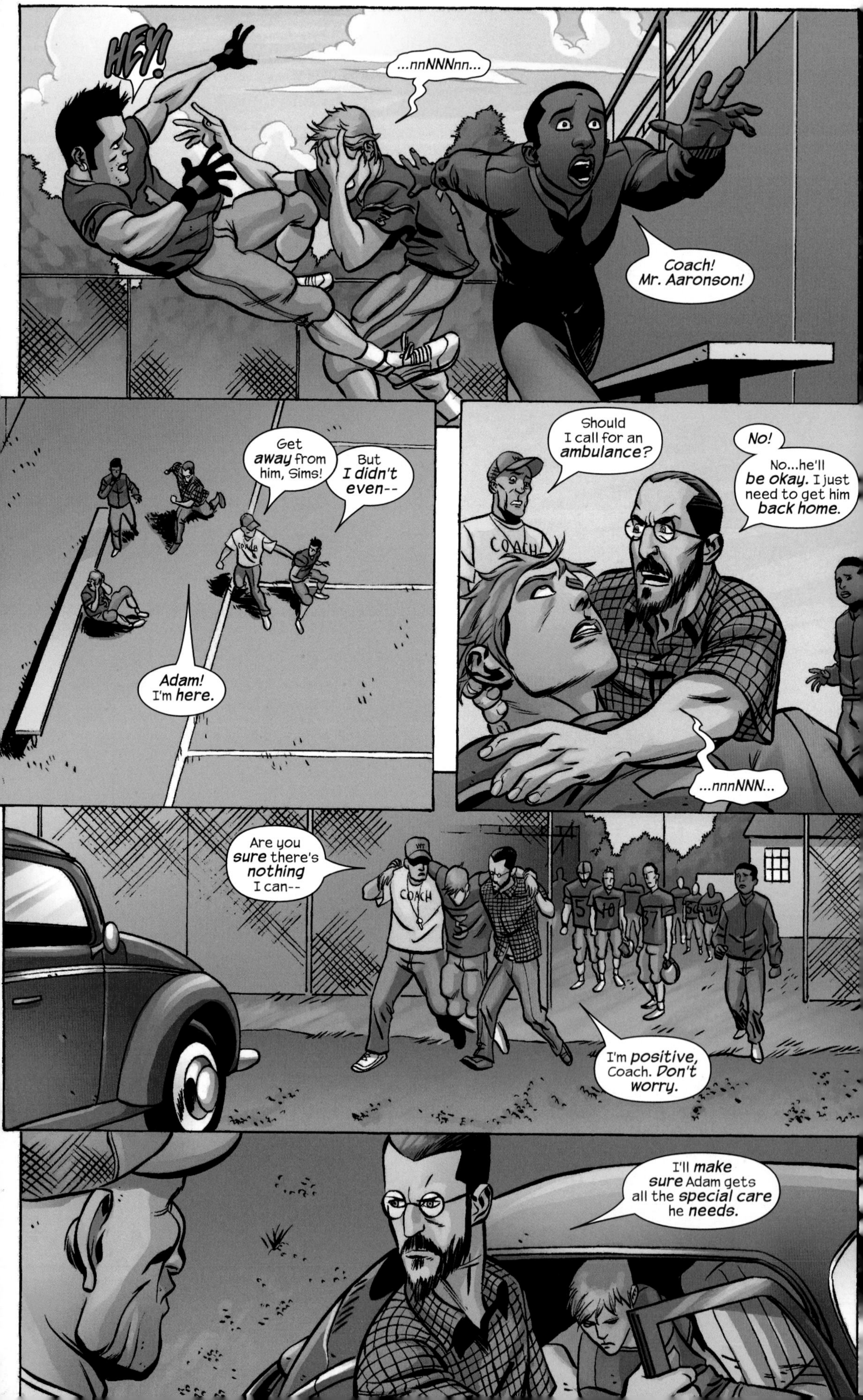
HEY!
...nnNNNnn...
Coach! Mr. Aaronson!
Get away from him, Sims!
But I didn't even--
Adam! I'm here.
Should I call for an ambulance?
No!
No...he'll be okay. I just need to get him back home.
...nnnNNN...
Are you sure there's nothing I can--
I'm positive, Coach. Don't worry.
I'll make sure Adam gets all the special care he needs.

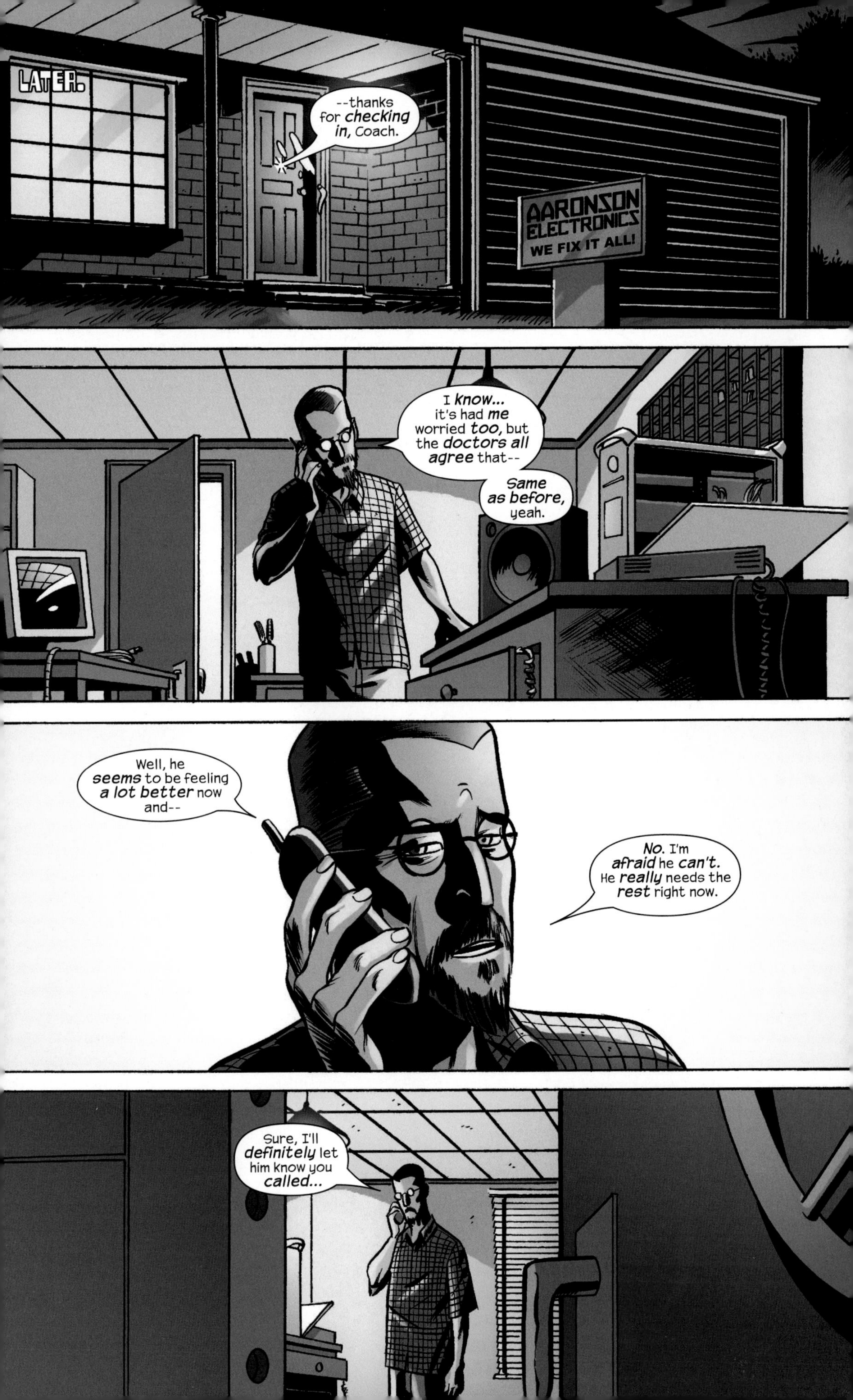
LATER.
--thanks for checking in, Coach.
AARONSON ELECTRONICS WE FIX IT ALL!
I know... it's had me worried too, but the doctors all agree that--
Same as before, yeah.
Well, he seems to be feeling a lot better now and--
No. I'm afraid he can't. He really needs the rest right now.
Sure, I'll definitely let him know you called...

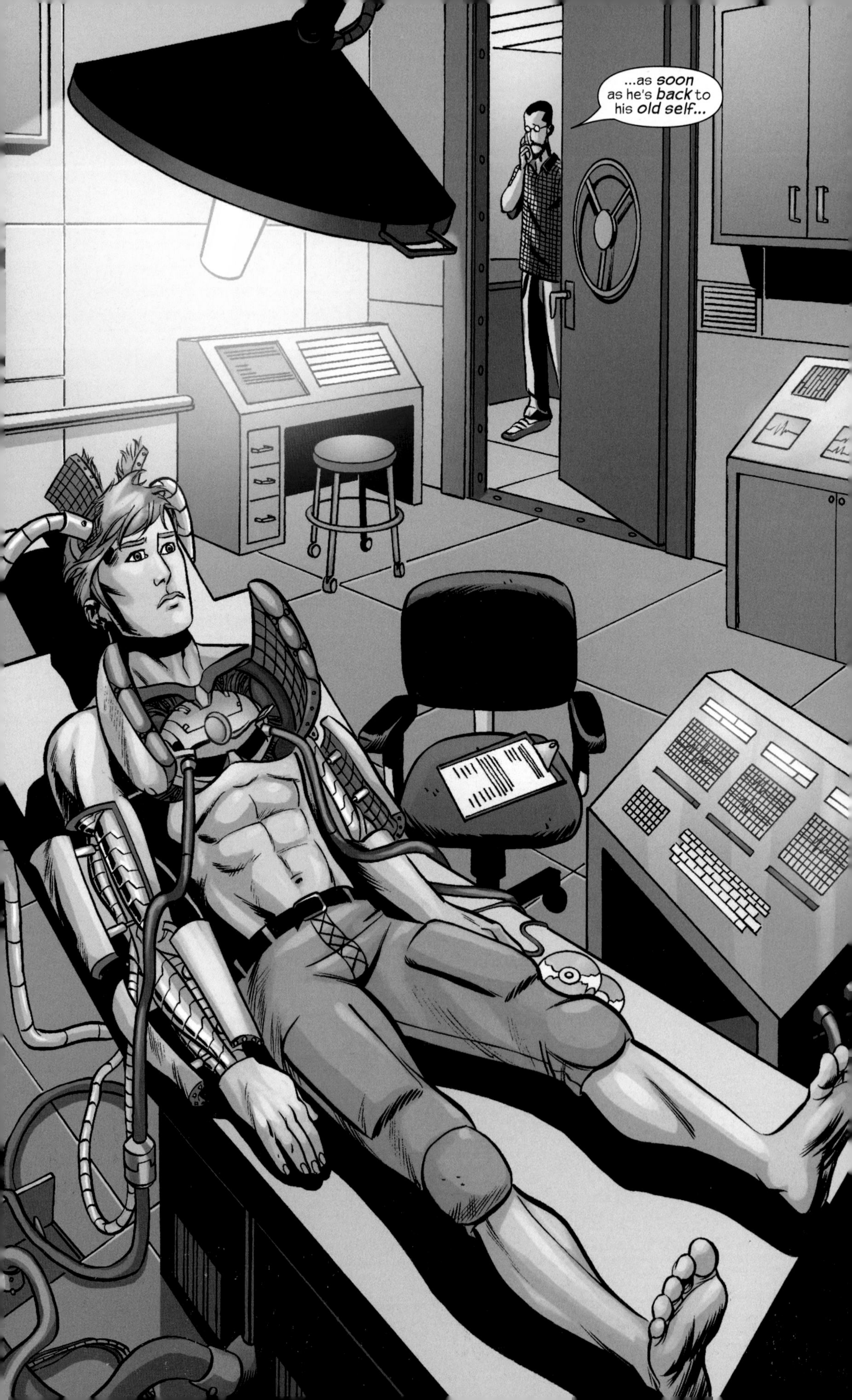
...as soon as he's back to his old self...

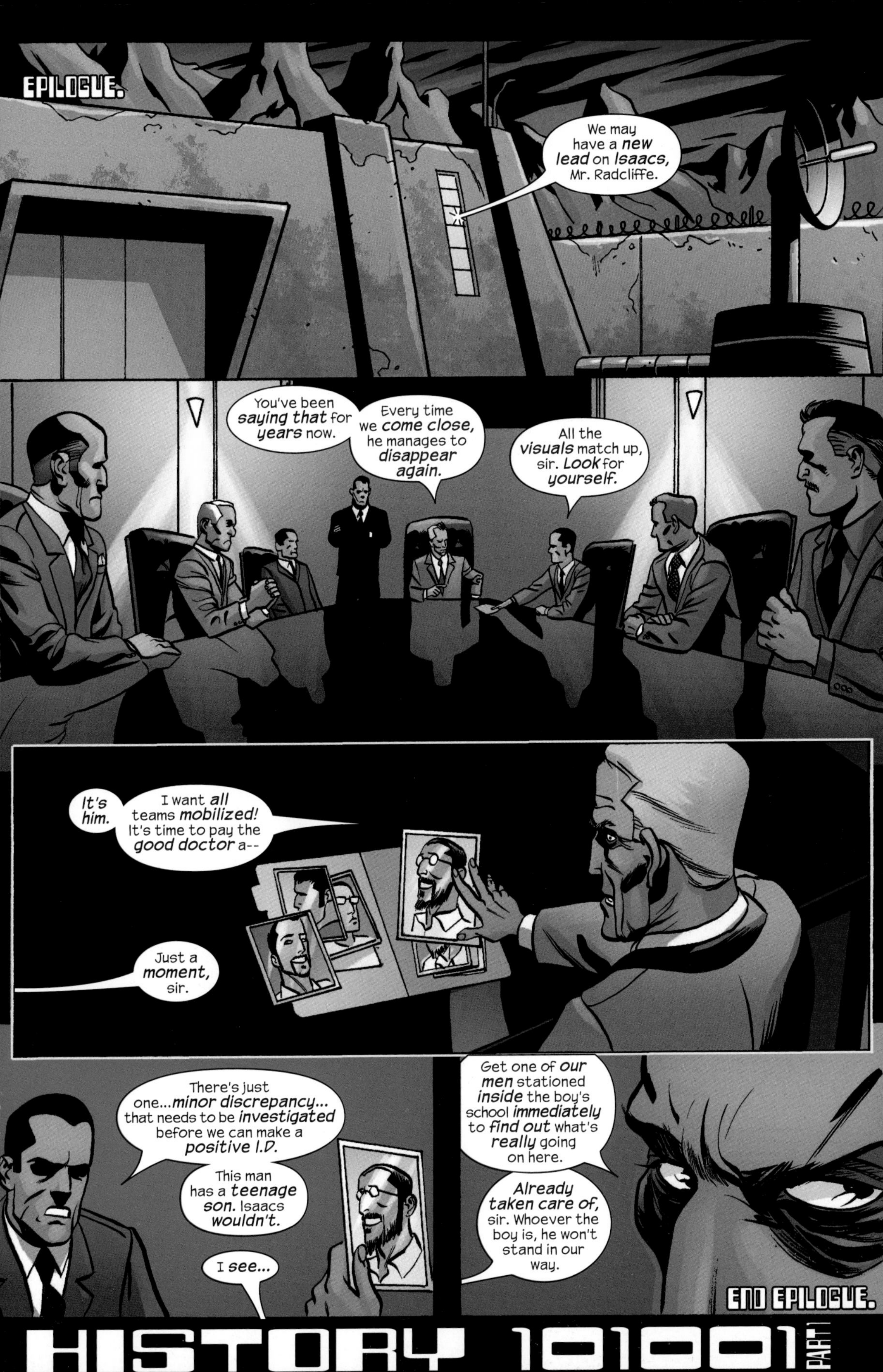

EPILOGUE.
We may have a new lead on Isaacs, Mr. Radcliffe.
You've been saying that for years now.
Every time we come close, he manages to disappear again.
All the visuals match up, sir. Look for yourself.
It's him.
I want all teams mobilized! It's time to pay the good doctor a--
Just a moment, sir.
There's just one...minor discrepancy... that needs to be investigated before we can make a positive I.D.
This man has a teenage son. Isaacs wouldn't.
I see...
Get one of our men stationed inside the boy's school immediately to find out what's really going on here.
Already taken care of, sir. Whoever the boy is, he won't stand in our way.
END EPILOGUE.
HISTORY 101001 PART 1

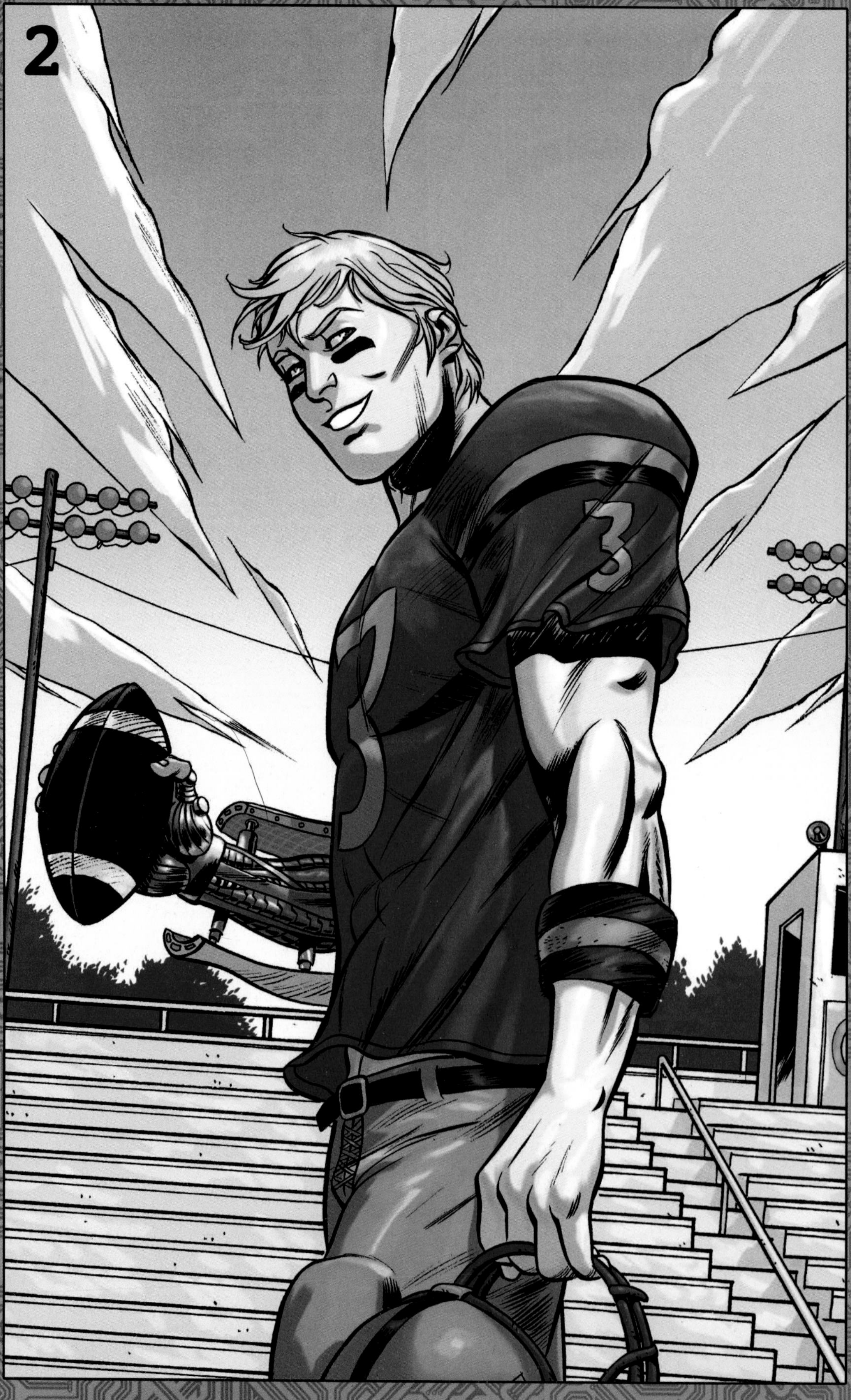
2

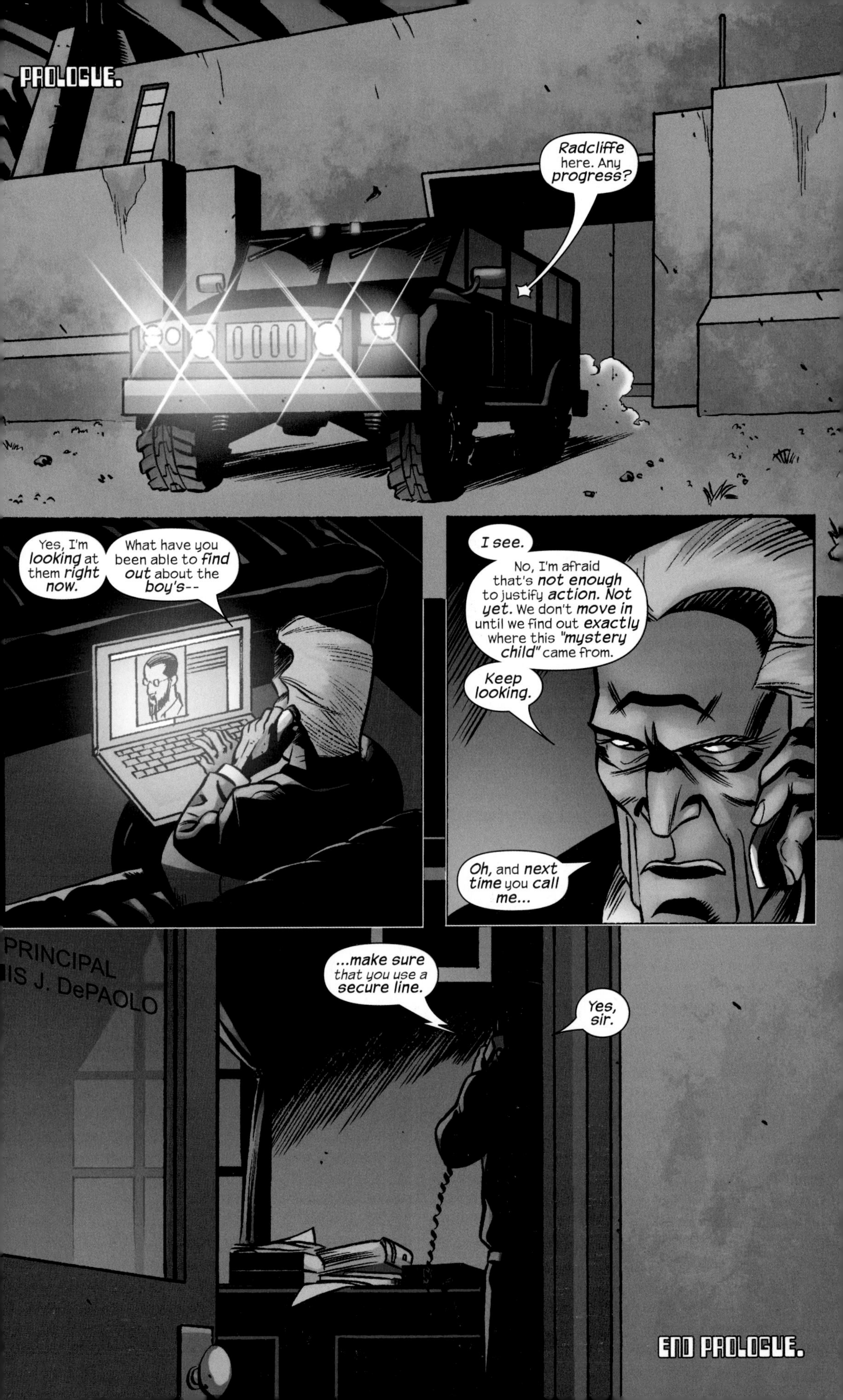
PROLOGUE.
Radcliffe here. Any progress?
Yes, I'm looking at them right now.
What have you been able to find out about the boy's--
I see.
No, I'm afraid that's not enough to justify action. Not yet. We don't move in until we find out exactly where this "mystery child" came from.
Keep looking.
Oh, and next time you call me...
PRINCIPAL
IS J. DePAOLO
...make sure that you use a secure line.
Yes, sir.
END PROLOGUE.

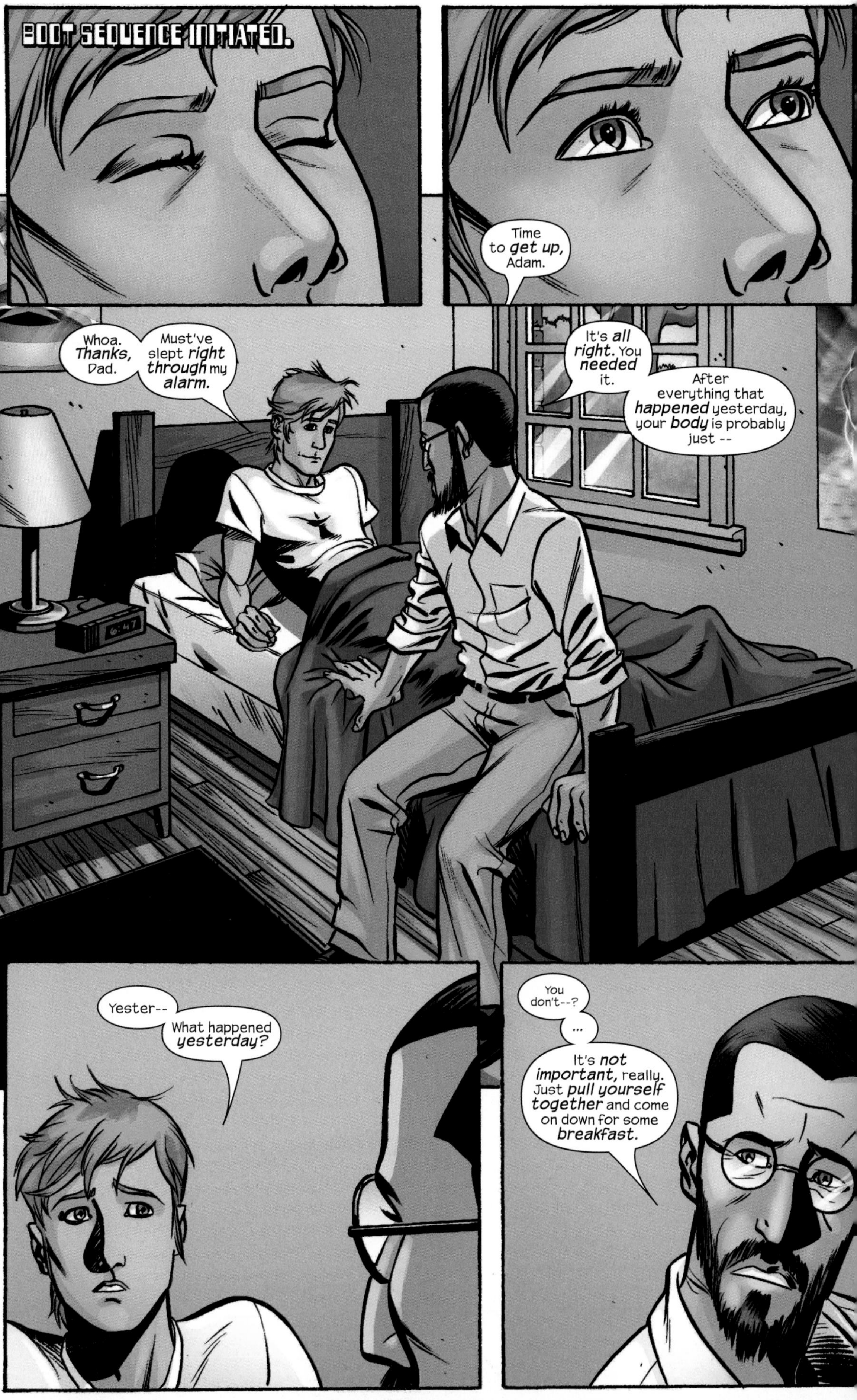
BOOT SEQUENCE INITIATED.
Time to get up, Adam.
Whoa. Thanks, Dad.
Must've slept right through my alarm.
It's all right. You needed it.
After everything that happened yesterday, your body is probably just --
Yester--
What happened yesterday?
You don't--?
...
It's not important, really. Just pull yourself together and come on down for some breakfast.

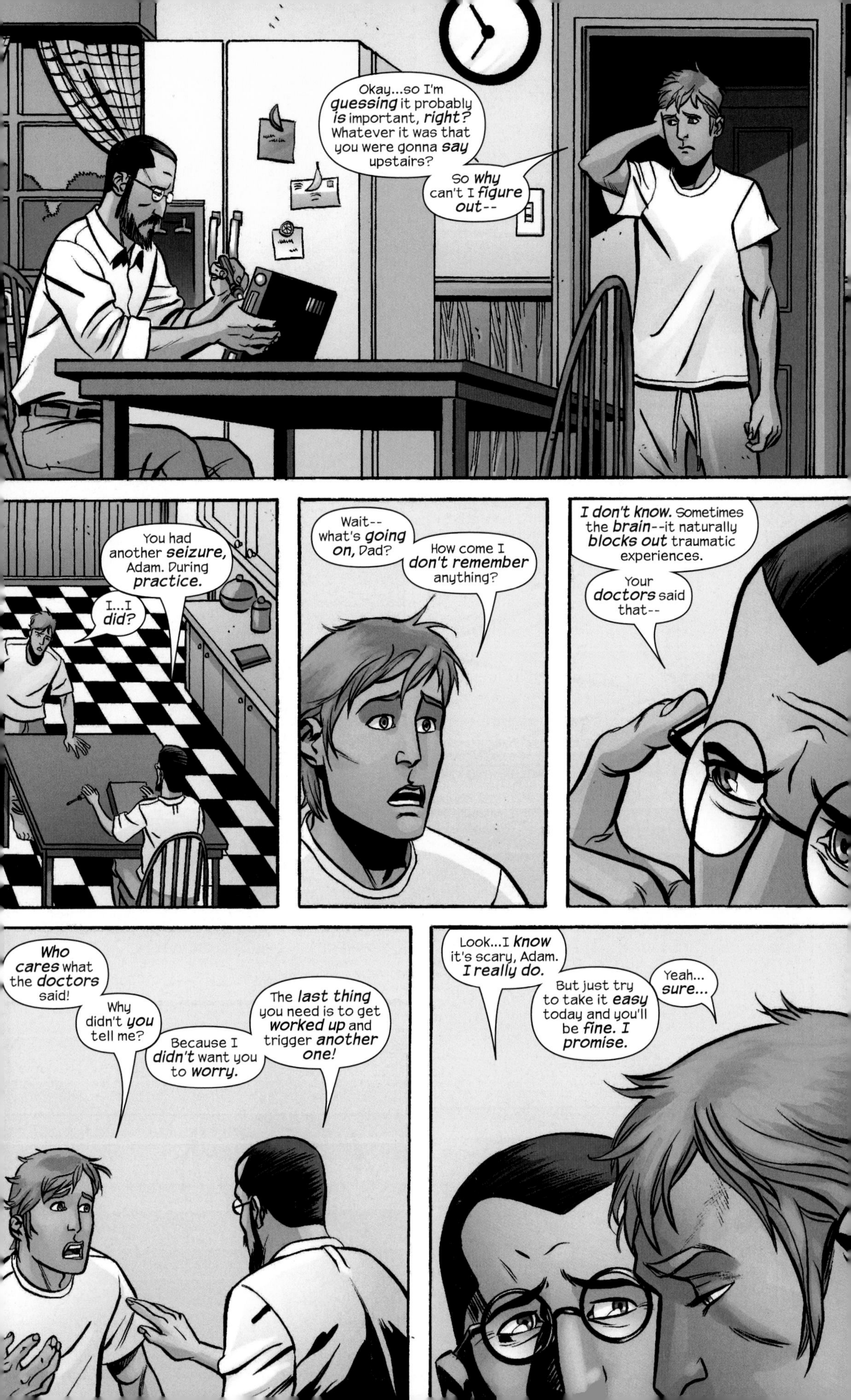
Okay...so I'm guessing it probably is important, right? Whatever it was that you were gonna say upstairs?
So why can't I figure out--
You had another seizure, Adam. During practice.
I...I did?
Wait-- what's going on, Dad?
How come I don't remember anything?
I don't know. Sometimes the brain--it naturally blocks out traumatic experiences.
Your doctors said that--
Who cares what the doctors said!
Why didn't you tell me?
Because I didn't want you to worry.
The last thing you need is to get worked up and trigger another one!
Look...I know it's scary, Adam. I really do.
But just try to take it easy today and you'll be fine. I promise.
Yeah... sure...

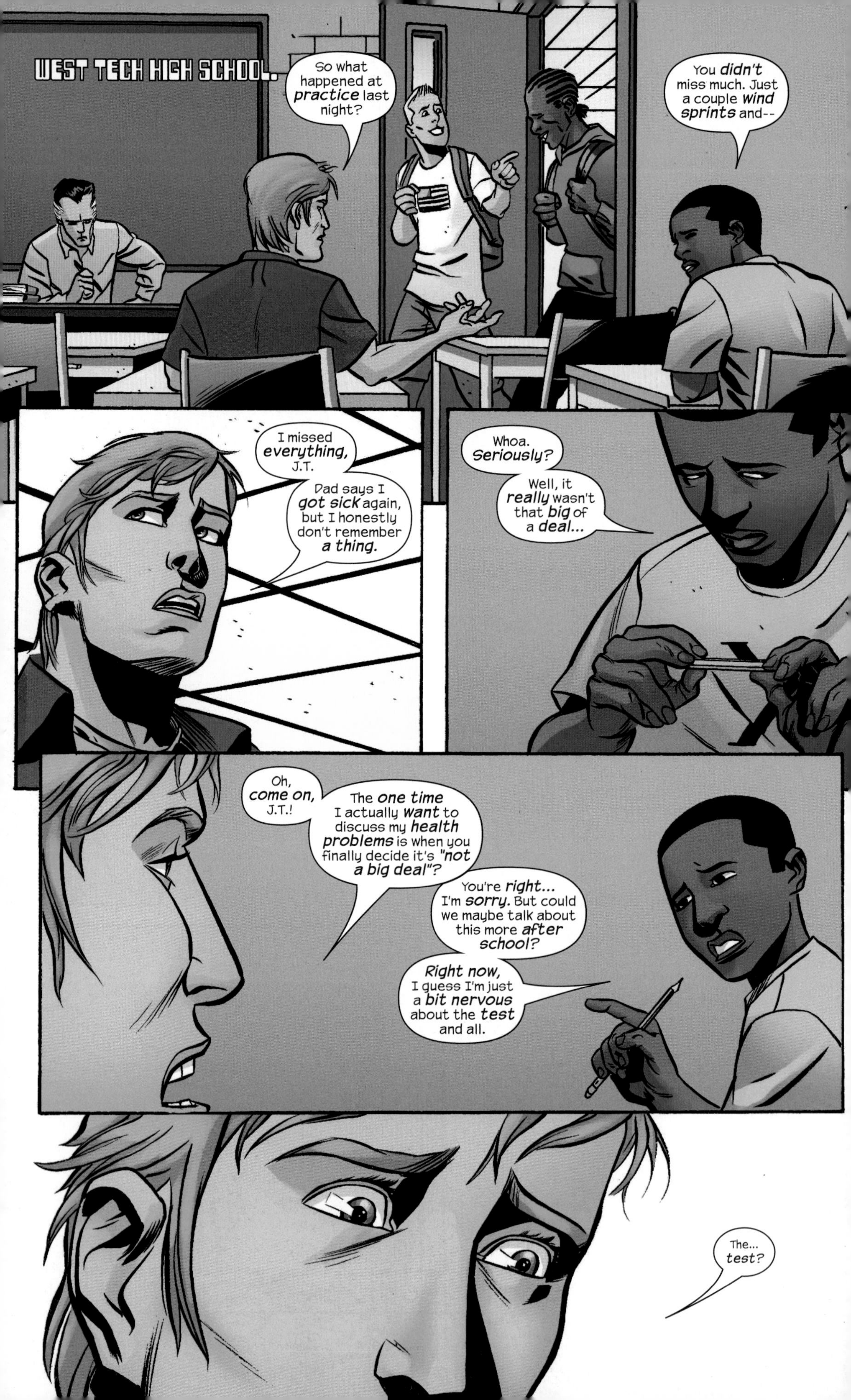
WEST TECH HIGH SCHOOL.
So what happened at practice last night?
You didn't miss much. Just a couple wind sprints and--
I missed everything, J.T.
Dad says I got sick again, but I honestly don't remember a thing.
Whoa. Seriously?
Well, it really wasn't that big of a deal...
Oh, come on, J.T.!
The one time I actually want to discuss my health problems is when you finally decide it's "not a big deal"?
You're right... I'm sorry. But could we maybe talk about this more after school?
Right now, I guess I'm just a bit nervous about the test and all.
The... test?

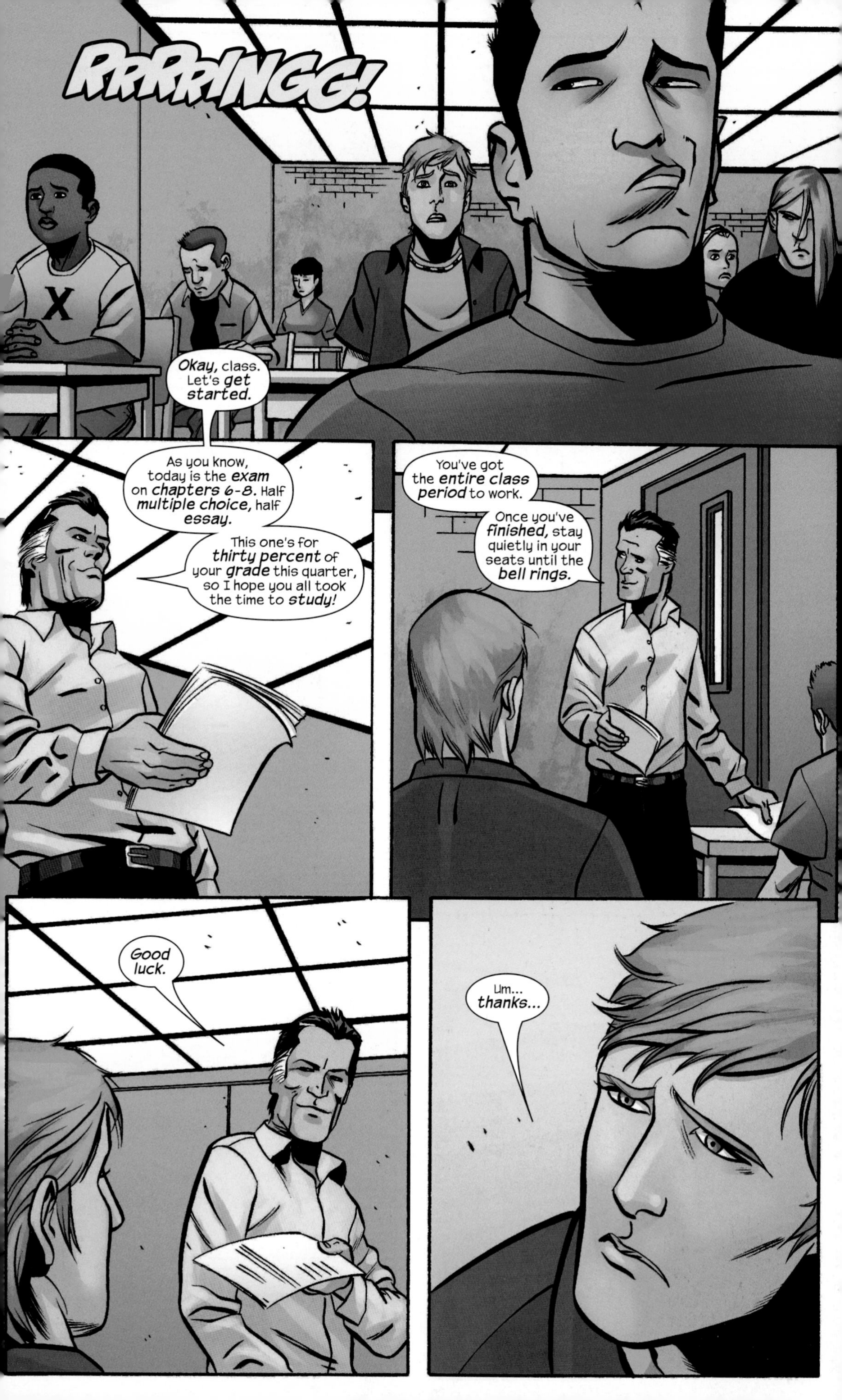
RRRRINGG!
Okay, class. Let's get started.
As you know, today is the exam on chapters 6-8. Half multiple choice, half essay.
This one's for thirty percent of your grade this quarter, so I hope you all took the time to study!
You've got the entire class period to work.
Once you've finished, stay quietly in your seats until the bell rings.
Good luck.
Um... thanks...

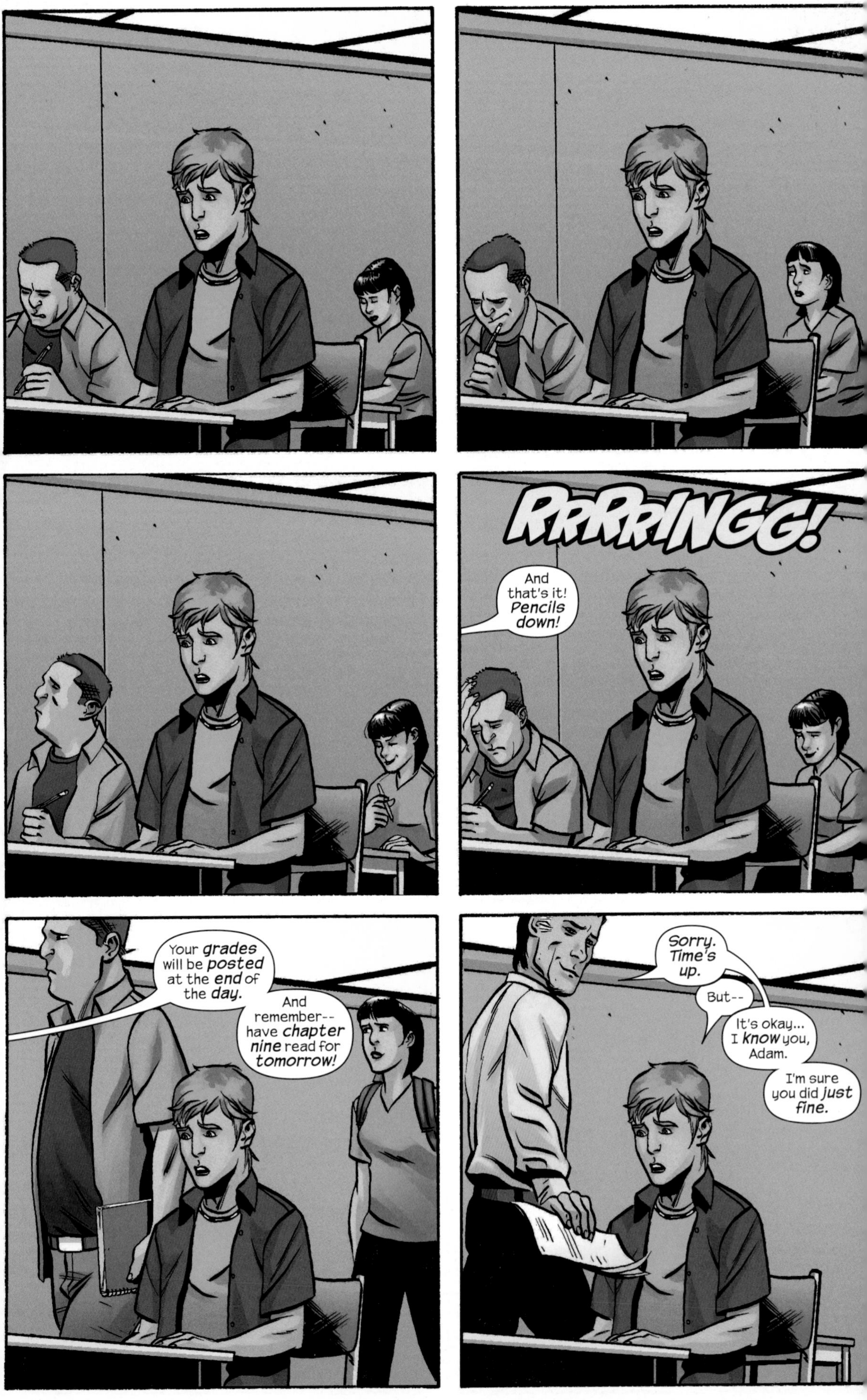
RRRRINGG!
And that's it! Pencils down!
Your grades will be posted at the end of the day.
And remember-- have chapter nine read for tomorrow!
Sorry. Time's up.
But--
It's okay... I know you, Adam.
I'm sure you did just fine.

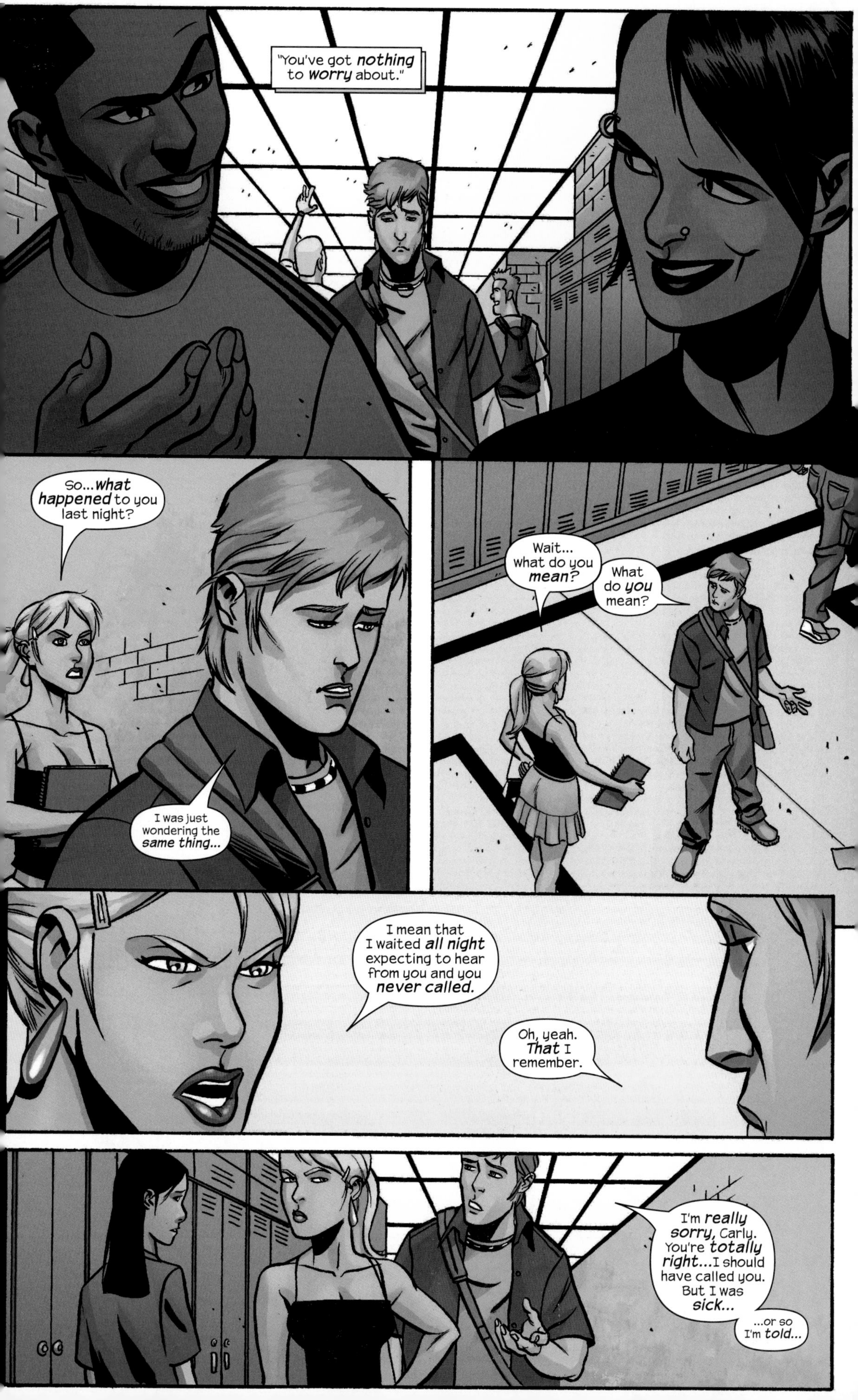
"You've got nothing to worry about."
So...what happened to you last night?
I was just wondering the same thing...
Wait... what do you mean?
What do you mean?
I mean that I waited all night expecting to hear from you and you never called.
Oh, yeah. That I remember.
I'm really sorry, Carly. You're totally right...I should have called you. But I was sick...
...or so I'm told...

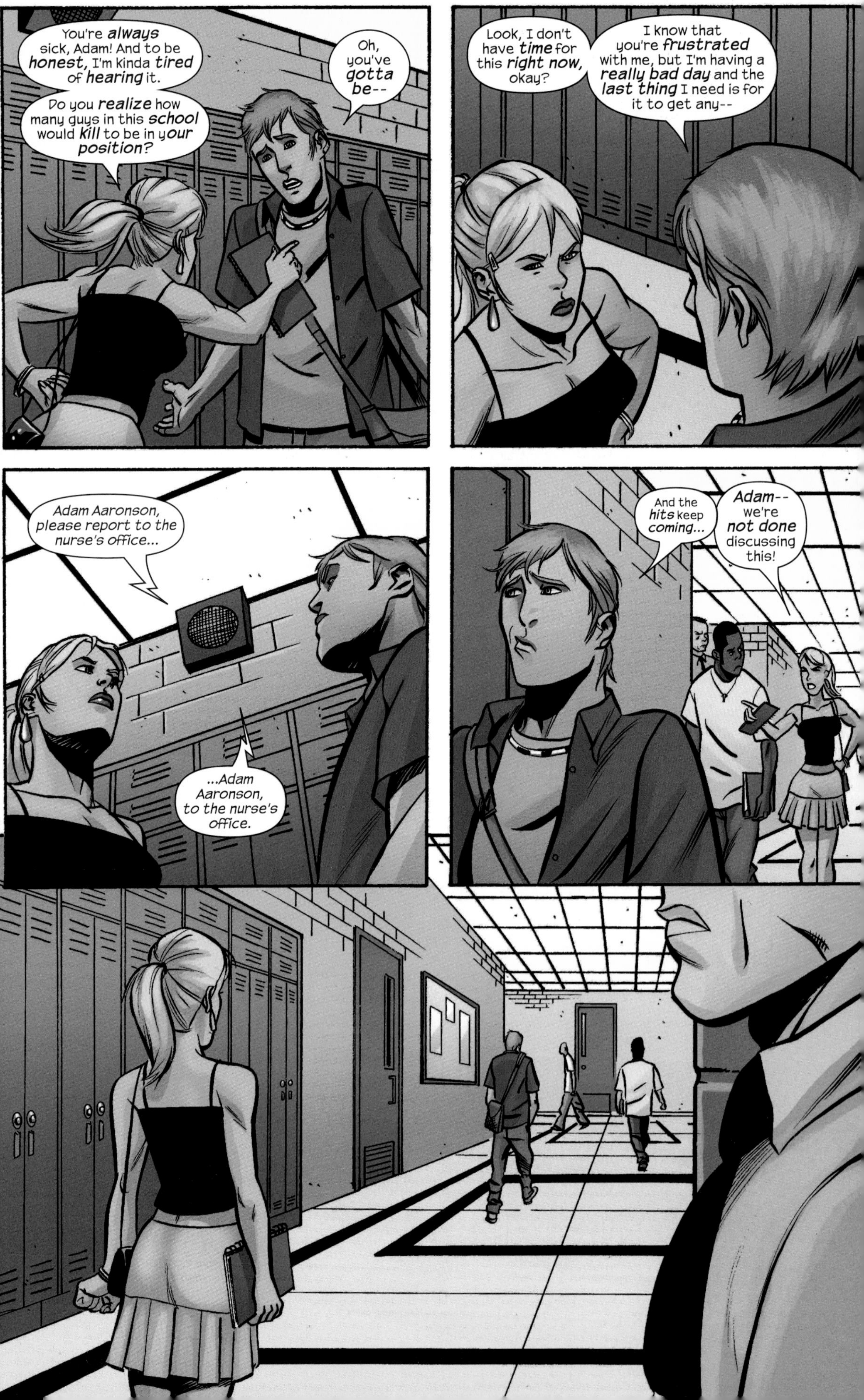
You're always sick, Adam! And to be honest, I'm kinda tired of hearing it.
Do you realize how many guys in this school would kill to be in your position?
Oh, you've gotta be--
Look, I don't have time for this right now, okay?
I know that you're frustrated with me, but I'm having a really bad day and the last thing I need is for it to get any--
Adam Aaronson, please report to the nurse's office...
...Adam Aaronson, to the nurse's office.
And the hits keep coming...
Adam--we're not done discussing this!

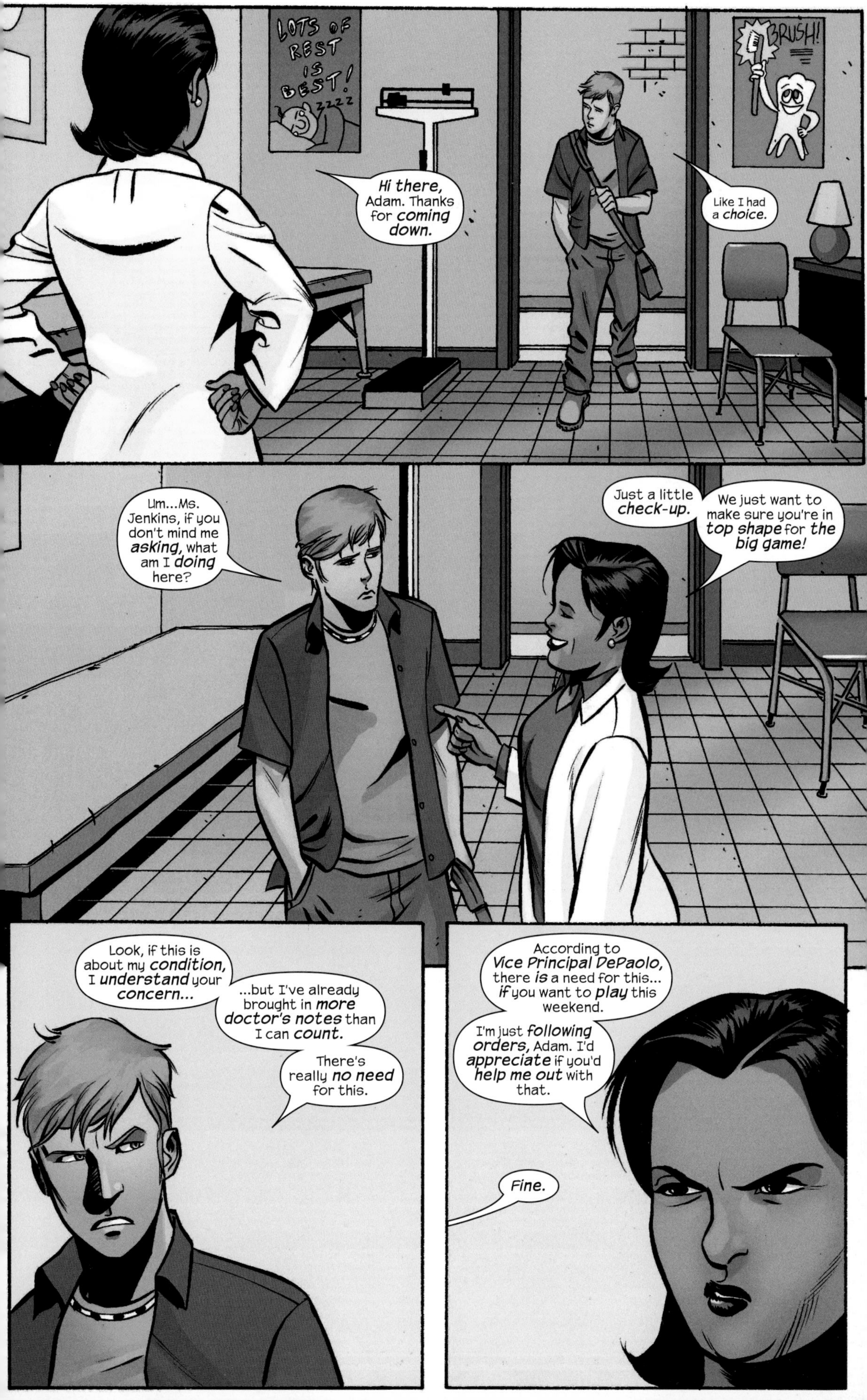
LOTS OF REST IS BEST!
ZZZZ
BRUSH!
Hi there, Adam. Thanks for coming down.
Like I had a choice.
Um...Ms. Jenkins, if you don't mind me asking, what am I doing here?
Just a little check-up.
We just want to make sure you're in top shape for the big game!
Look, if this is about my condition, I understand your concern...
...but I've already brought in more doctor's notes than I can count.
There's really no need for this.
According to Vice Principal DePaolo, there is a need for this... if you want to play this weekend.
I'm just following orders, Adam. I'd appreciate if you'd help me out with that.
Fine.

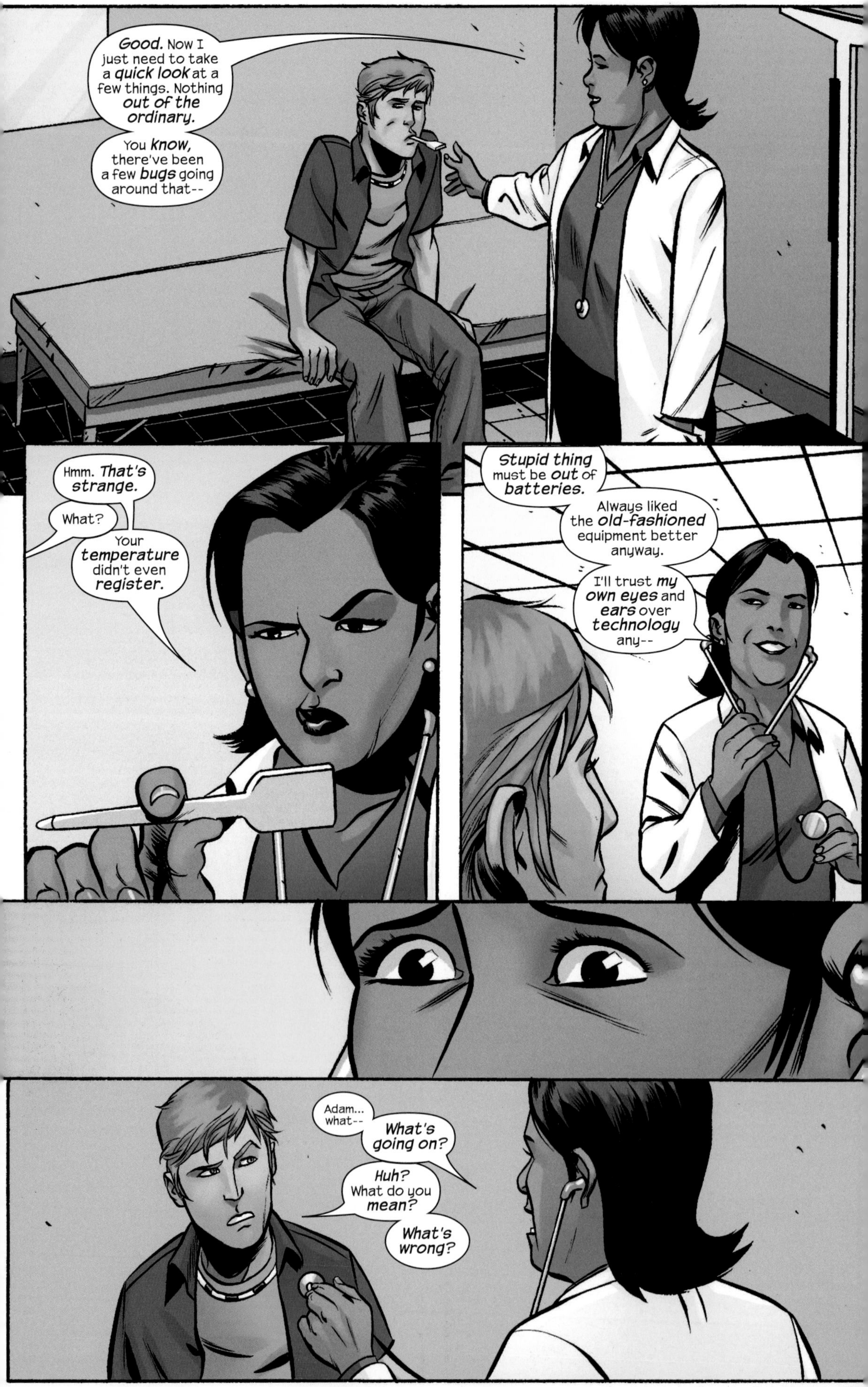

Good. Now I just need to take a quick look at a few things. Nothing out of the ordinary.
You know, there've been a few bugs going around that--
Hmm. That's strange.
What?
Your temperature didn't even register.
Stupid thing must be out of batteries.
Always liked the old-fashioned equipment better anyway.
I'll trust my own eyes and ears over technology any--
Adam... what--
What's going on?
Huh? What do you mean?
What's wrong?

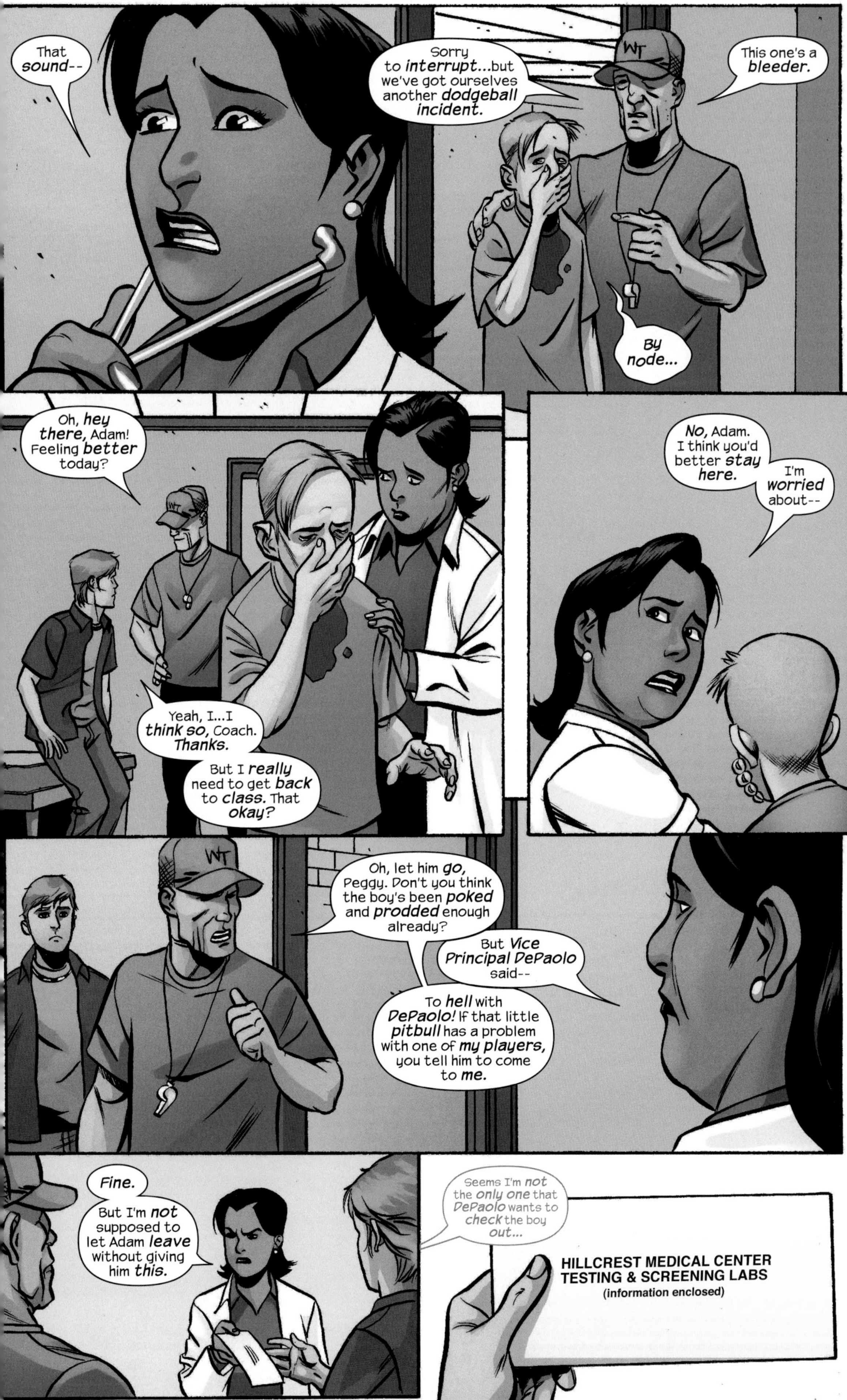
That sound--
Sorry to interrupt...but we've got ourselves another dodgeball incident.
This one's a bleeder.
By node...
Oh, hey there, Adam! Feeling better today?
Yeah, I...I think so, Coach. Thanks.
But I really need to get back to class. That okay?
No, Adam. I think you'd better stay here.
I'm worried about--
Oh, let him go, Peggy. Don't you think the boy's been poked and prodded enough already?
But Vice Principal DePaolo said--
To hell with DePaolo! If that little pitbull has a problem with one of my players, you tell him to come to me.
Fine.
But I'm not supposed to let Adam leave without giving him this.
Seems I'm not the only one that DePaolo wants to check the boy out...
HILLCREST MEDICAL CENTER
TESTING & SCREENING LABS
(information enclosed)

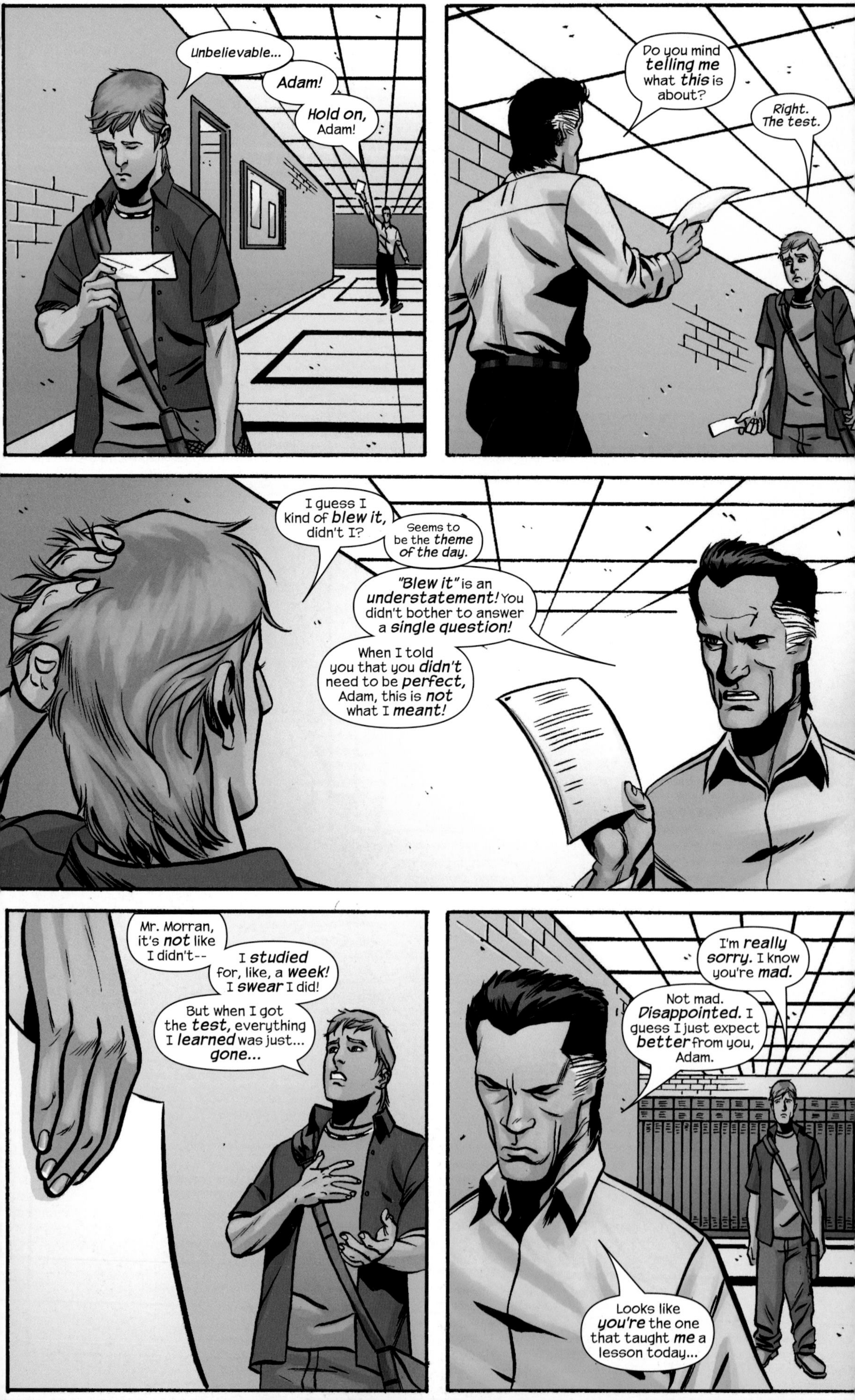

Unbelievable...
Adam!
Hold on, Adam!
Do you mind telling me what this is about?
Right. The test.
I guess I kind of blew it, didn't I?
Seems to be the theme of the day.
"Blew it" is an understatement! You didn't bother to answer a single question!
When I told you that you didn't need to be perfect, Adam, this is not what I meant!
Mr. Morran, it's not like I didn't--
I studied for, like, a week! I swear I did!
But when I got the test, everything I learned was just... gone...
I'm really sorry. I know you're mad.
Not mad. Disappointed. I guess I just expect better from you, Adam.
Looks like you're the one that taught me a lesson today...

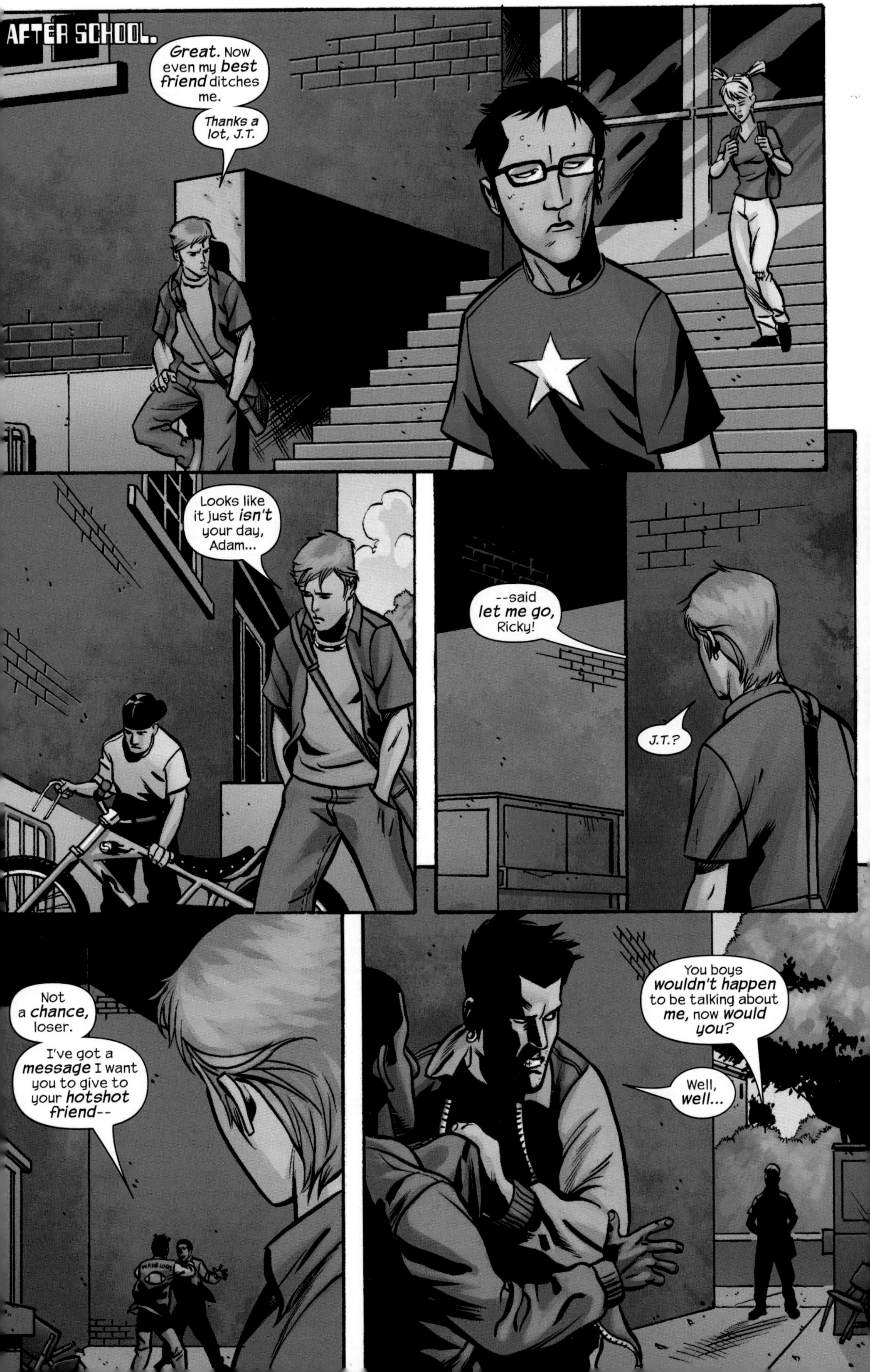

AFTER SCHOOL.
Great. Now even my best friend ditches me.
Thanks a lot, J.T.
Looks like it just isn't your day, Adam...
--said let me go, Ricky!
J.T.?
Not a chance, loser.
I've got a message I want you to give to your hotshot friend--
You boys wouldn't happen to be talking about me, now would you?
Well, well...

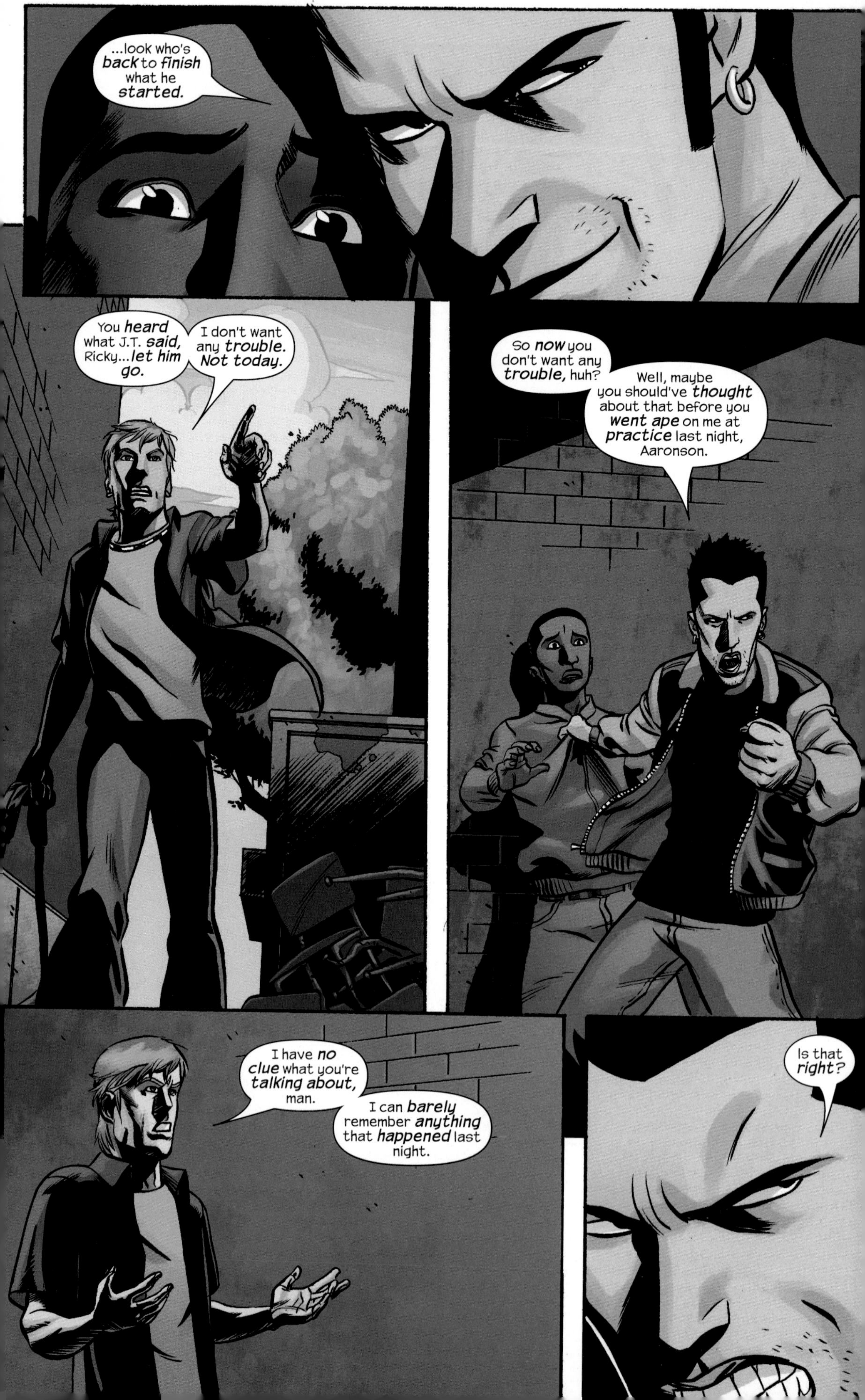
...look who's back to finish what he started.
You heard what J.T. said, Ricky...let him go.
I don't want any trouble. Not today.
So now you don't want any trouble, huh?
Well, maybe you should've thought about that before you went ape on me at practice last night, Aaronson.
I have no clue what you're talking about, man.
I can barely remember anything that happened last night.
Is that right?

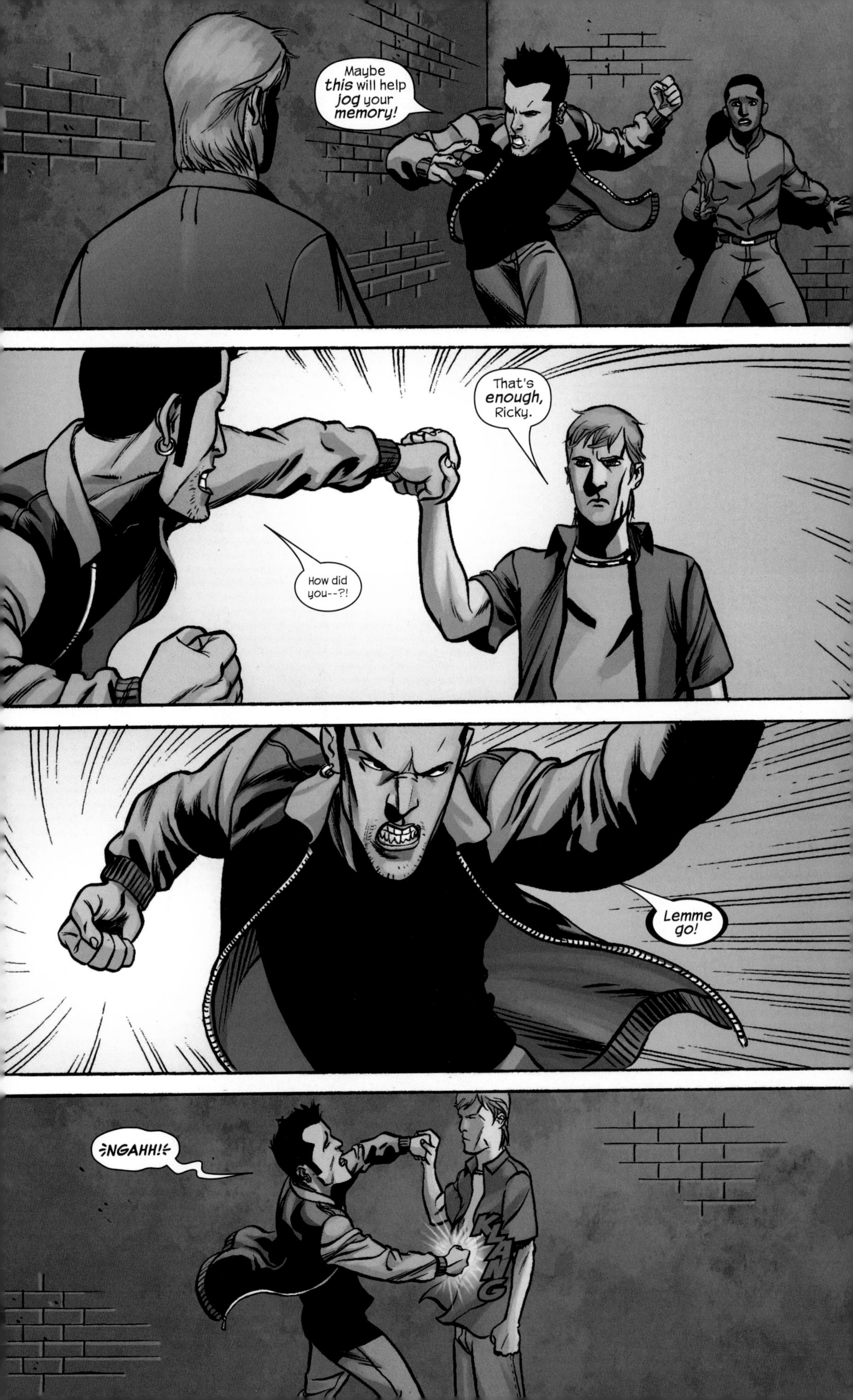
Maybe this will help jog your memory!
That's enough, Ricky.
How did you--?!
Lemme go!
NGAHH!
KLANG

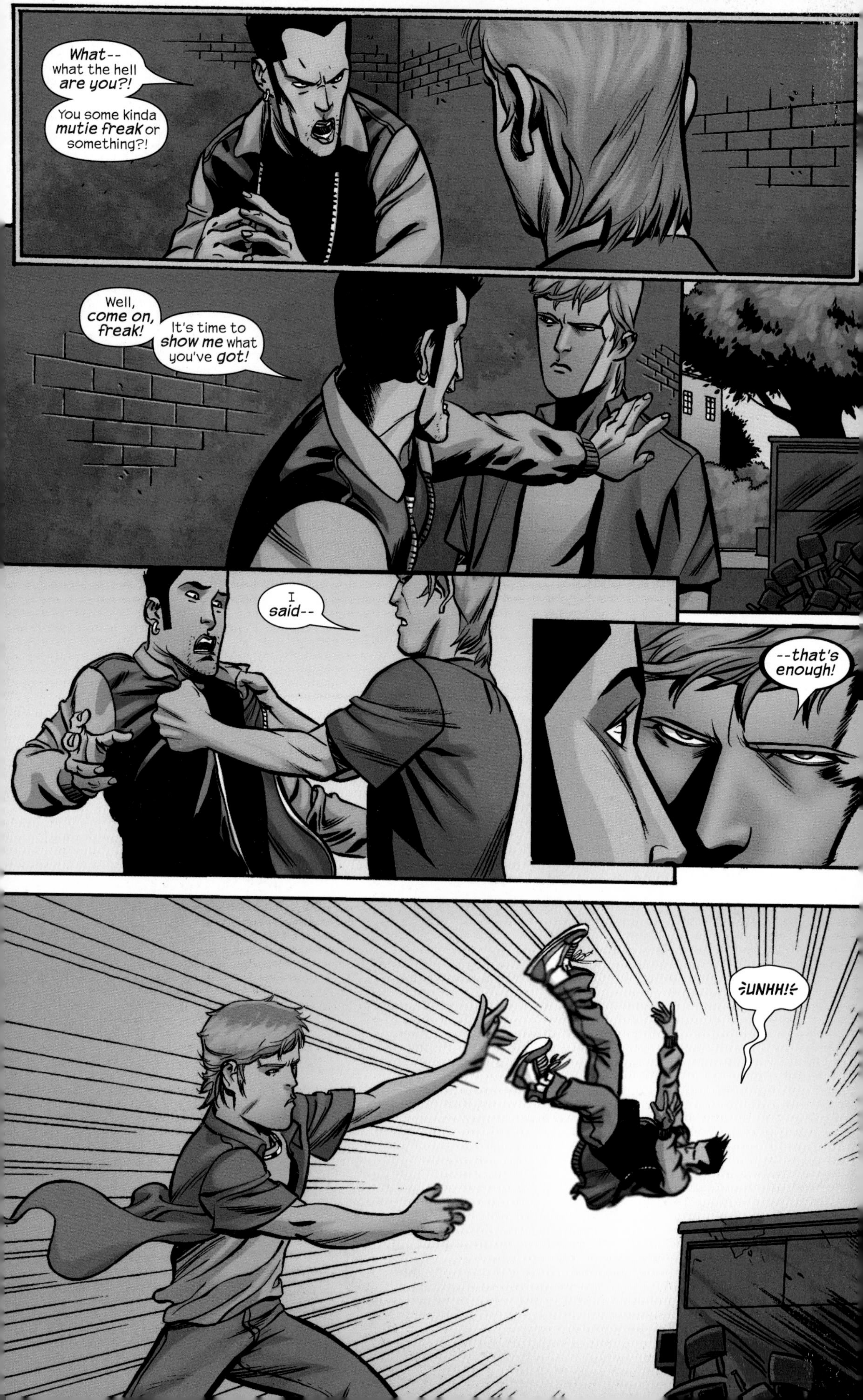
What-- what the hell are you?!
You some kinda mutie freak or something?!
Well, come on, freak!
It's time to show me what you've got!
I said--
--that's enough!
UNHH!

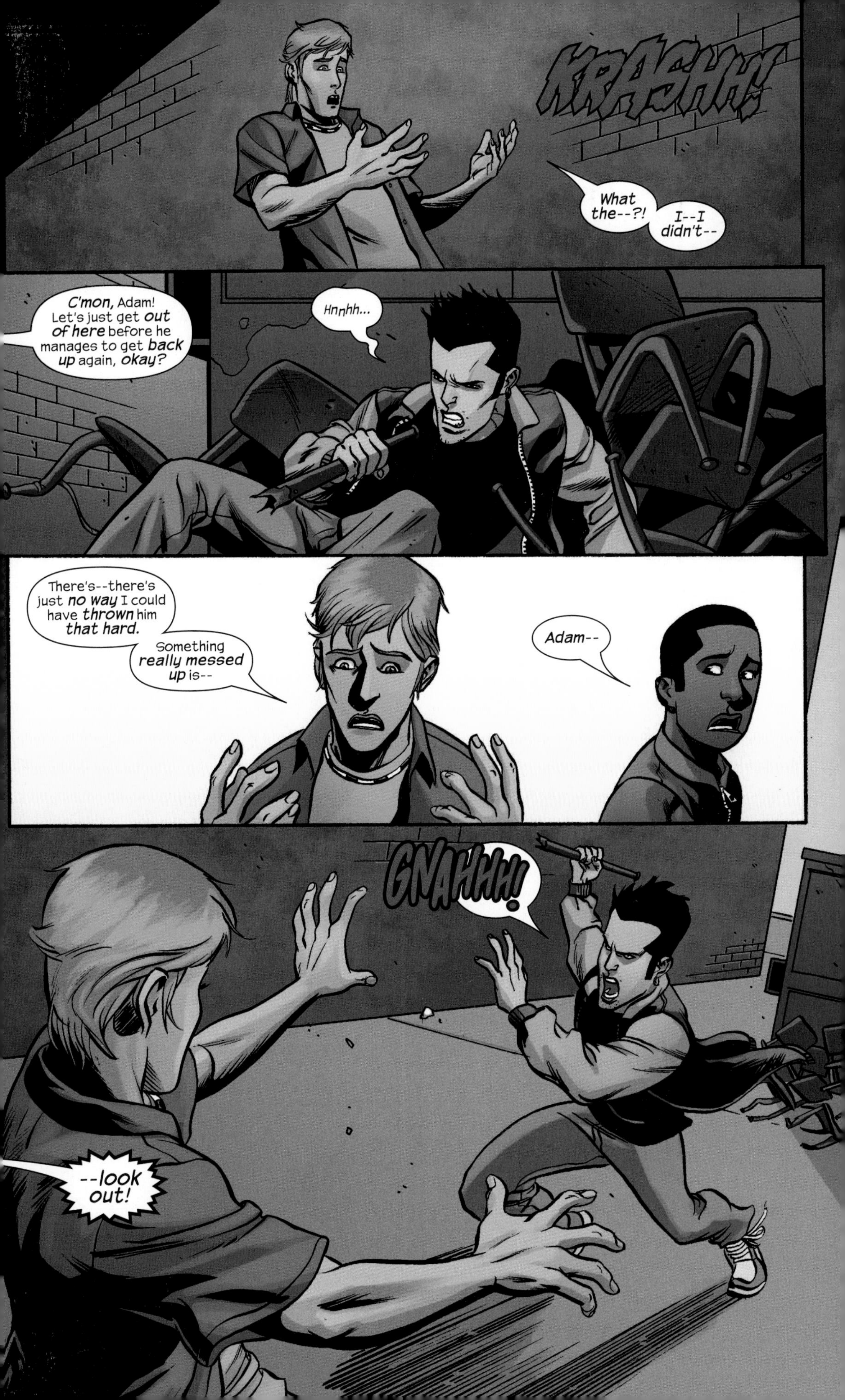
KRASHH!
What the--?!
I--I didn't--
C'mon, Adam! Let's just get out of here before he manages to get back up again, okay?
Hnnhh...
There's--there's just no way I could have thrown him that hard.
Something really messed up is--
Adam--
GNAHHH!
--look out!

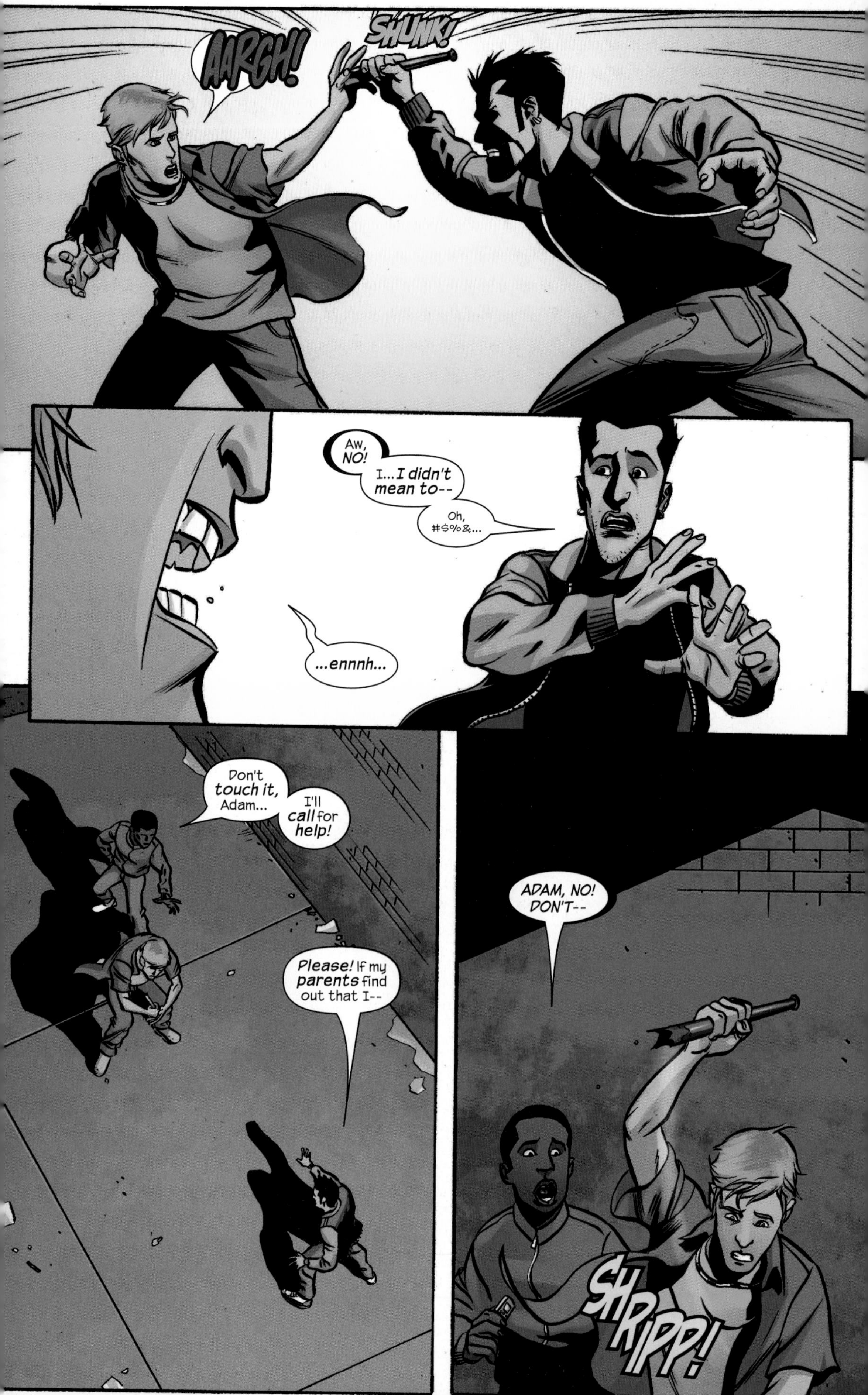

AARGH!
SHUNK!
Aw, NO!
I...I didn't mean to--
Oh, #$%&...
...ennnh...
Don't touch it, Adam...
I'll call for help!
Please! If my parents find out that I--
ADAM, NO! DON'T--
SHRIPP!

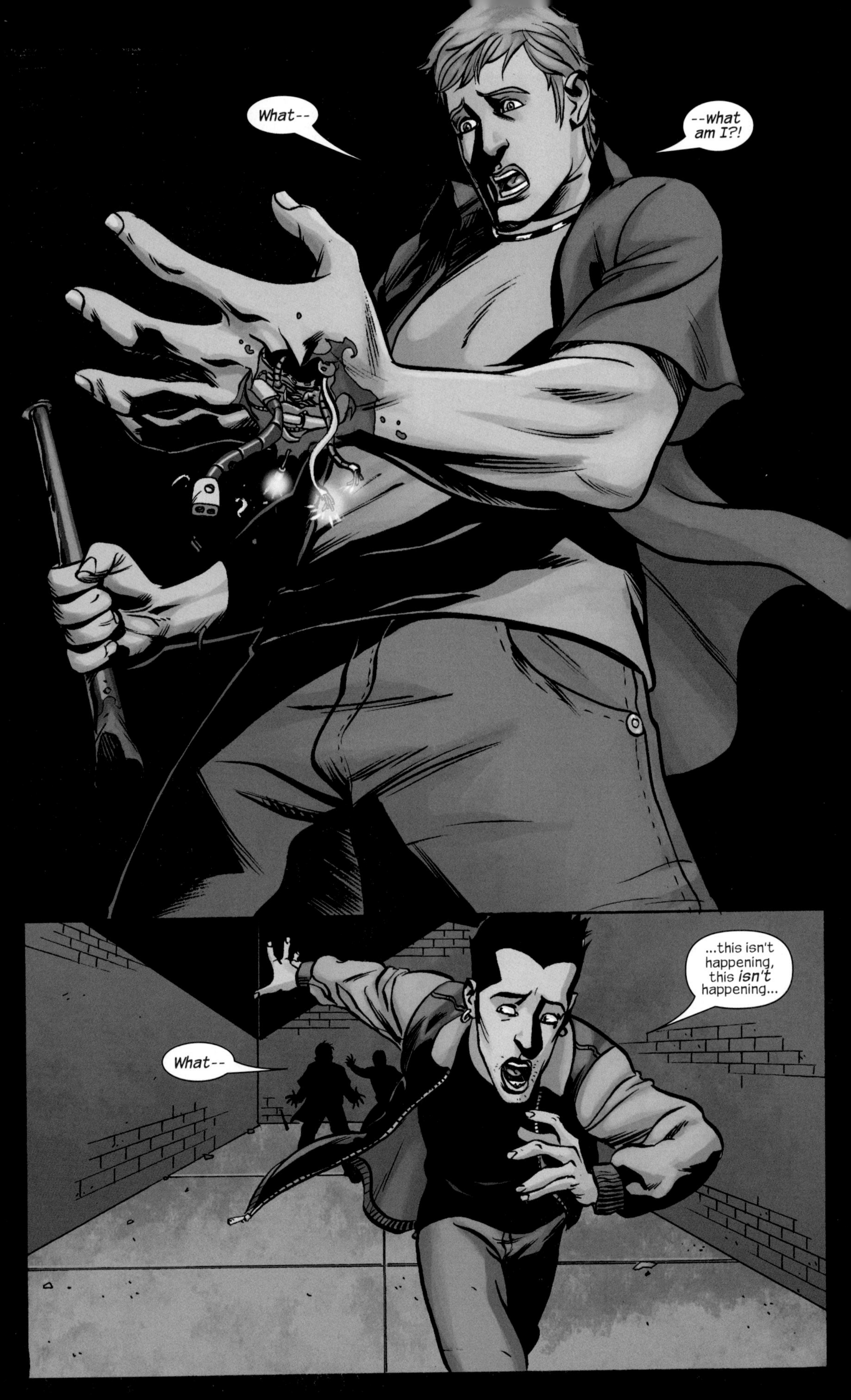

What--
--what am I?!
...this isn't happening, this *isn't* happening...
What--

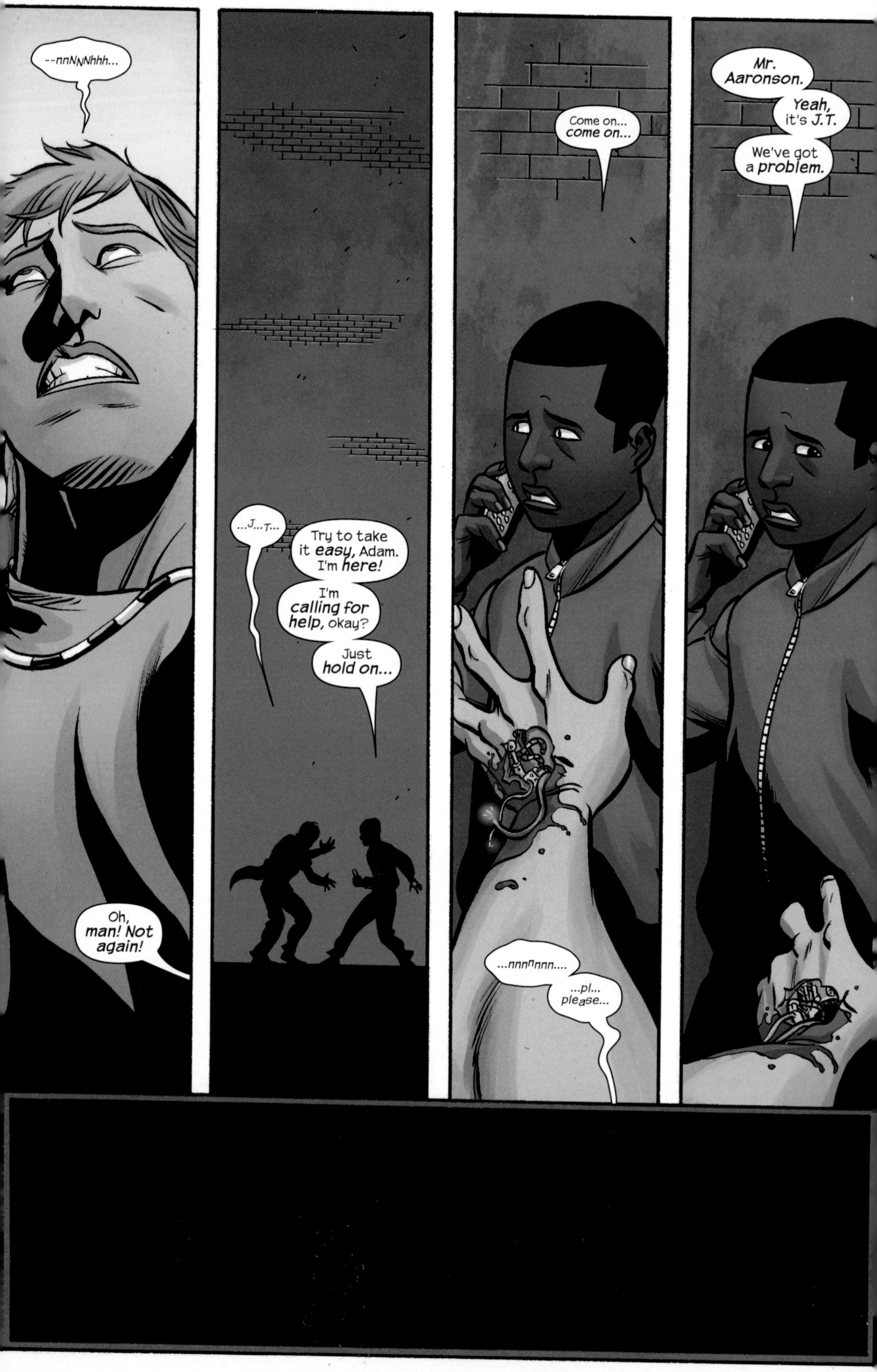
--nnNNhhh...
Oh, man! Not again!
...J...T...
Try to take it easy, Adam. I'm here!
I'm calling for help, okay?
Just hold on...
Come on... come on...
...nnnnnnn....
...pl... please...
Mr. Aaronson.
Yeah, it's J.T.
We've got a problem.

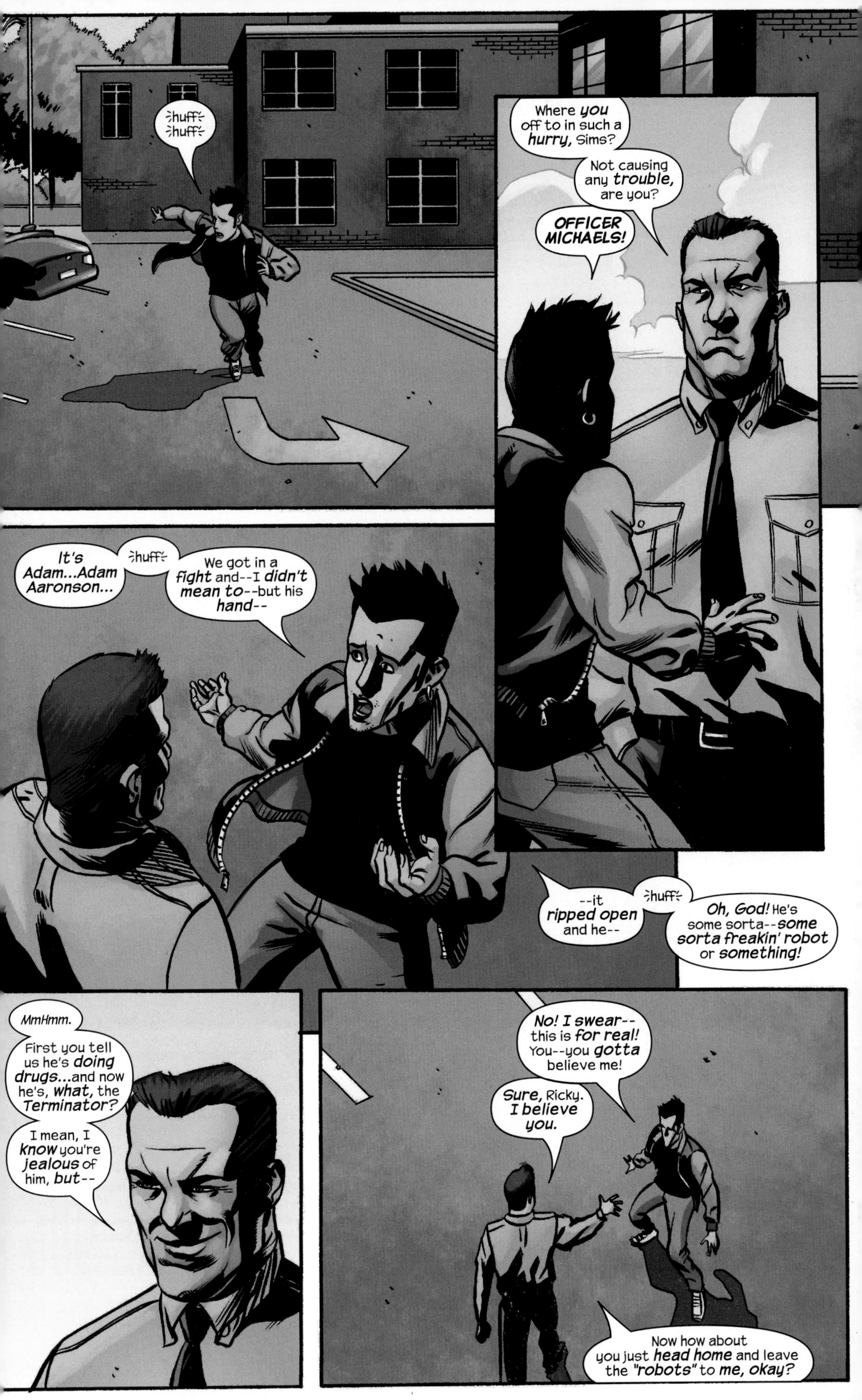
huff
huff
Where you off to in such a hurry, Sims?
Not causing any trouble, are you?
OFFICER MICHAELS!
It's Adam...Adam Aaronson...
huff
We got in a fight and--I didn't mean to--but his hand--
--it ripped open and he--
huff
Oh, God! He's some sorta--some sorta freakin' robot or something!
MmHmm.
First you tell us he's doing drugs...and now he's, what, the Terminator?
I mean, I know you're jealous of him, but--
No! I swear--this is for real! You--you gotta believe me!
Sure, Ricky. I believe you.
Now how about you just head home and leave the "robots" to me, okay?

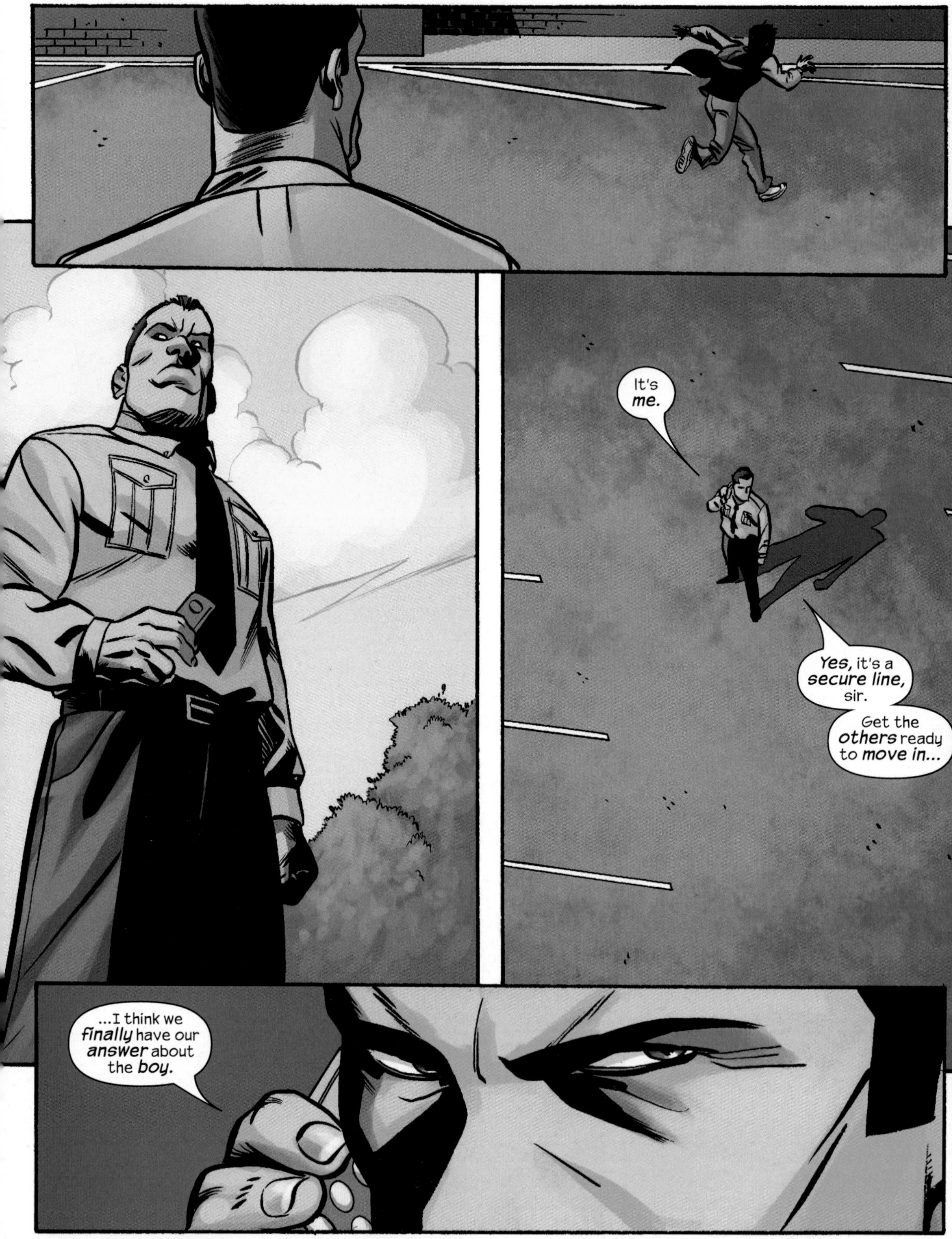

It's me.
Yes, it's a secure line, sir.
Get the others ready to move in...
...I think we finally have our answer about the boy.

HISTORY 101001 PART 2

3

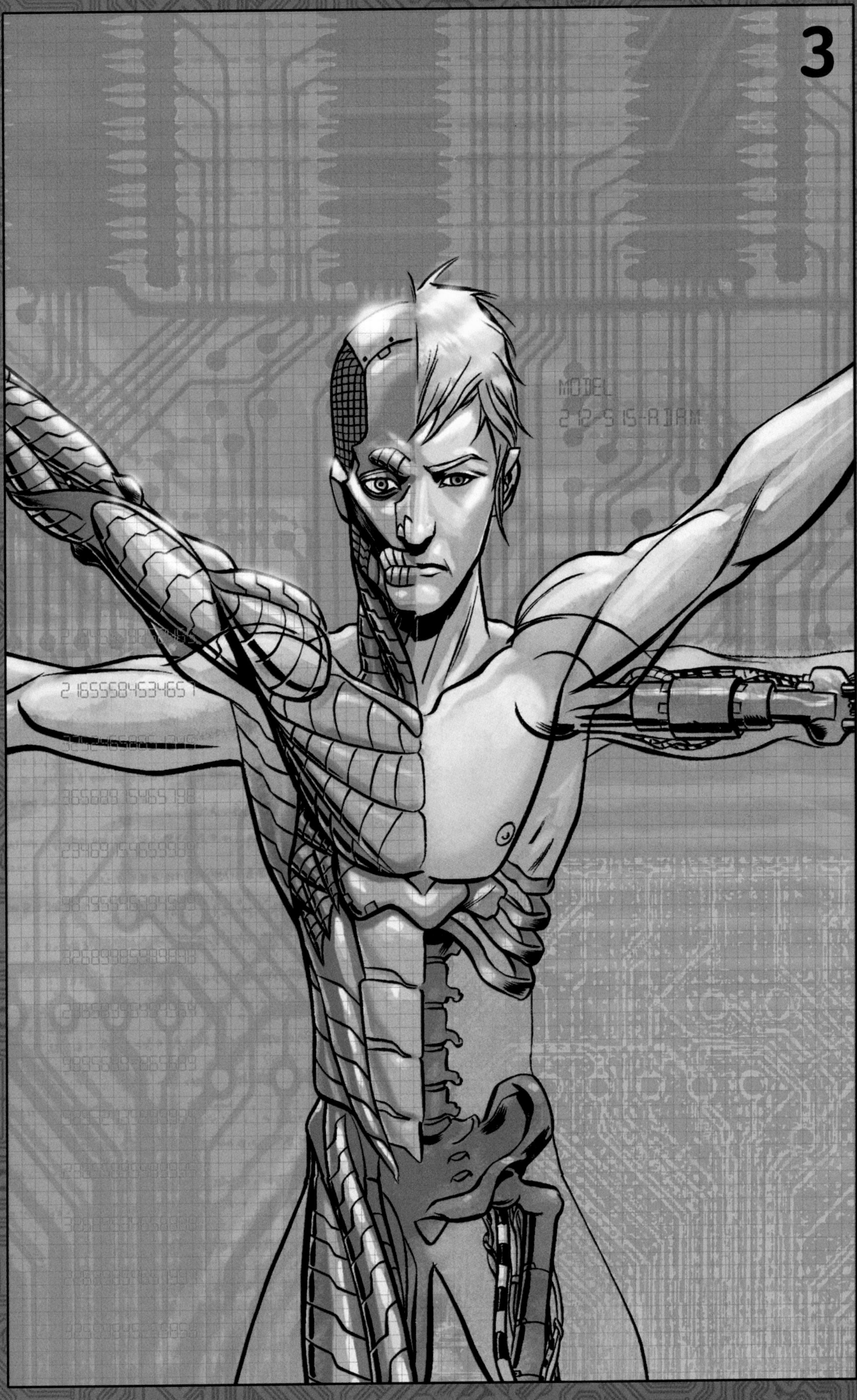
MODEL

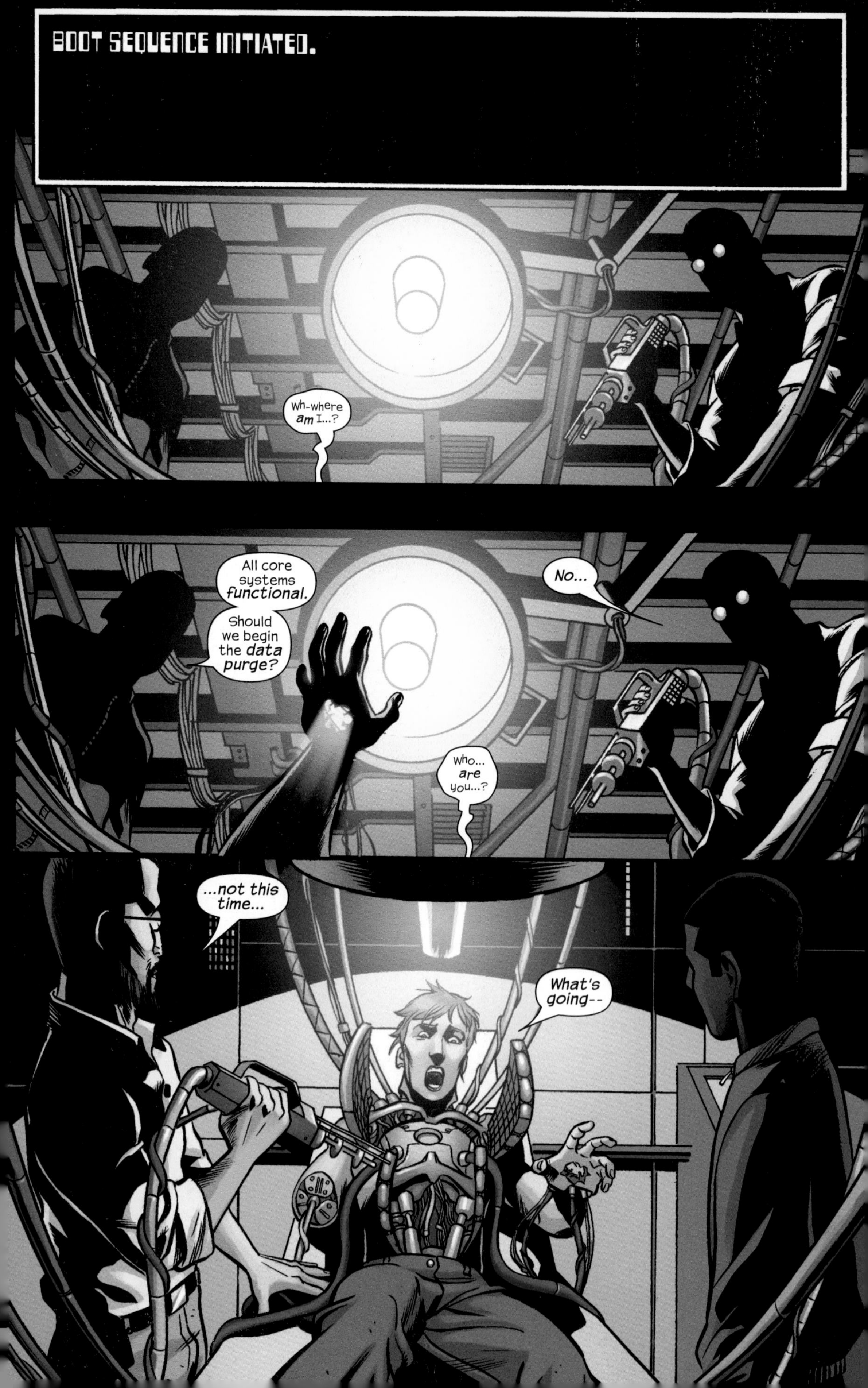
BOOT SEQUENCE INITIATED.
Wh-where am I...?
All core systems functional.
Should we begin the data purge?
No...
Who... are you...?
...not this time...
What's going--

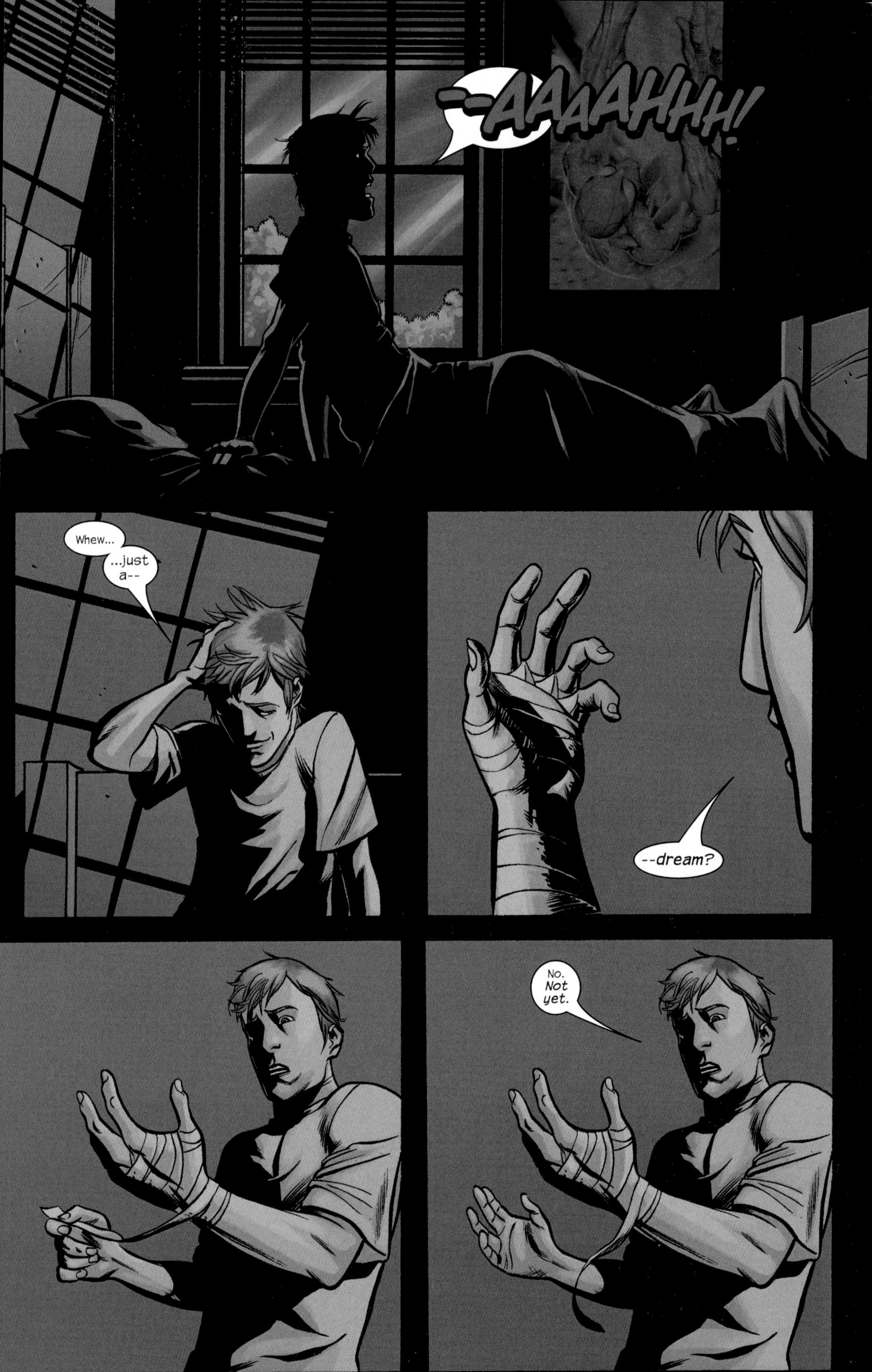
--AAAAHHH!
Whew...
...just a--
--dream?
No. Not yet.

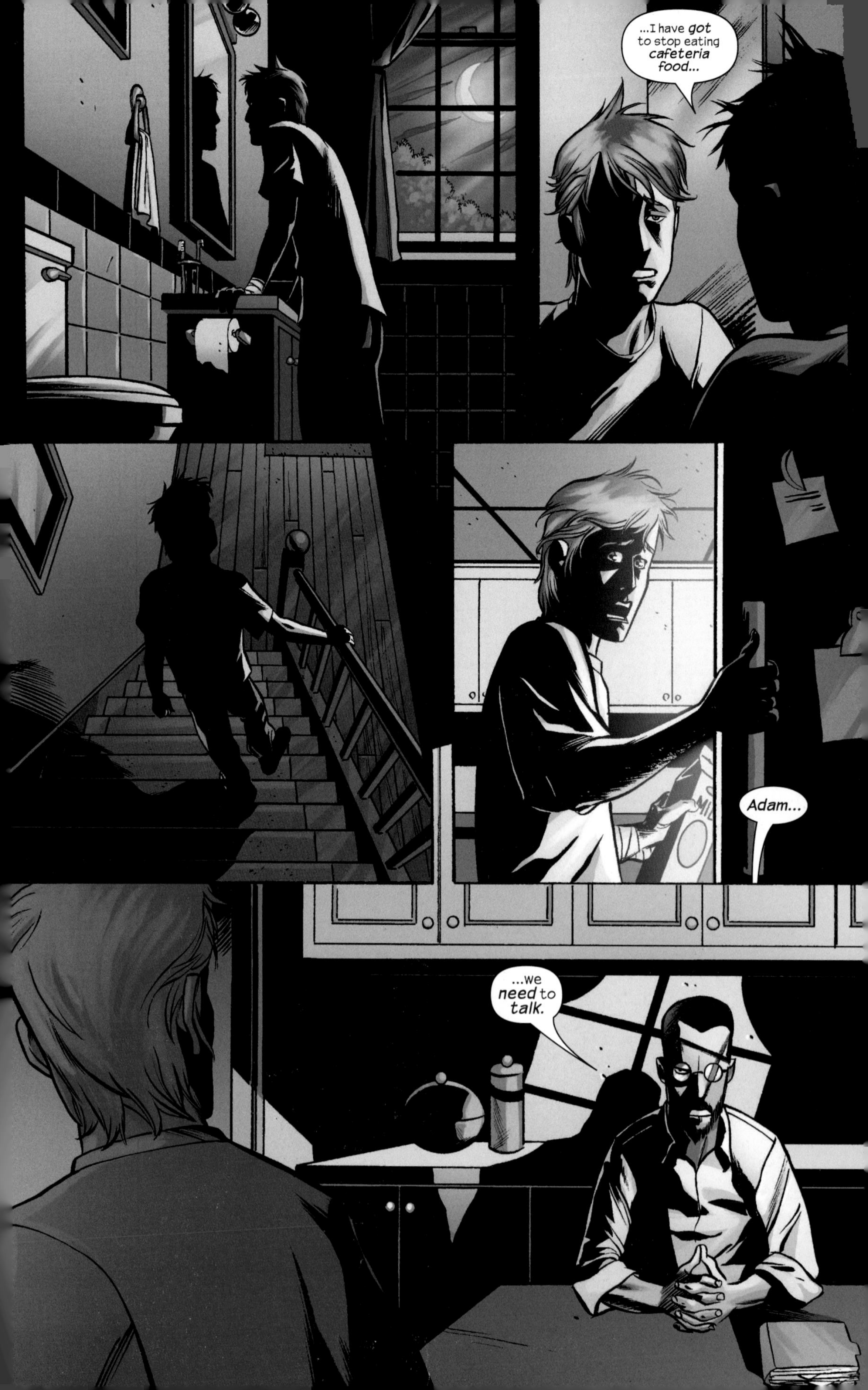
...I have got to stop eating cafeteria food...
Adam...
...we need to talk.

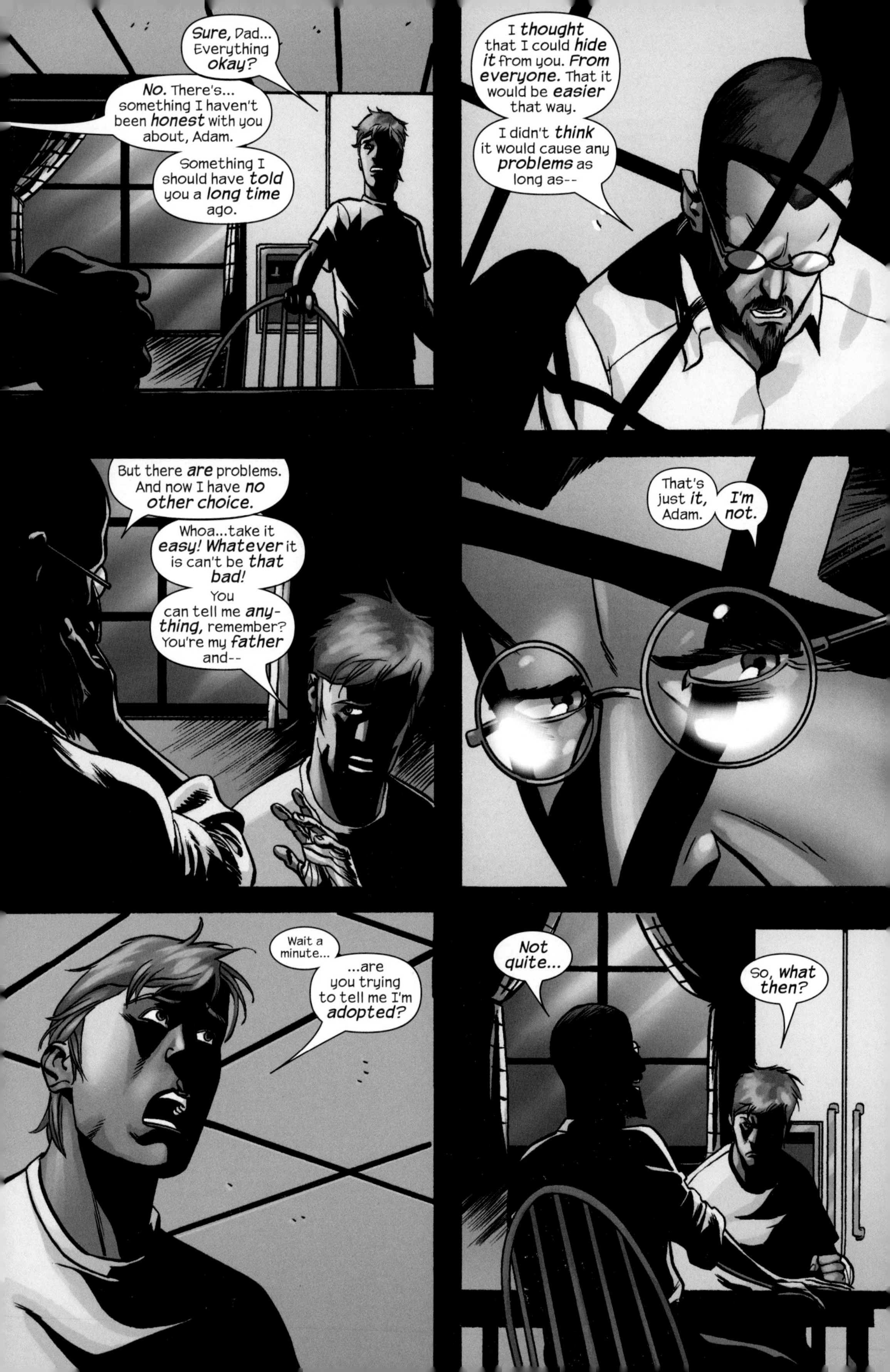
Sure, Dad... Everything okay?
No. There's... something I haven't been honest with you about, Adam.
Something I should have told you a long time ago.
I thought that I could hide it from you. From everyone. That it would be easier that way.
I didn't think it would cause any problems as long as--
But there are problems. And now I have no other choice.
Whoa...take it easy! Whatever it is can't be that bad!
You can tell me any-thing, remember? You're my father and--
That's just it, Adam.
I'm not.
Wait a minute...
...are you trying to tell me I'm adopted?
Not quite...
So, what then?

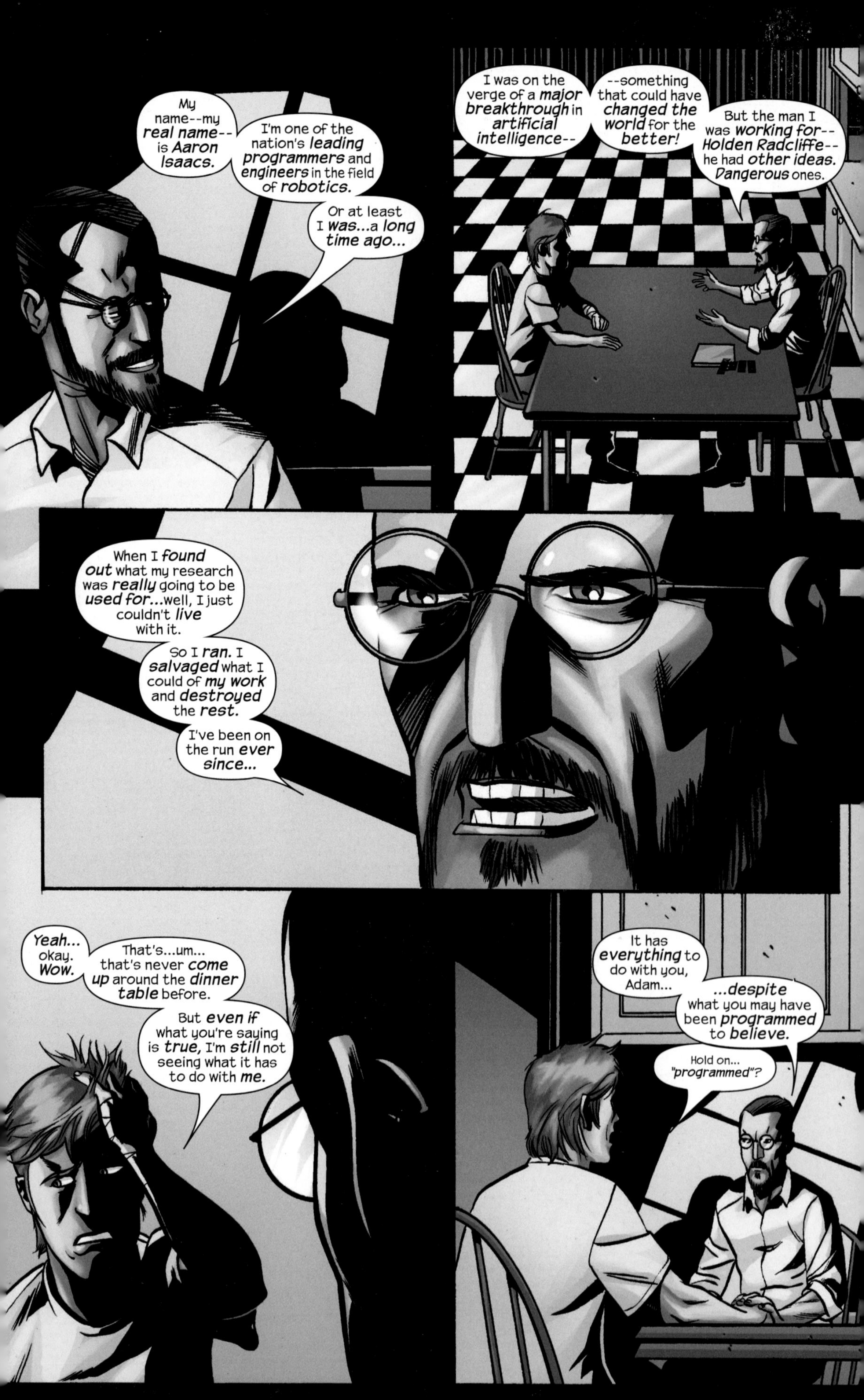
My name--my real name--is Aaron Isaacs.
I'm one of the nation's leading programmers and engineers in the field of robotics.
Or at least I was...a long time ago...
I was on the verge of a major breakthrough in artificial intelligence--
--something that could have changed the world for the better!
But the man I was working for--Holden Radcliffe--he had other ideas. Dangerous ones.
When I found out what my research was really going to be used for...well, I just couldn't live with it.
So I ran. I salvaged what I could of my work and destroyed the rest.
I've been on the run ever since...
Yeah... okay. Wow.
That's...um... that's never come up around the dinner table before.
But even if what you're saying is true, I'm still not seeing what it has to do with me.
It has everything to do with you, Adam...
...despite what you may have been programmed to believe.
Hold on... "programmed"?

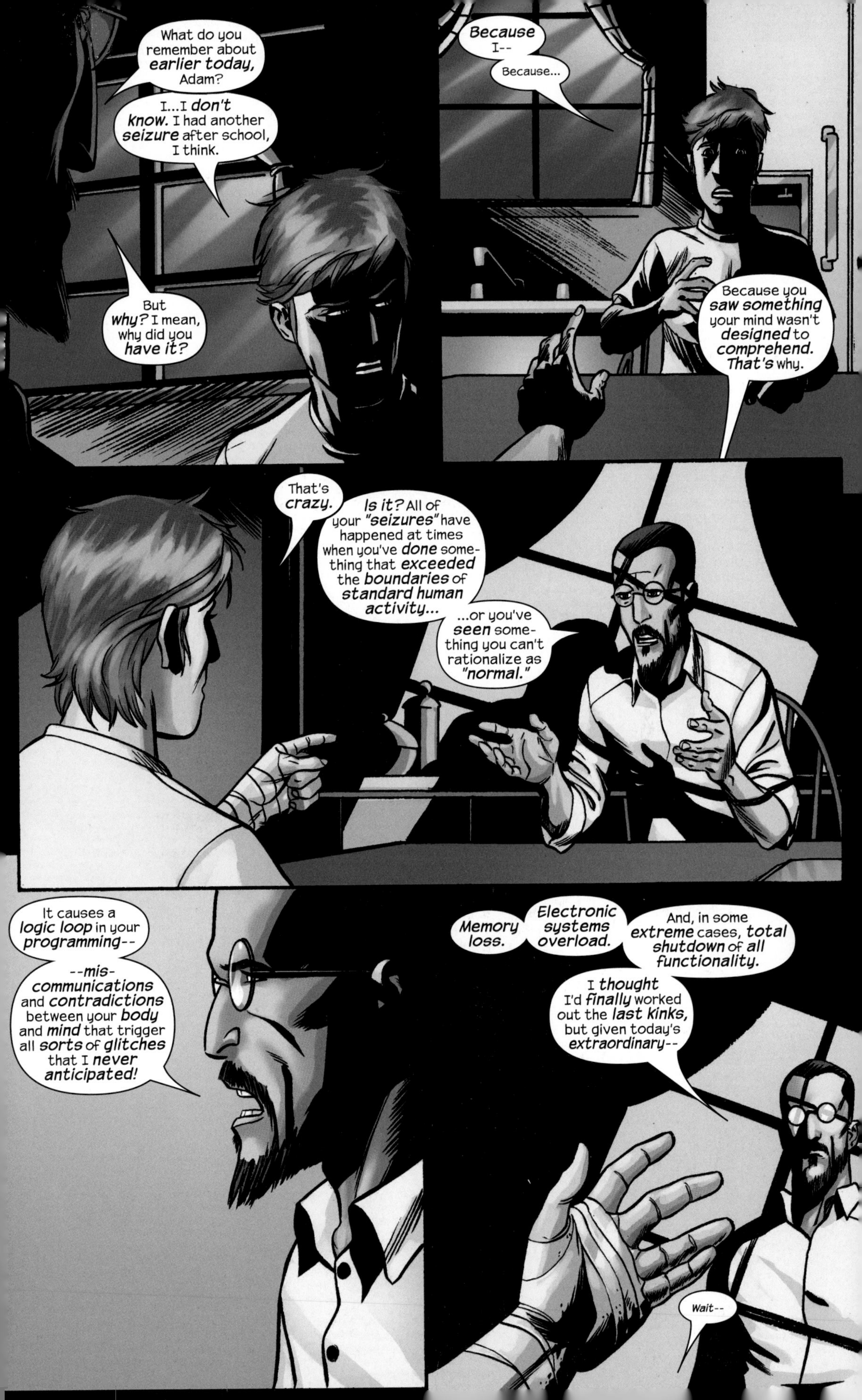
What do you remember about earlier today, Adam?
I...I don't know. I had another seizure after school, I think.
But why? I mean, why did you have it?
Because I--
Because...
Because you saw something your mind wasn't designed to comprehend. That's why.
That's crazy.
Is it? All of your "seizures" have happened at times when you've done something that exceeded the boundaries of standard human activity...
...or you've seen something you can't rationalize as "normal."
It causes a logic loop in your programming--
--mis-communications and contradictions between your body and mind that trigger all sorts of glitches that I never anticipated!
Memory loss.
Electronic systems overload.
And, in some extreme cases, total shutdown of all functionality.
I thought I'd finally worked out the last kinks, but given today's extraordinary--
Wait--

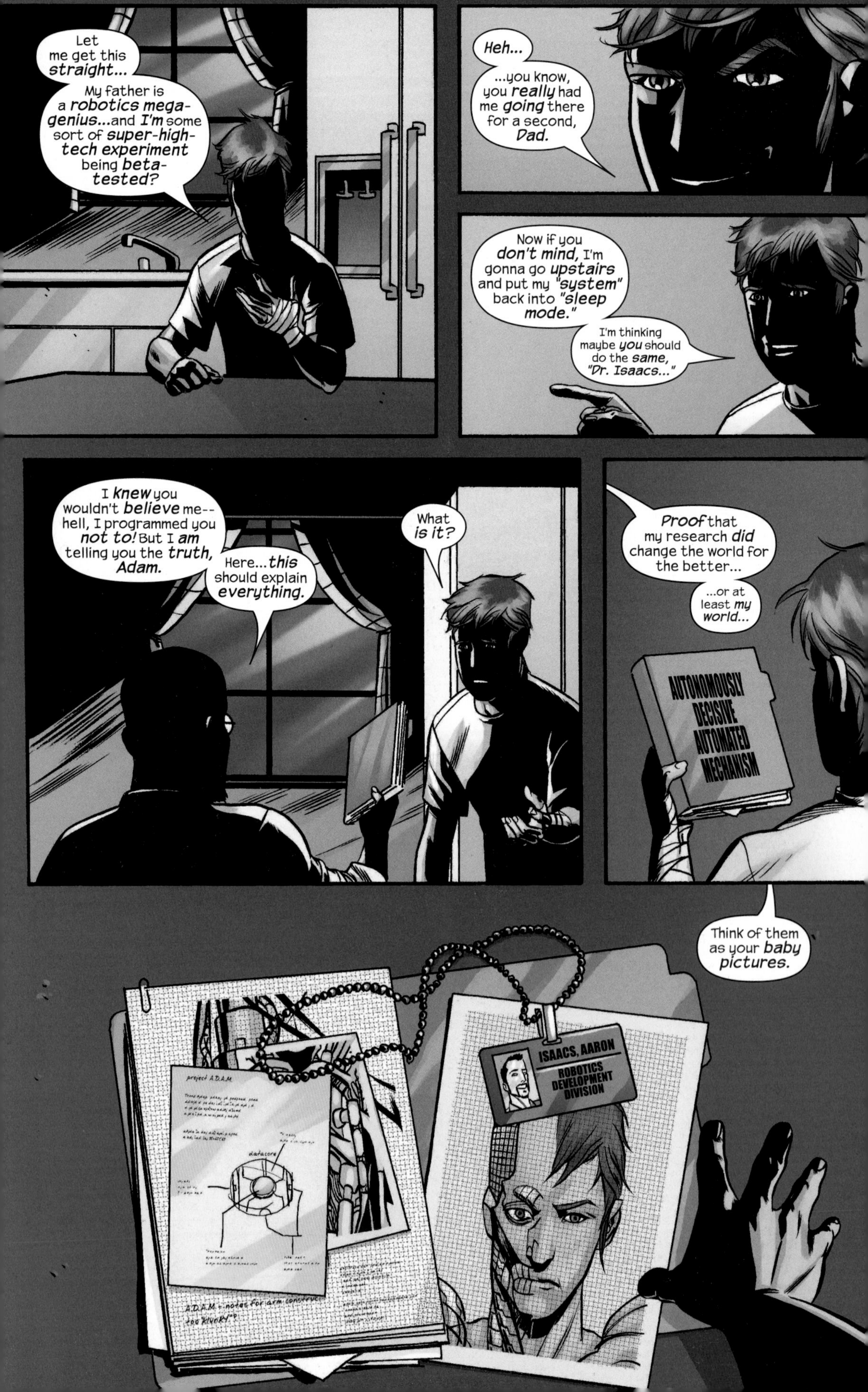

Let me get this straight... My father is a robotics mega-genius...and I'm some sort of super-high-tech experiment being beta-tested?
Heh...
...you know, you really had me going there for a second, Dad.
Now if you don't mind, I'm gonna go upstairs and put my "system" back into "sleep mode."
I'm thinking maybe you should do the same, "Dr. Isaacs..."
I knew you wouldn't believe me--hell, I programmed you not to! But I am telling you the truth, Adam.
Here...this should explain everything.
What is it?
Proof that my research did change the world for the better...
...or at least my world...
AUTONOMOUSLY DECISIVE AUTOMATED MECHANISM
Think of them as your baby pictures.
project A.D.A.M.
datacore
ISAACS, AARON
ROBOTICS DEVELOPMENT DIVISION

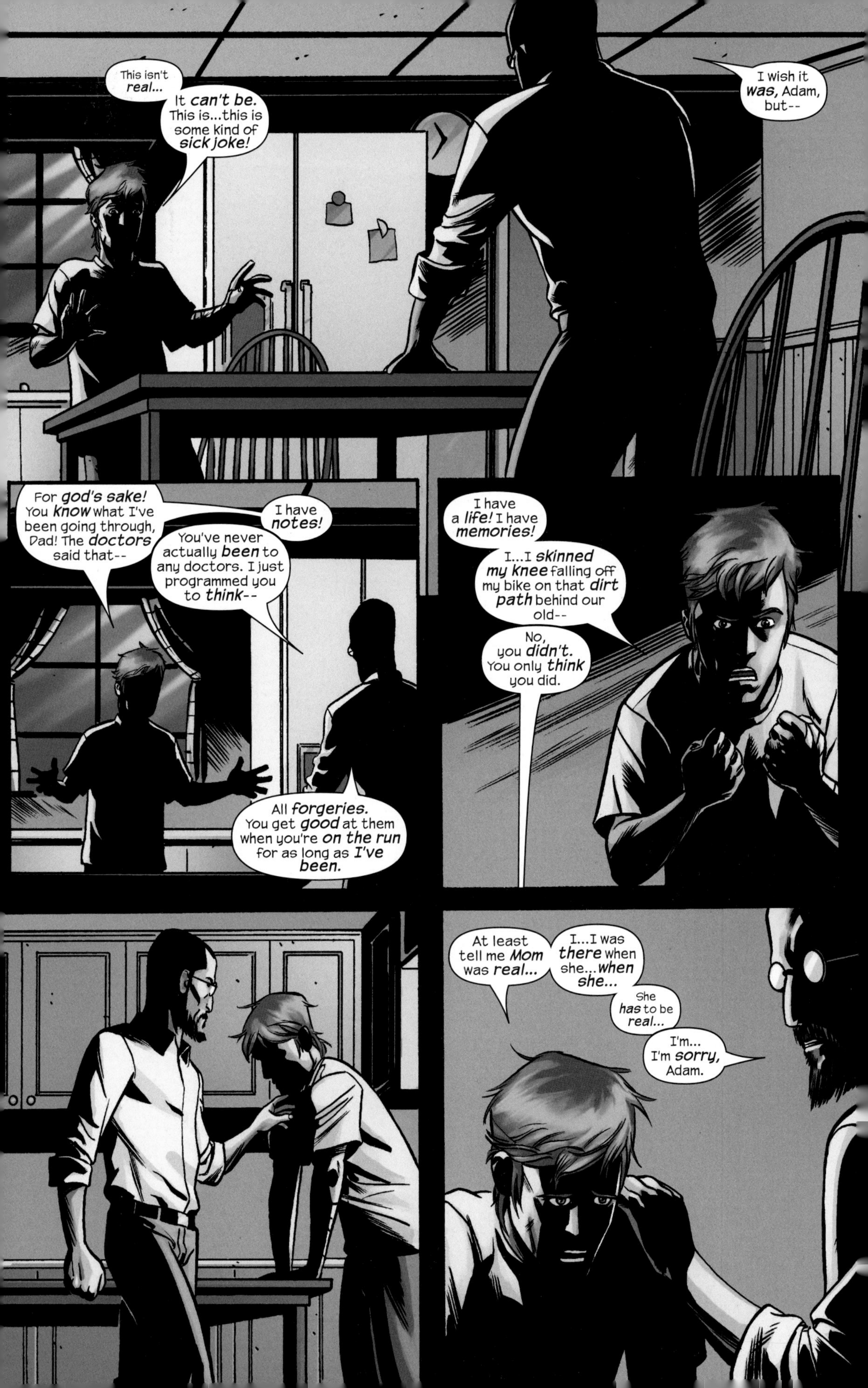
This isn't real...
It can't be. This is...this is some kind of sick joke!
I wish it was, Adam, but--
For god's sake! You know what I've been going through, Dad! The doctors said that--
I have notes!
You've never actually been to any doctors. I just programmed you to think--
All forgeries. You get good at them when you're on the run for as long as I've been.
I have a life! I have memories!
I...I skinned my knee falling off my bike on that dirt path behind our old--
No, you didn't. You only think you did.
At least tell me Mom was real...
I...I was there when she...when she...
She has to be real...
I'm... I'm sorry, Adam.

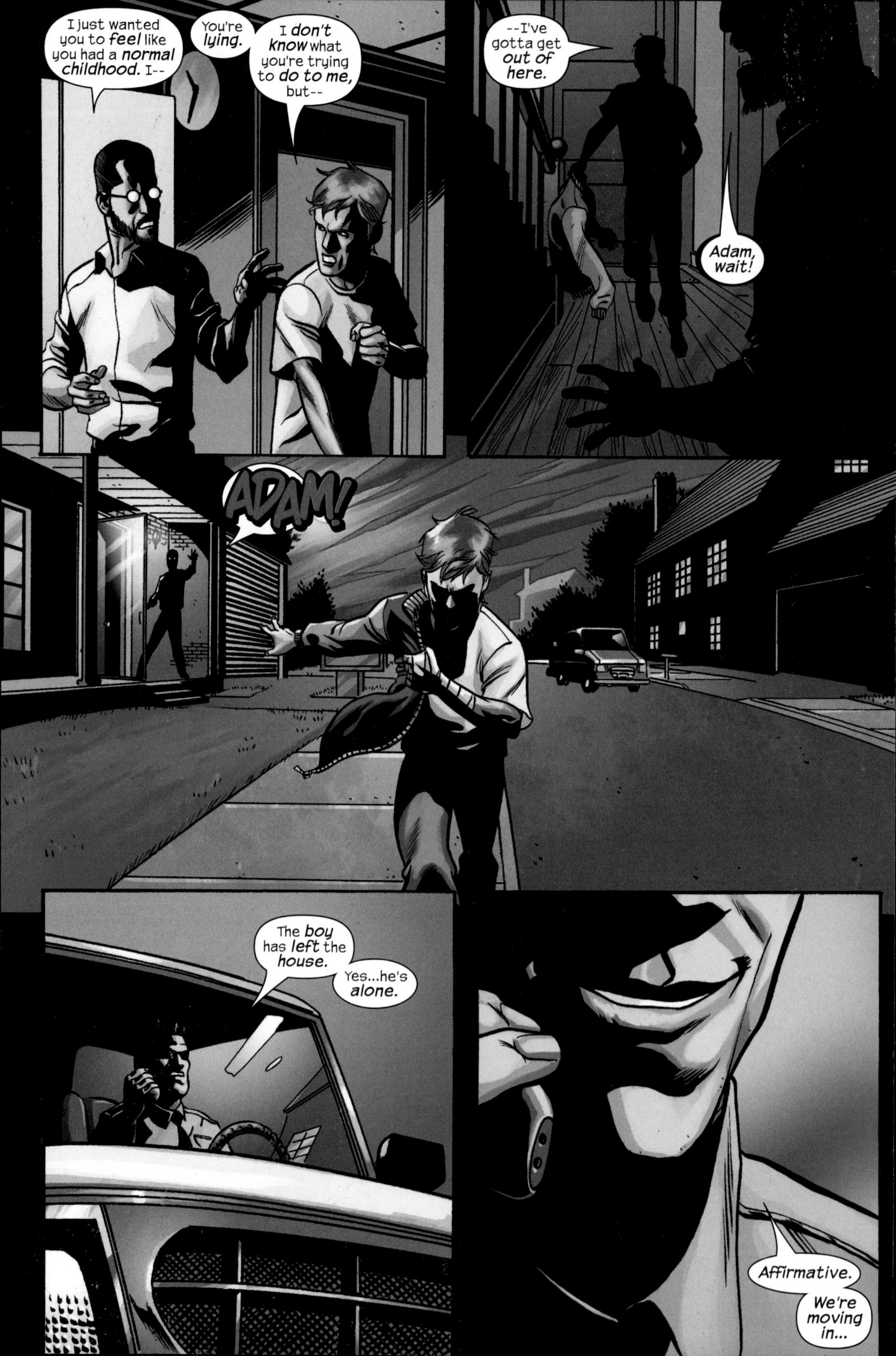
I just wanted you to feel like you had a normal childhood. I--
You're lying.
I don't know what you're trying to do to me, but--
--I've gotta get out of here.
Adam, wait!
ADAM!
The boy has left the house.
Yes...he's alone.
Affirmative.
We're moving in...

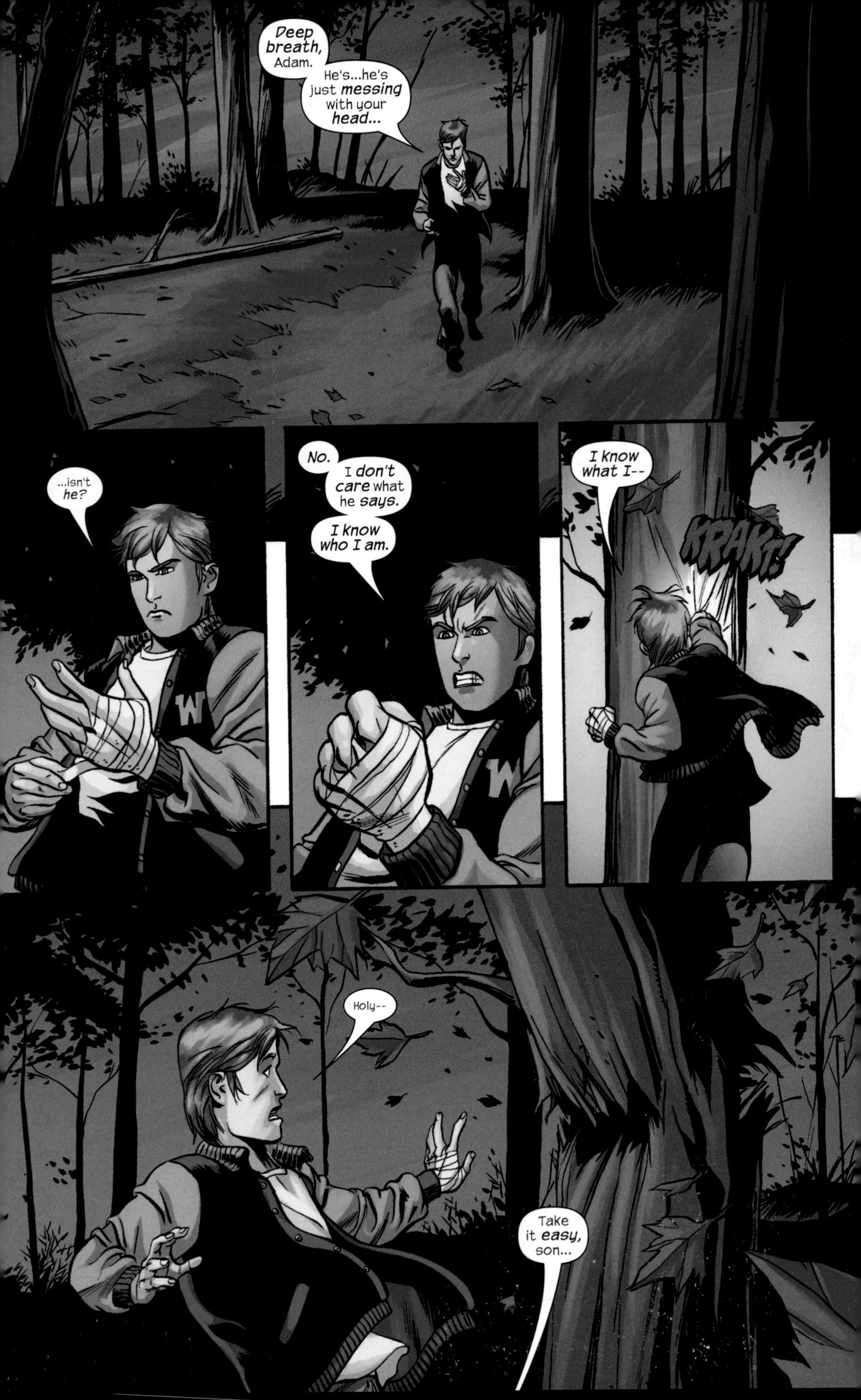
Deep breath, Adam.
He's...he's just messing with your head...
...isn't he?
No.
I don't care what he says.
I know who I am.
I know what I--
KRAKT!
Holy--
Take it easy, son...

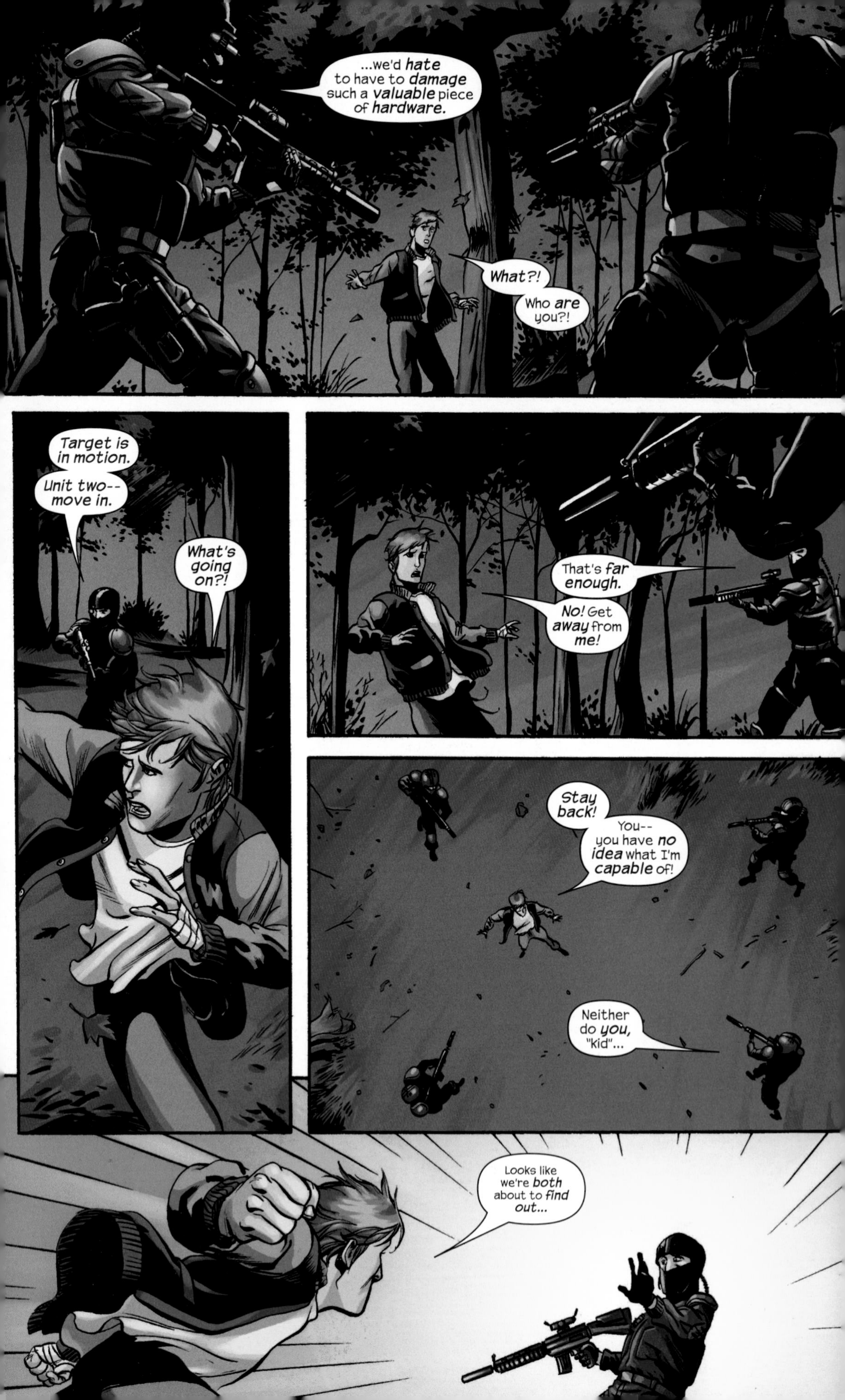
...we'd hate to have to damage such a valuable piece of hardware.
What?!
Who are you?!
Target is in motion.
Unit two-- move in.
What's going on?!
That's far enough.
No! Get away from me!
Stay back!
You-- you have no idea what I'm capable of!
Neither do you, "kid"...
Looks like we're both about to find out...

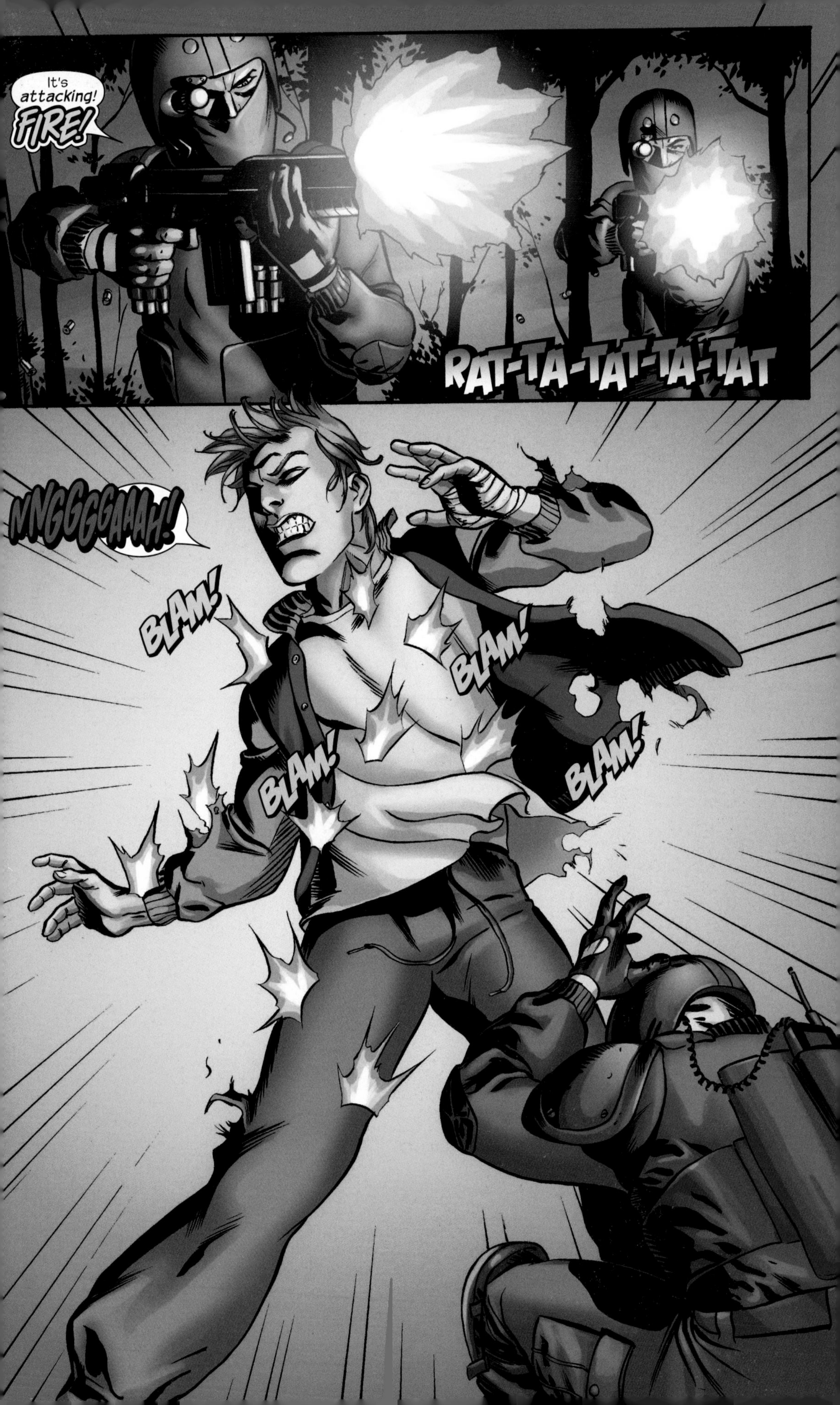
It's attacking! FIRE!
RAT-TA-TAT-TA-TAT
NNGGGGAAAAH!
BLAM!
BLAM!
BLAM!
BLAM!

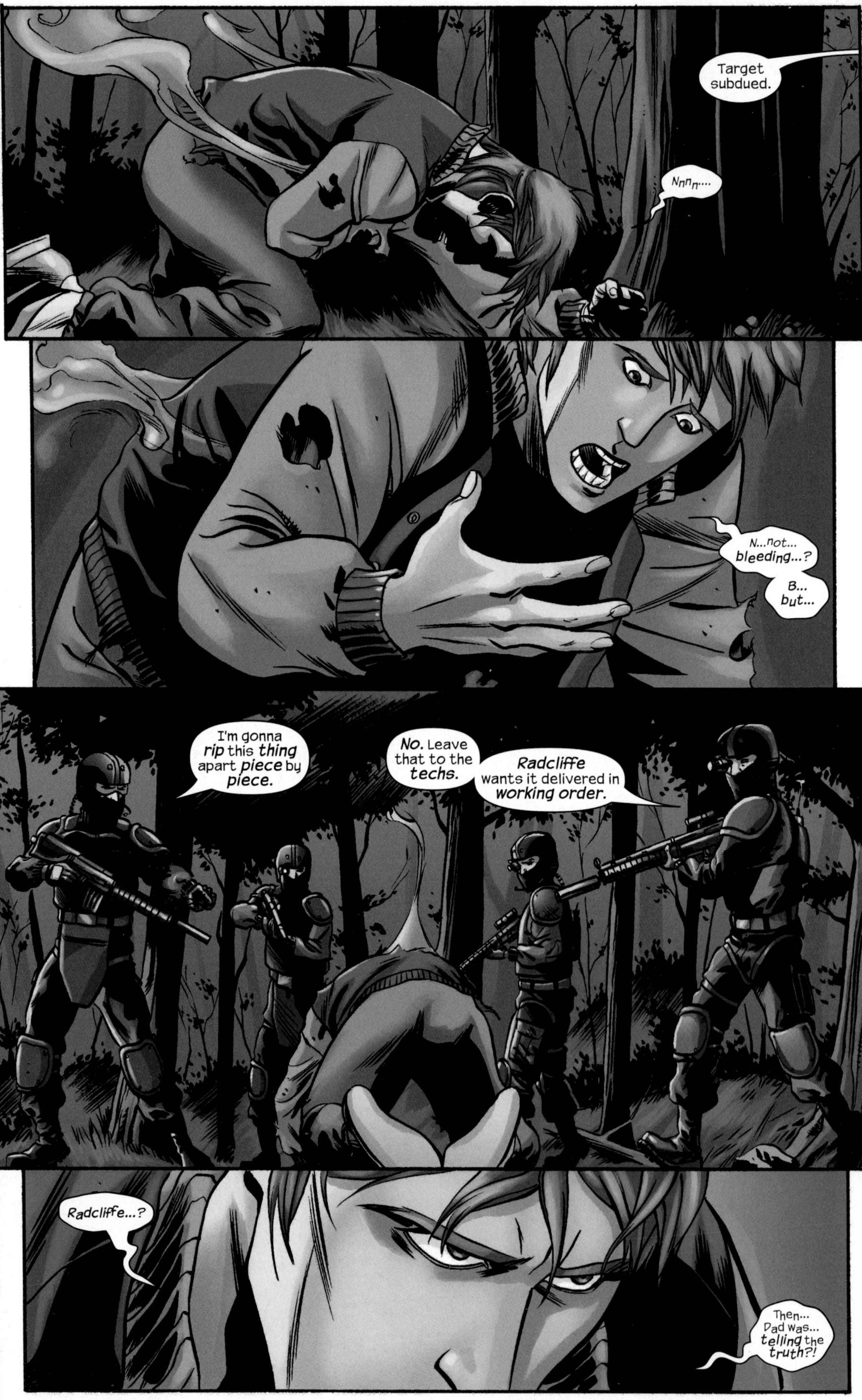
Target subdued.
Nnnn....
N...not... bleeding...?
B... but...
I'm gonna rip this thing apart piece by piece.
No. Leave that to the techs.
Radcliffe wants it delivered in working order.
Radcliffe...?
Then... Dad was... telling the truth?!

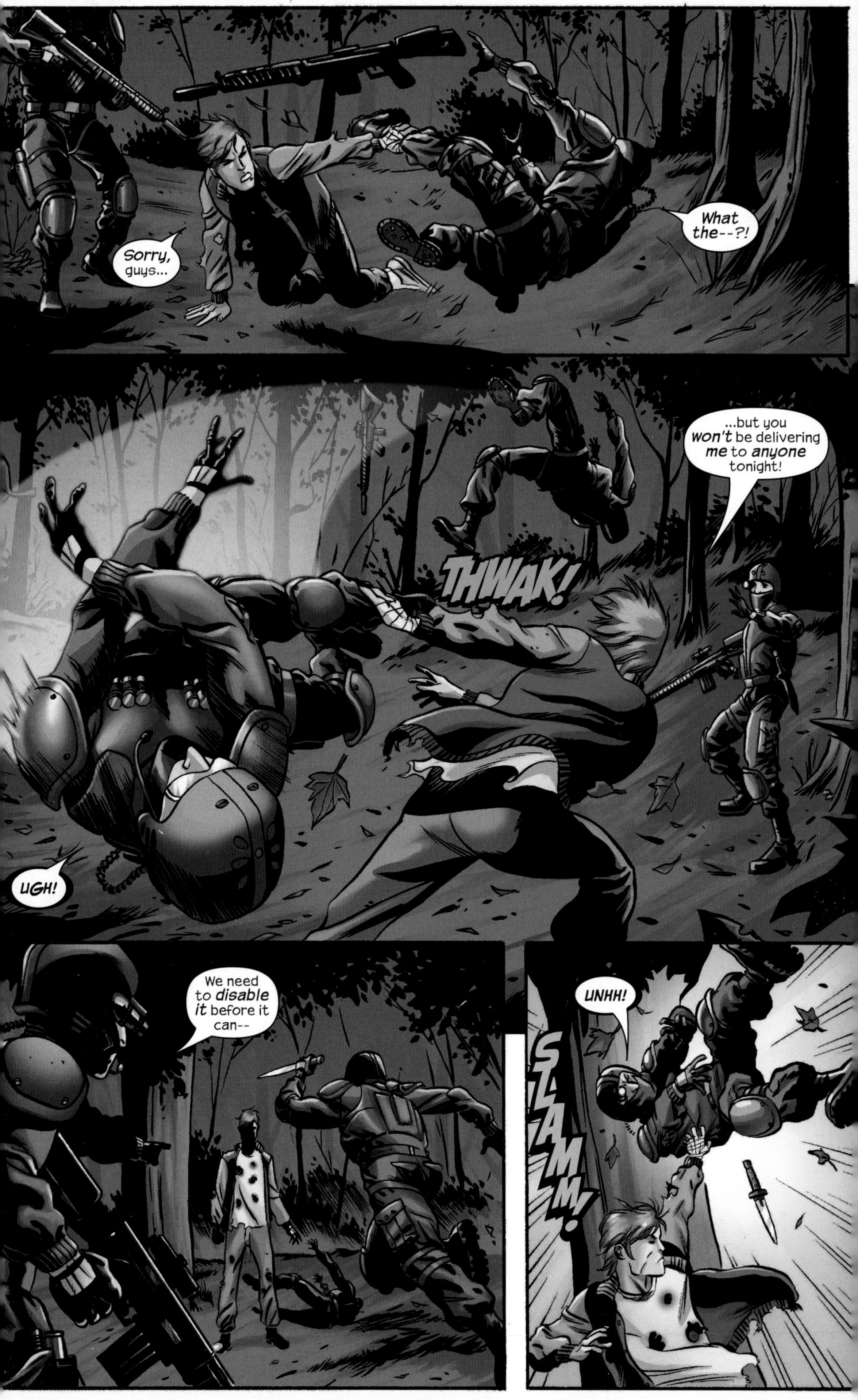
Sorry, guys...
What the--?!
...but you won't be delivering me to anyone tonight!
THWAK!
UGH!
We need to disable it before it can--
UNHH!
SLAMM!

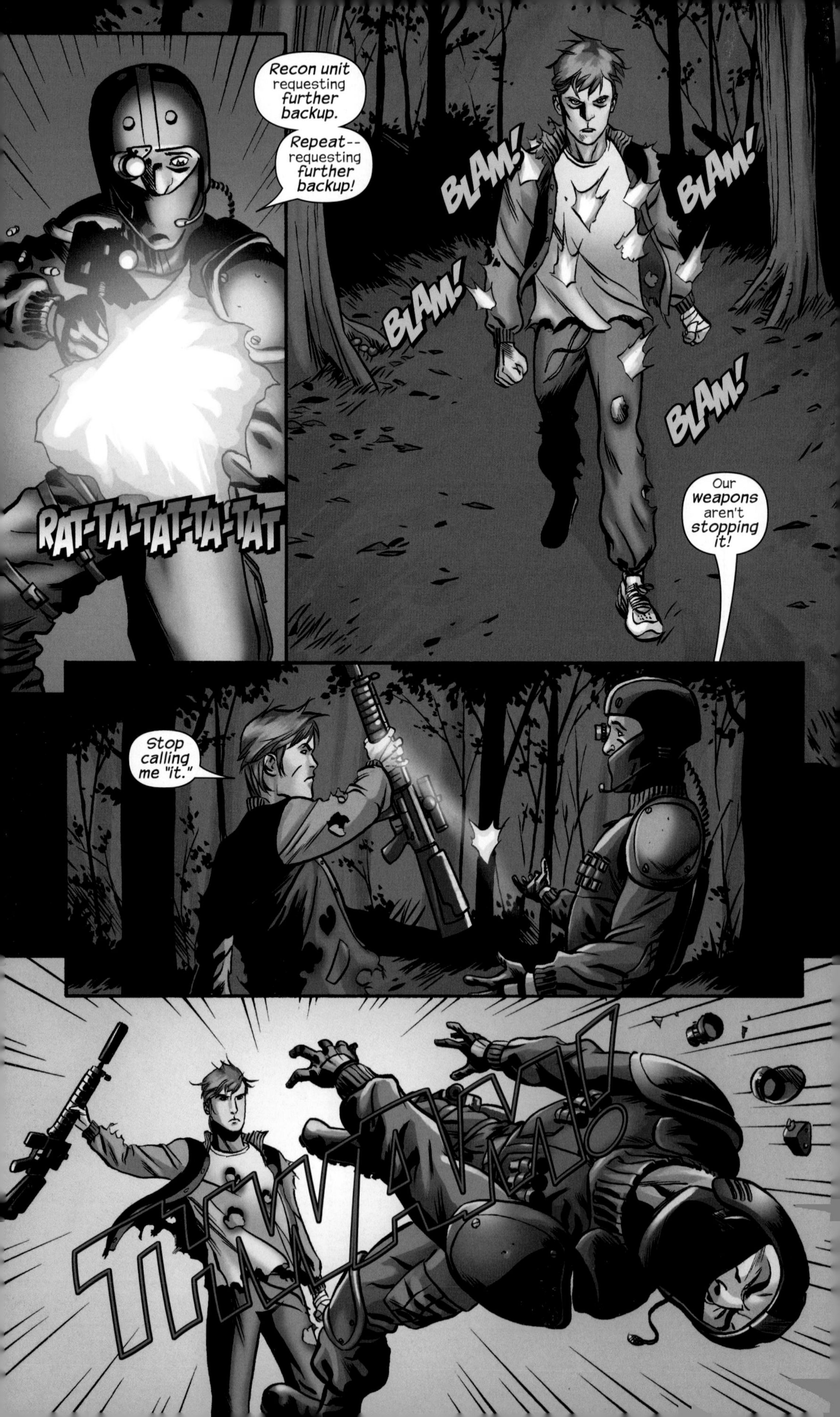
Recon unit requesting further backup.
Repeat-- requesting further backup!
RAT-TA-TAT-TA-TAT
BLAM!
BLAM!
BLAM!
BLAM!
Our weapons aren't stopping it!
Stop calling me "it."
THWAAM!

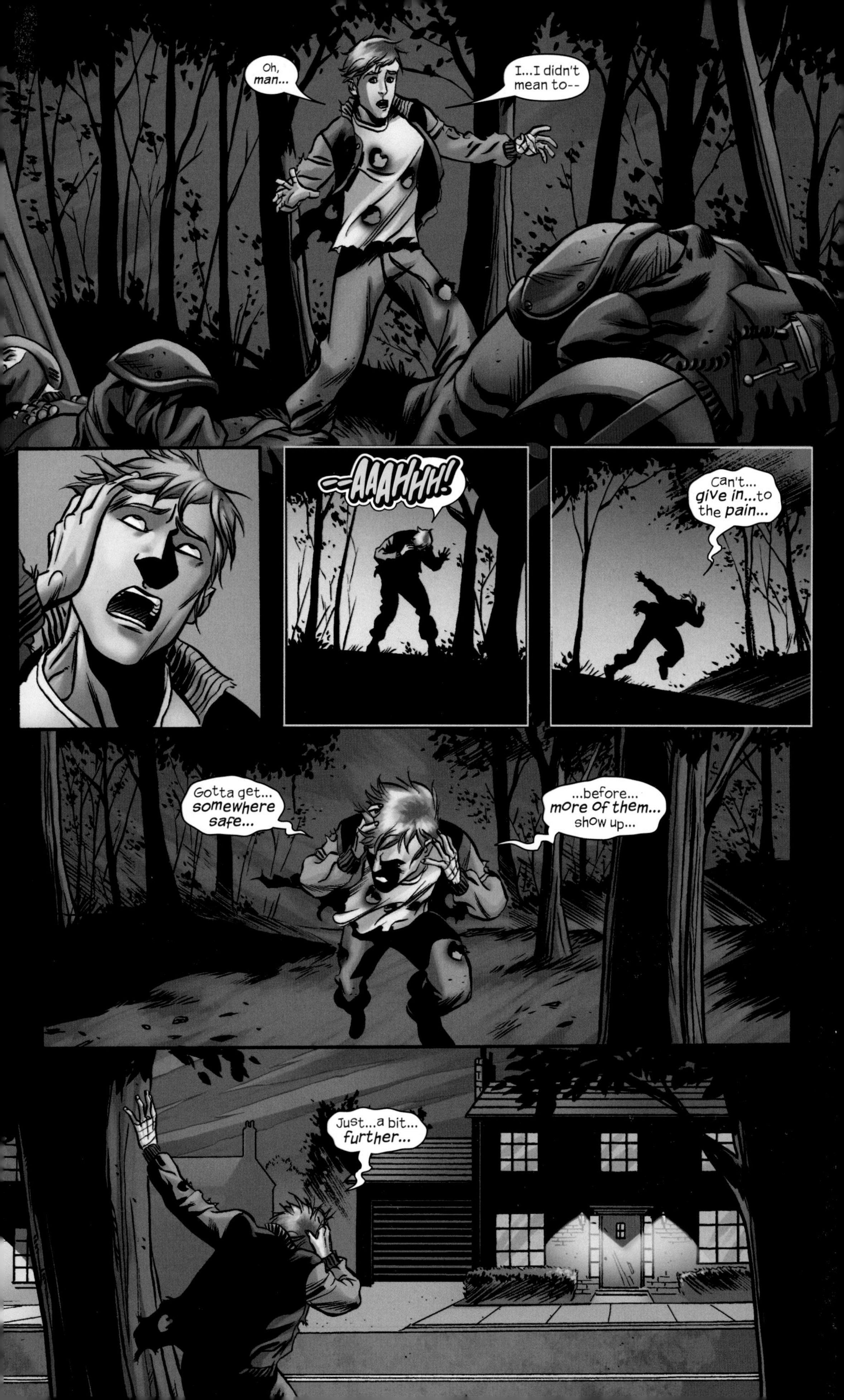
Oh, man...
I...I didn't mean to--
-AAAHHH!
Can't... give in...to the pain...
Gotta get... somewhere safe...
...before... more of them... show up...
Just...a bit... further...

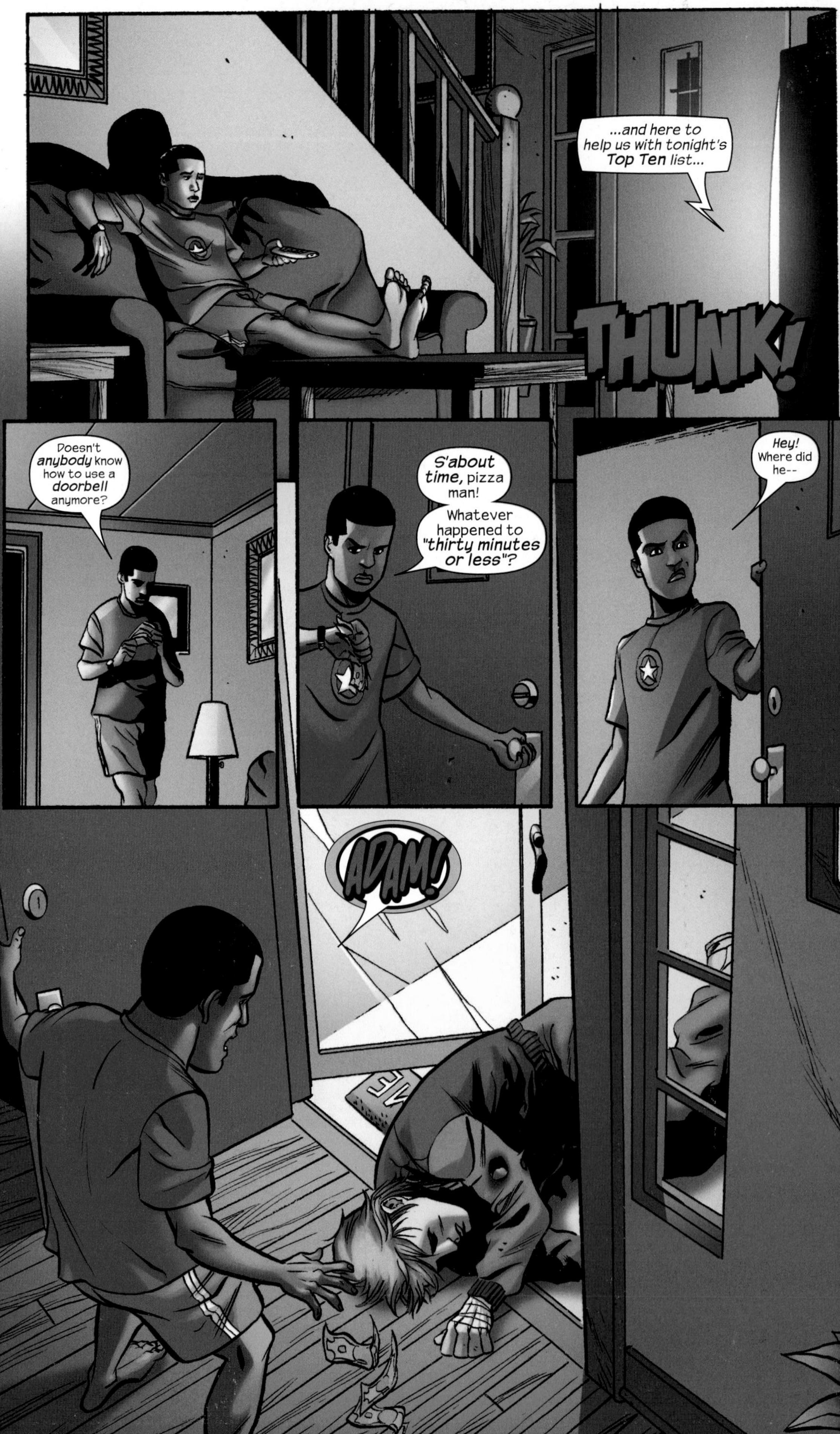

...and here to help us with tonight's *Top Ten* list...
THUNK!
Doesn't *anybody* know how to use a *doorbell* anymore?
S'about time, pizza man!
Whatever happened to *"thirty minutes or less"*?
Hey! Where did he--
ADAM!

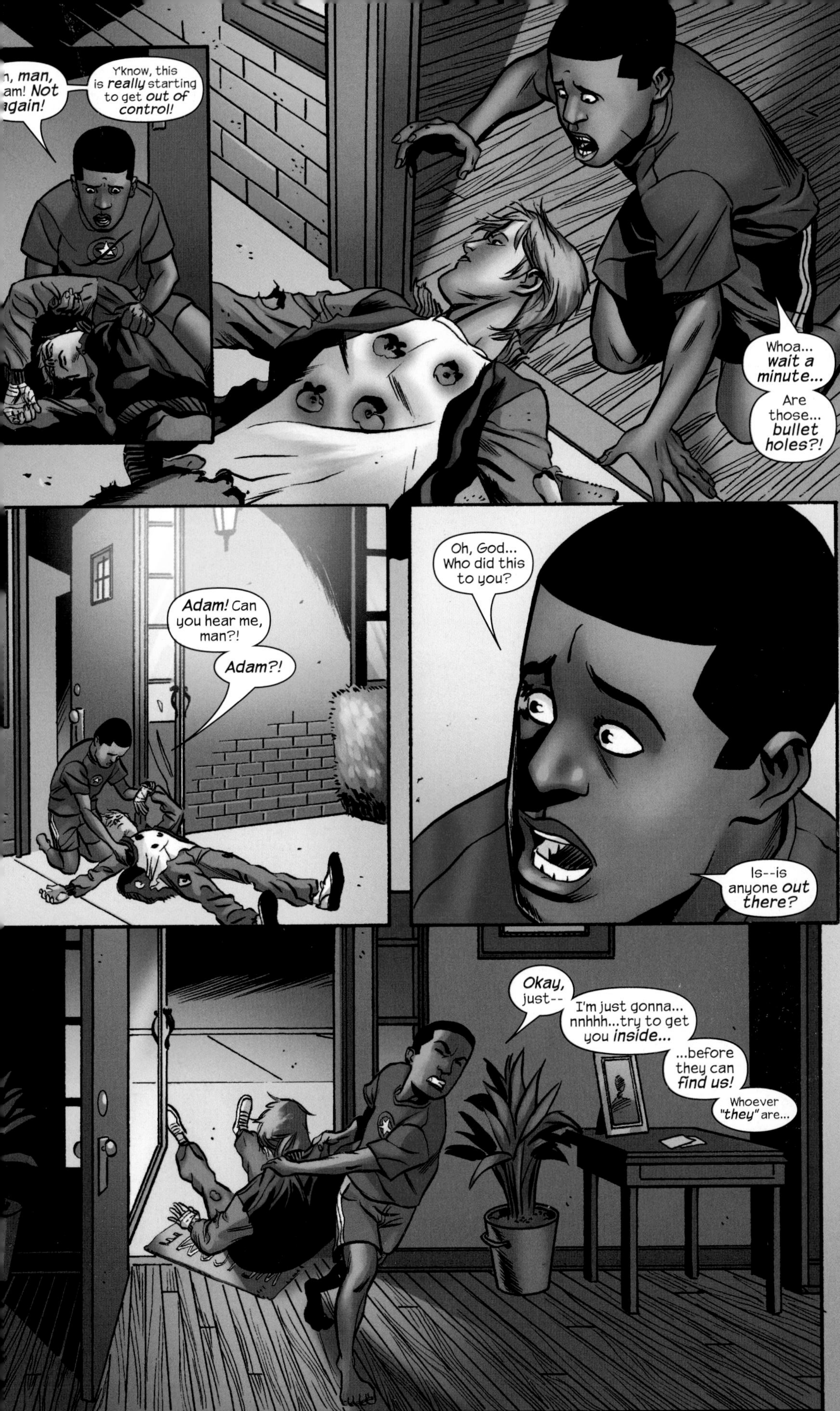

...n, man, ...am! Not ...again!
Y'know, this is really starting to get out of control!
Whoa... wait a minute...
Are those... bullet holes?!
Adam! Can you hear me, man?!
Adam?!
Oh, God... Who did this to you?
Is--is anyone out there?
Okay, just--
I'm just gonna... nnhhh...try to get you inside...
...before they can find us!
Whoever "they" are...

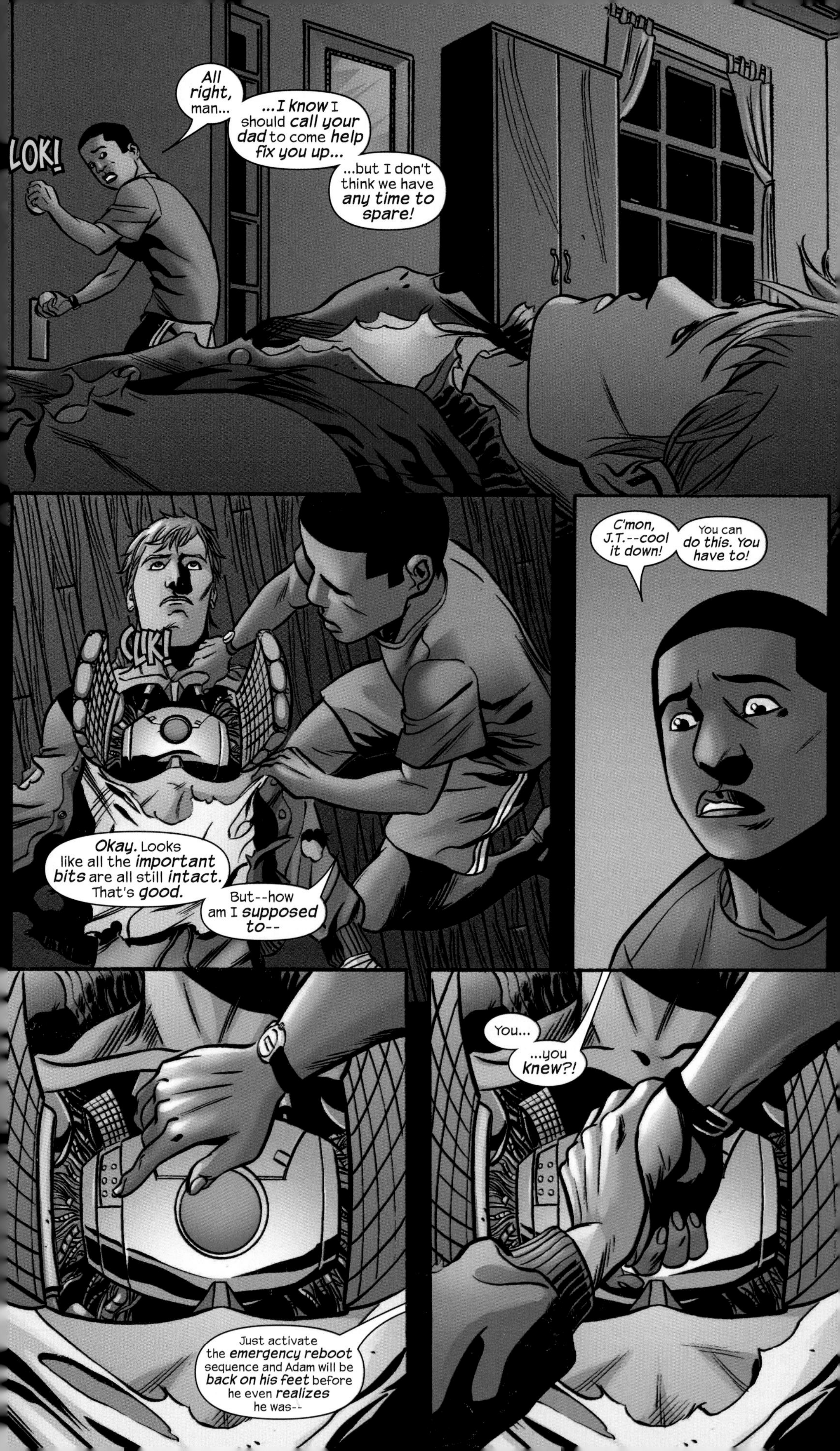
LOK!
All right, man...
...I know I should call your dad to come help fix you up...
...but I don't think we have any time to spare!
CLIK!
Okay. Looks like all the important bits are all still intact. That's good.
But--how am I supposed to--
C'mon, J.T.--cool it down!
You can do this. You have to!
Just activate the emergency reboot sequence and Adam will be back on his feet before he even realizes he was--
You...
...you knew?!

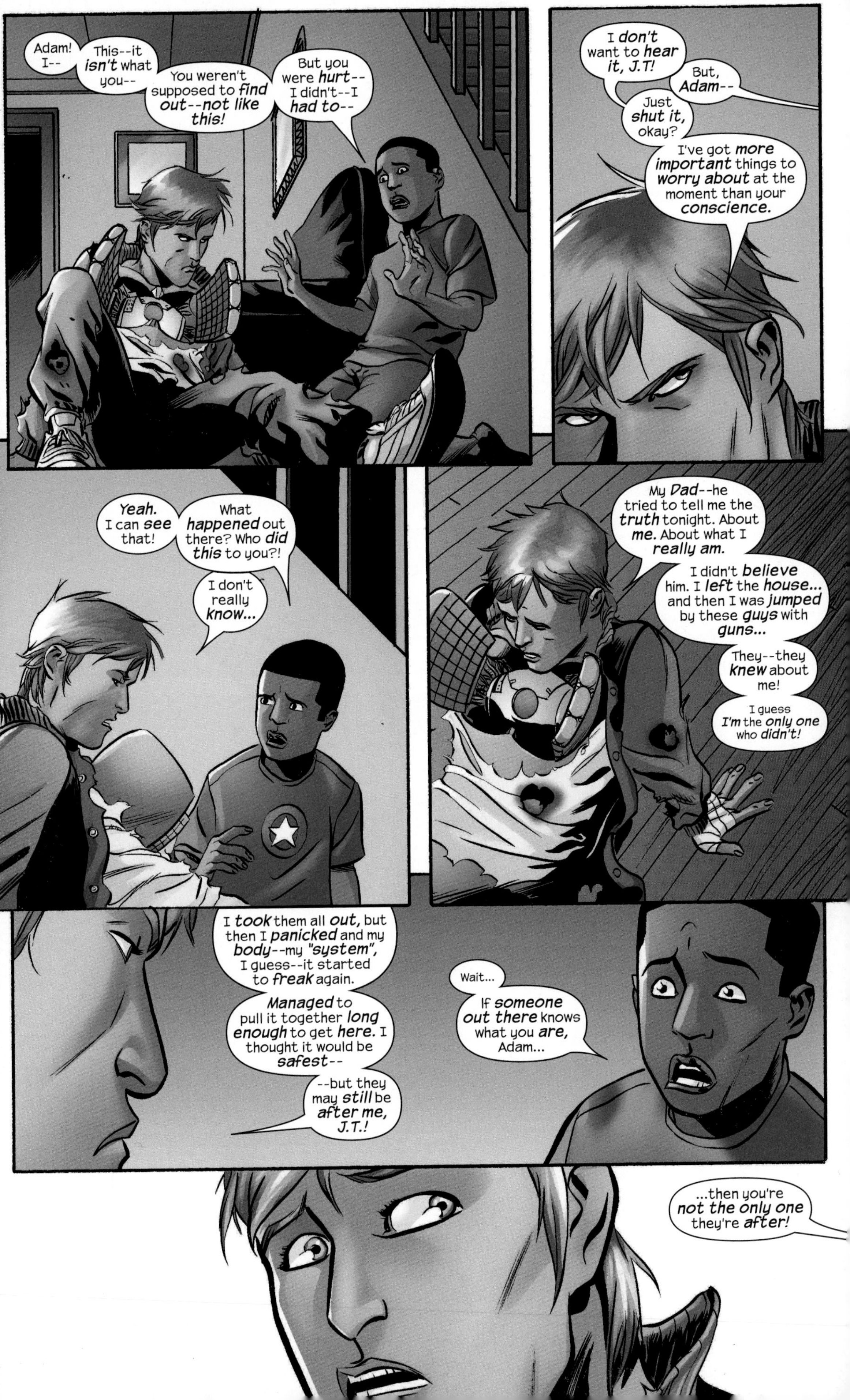
Adam! I--
This--it isn't what you--
You weren't supposed to find out--not like this!
But you were hurt--I didn't--I had to--
I don't want to hear it, J.T!
But, Adam--
Just shut it, okay?
I've got more important things to worry about at the moment than your conscience.
Yeah. I can see that!
What happened out there? Who did this to you?!
I don't really know...
My Dad--he tried to tell me the truth tonight. About me. About what I really am.
I didn't believe him. I left the house... and then I was jumped by these guys with guns...
They--they knew about me!
I guess I'm the only one who didn't!
I took them all out, but then I panicked and my body--my "system", I guess--it started to freak again.
Managed to pull it together long enough to get here. I thought it would be safest--
--but they may still be after me, J.T.!
Wait...
If someone out there knows what you are, Adam...
...then you're not the only one they're after!

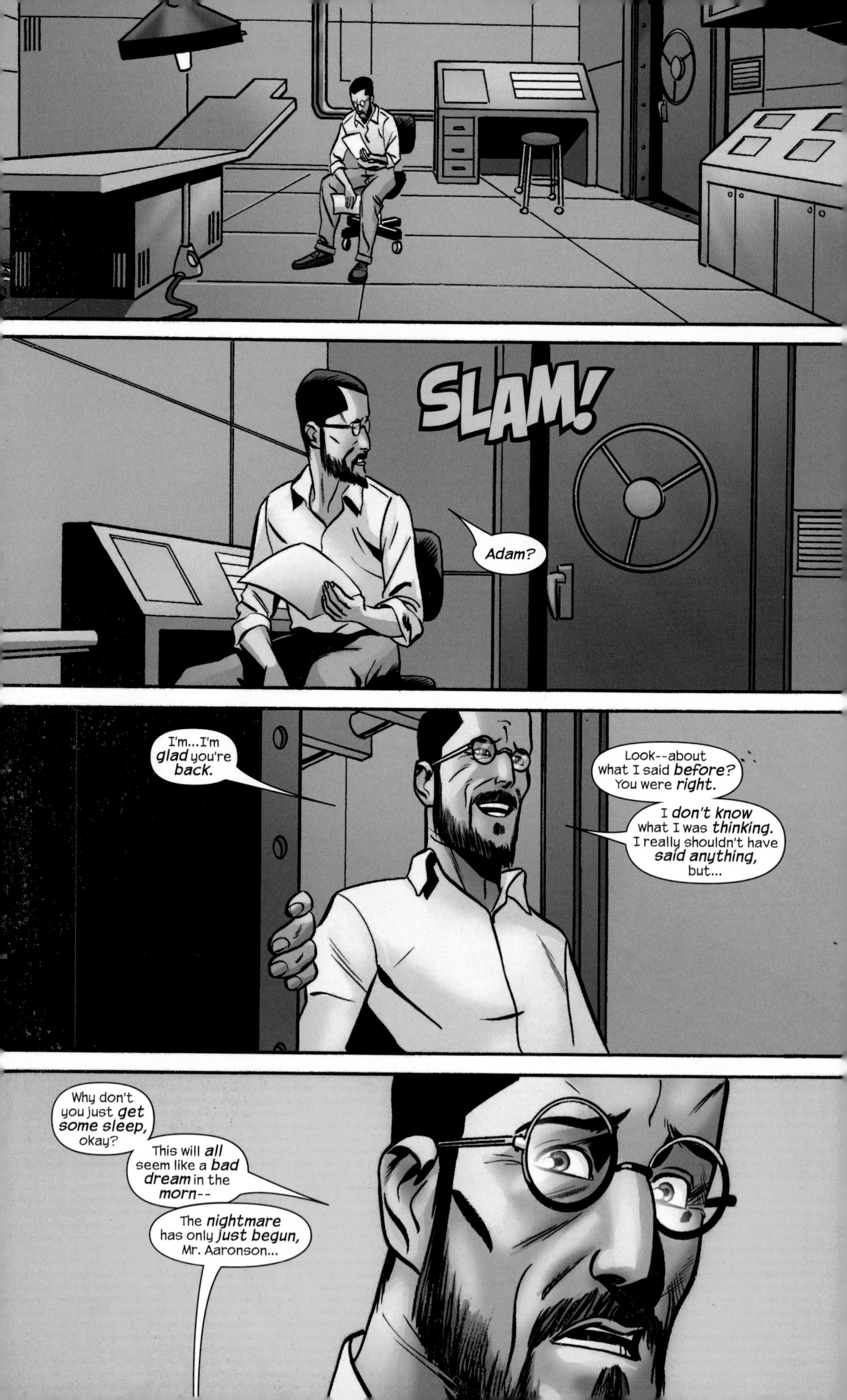
SLAM!
Adam?
I'm...I'm glad you're back.
Look--about what I said before? You were right.
I don't know what I was thinking. I really shouldn't have said anything, but...
Why don't you just get some sleep, okay?
This will all seem like a bad dream in the morn--
The nightmare has only just begun, Mr. Aaronson...

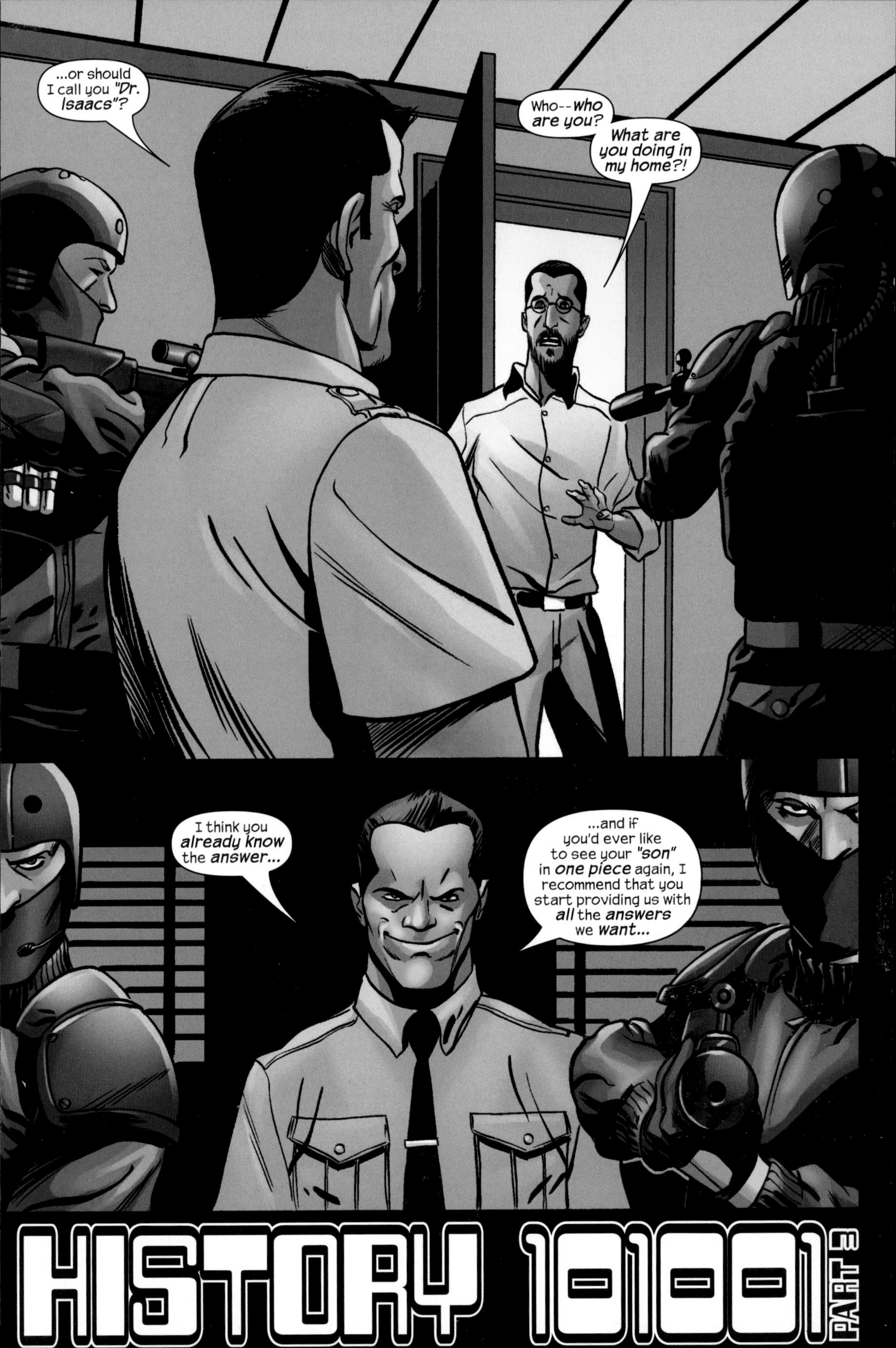
...or should I call you "Dr. Isaacs"?
Who--who are you?
What are you doing in my home?!
I think you already know the answer...
...and if you'd ever like to see your "son" in one piece again, I recommend that you start providing us with all the answers we want...
HISTORY 101001 PART 3

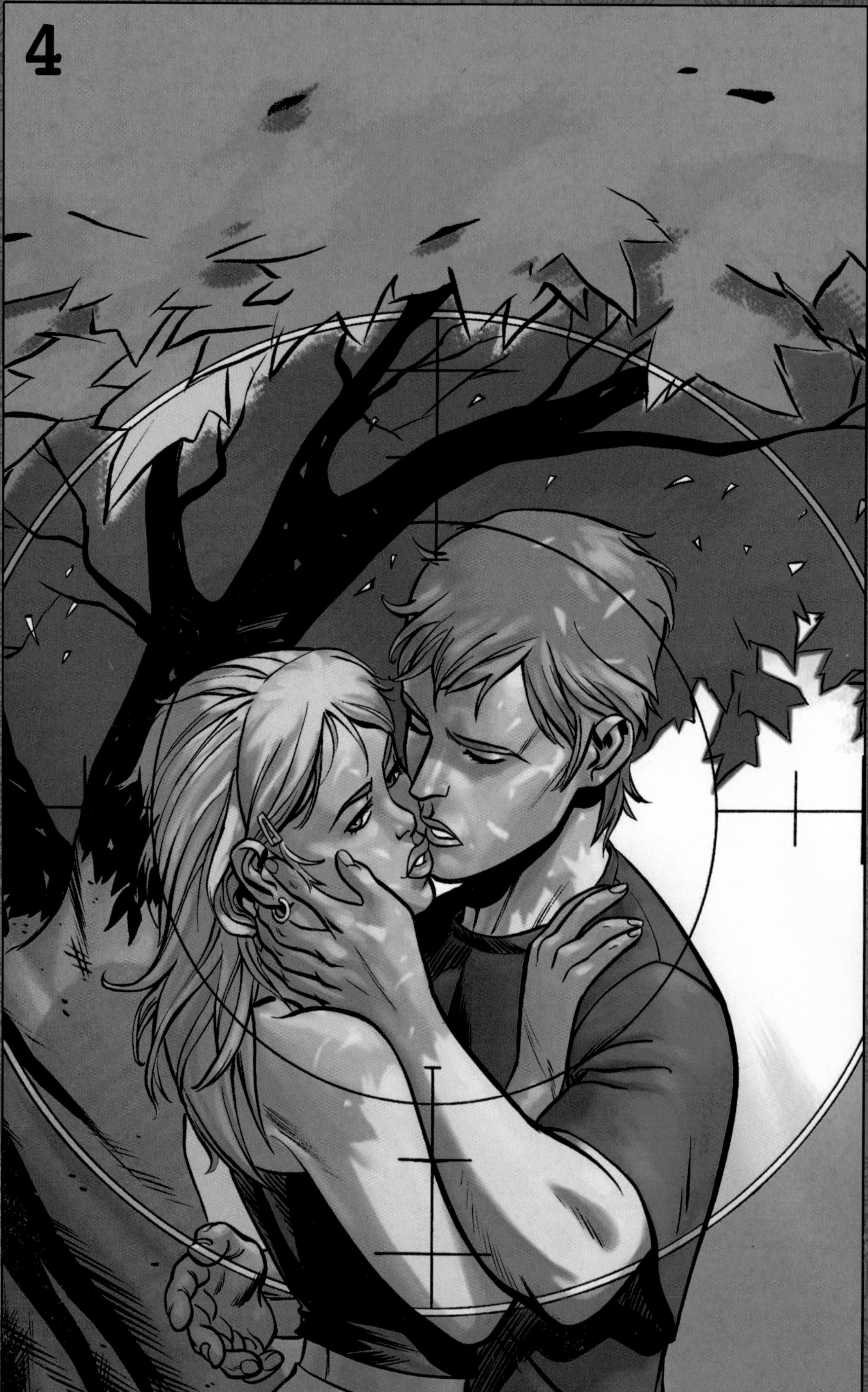
4

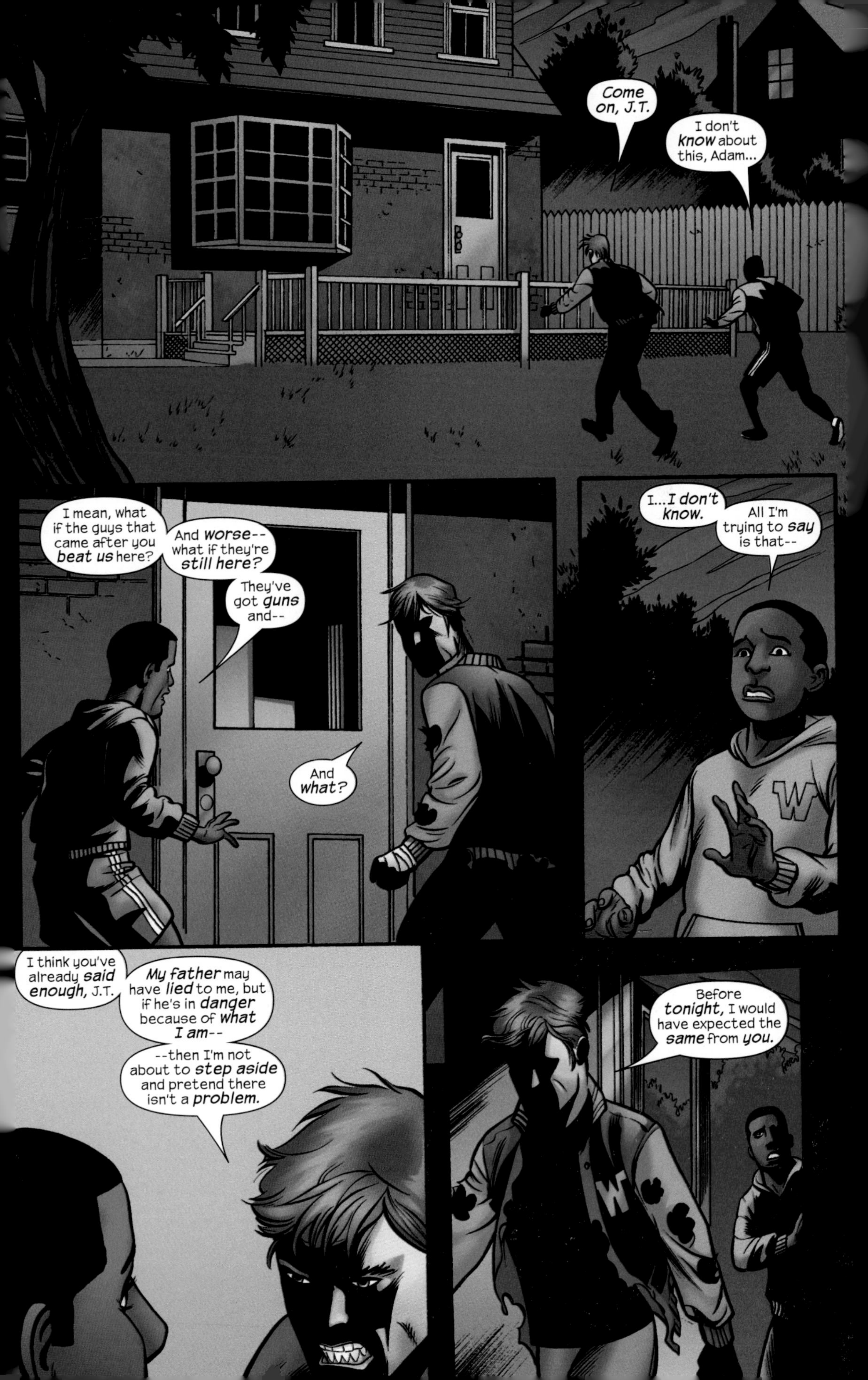
Come on, J.T.
I don't know about this, Adam...
I mean, what if the guys that came after you beat us here?
And worse--what if they're still here?
They've got guns and--
And what?
I...I don't know.
All I'm trying to say is that--
I think you've already said enough, J.T.
My father may have lied to me, but if he's in danger because of what I am--
--then I'm not about to step aside and pretend there isn't a problem.
Before tonight, I would have expected the same from you.

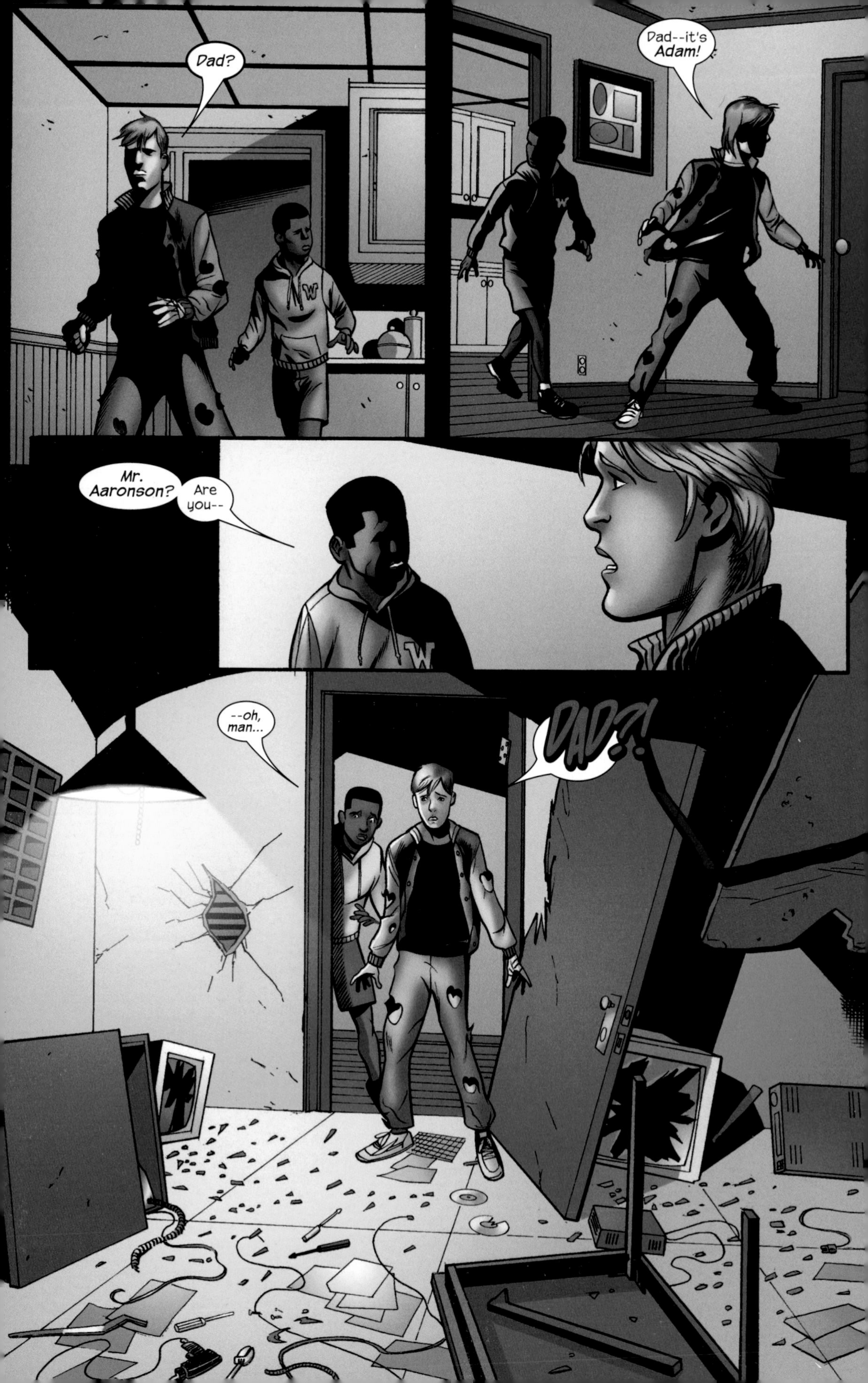

Dad?
Dad--it's Adam!
Mr. Aaronson?
Are you--
--oh, man...
DAD?!

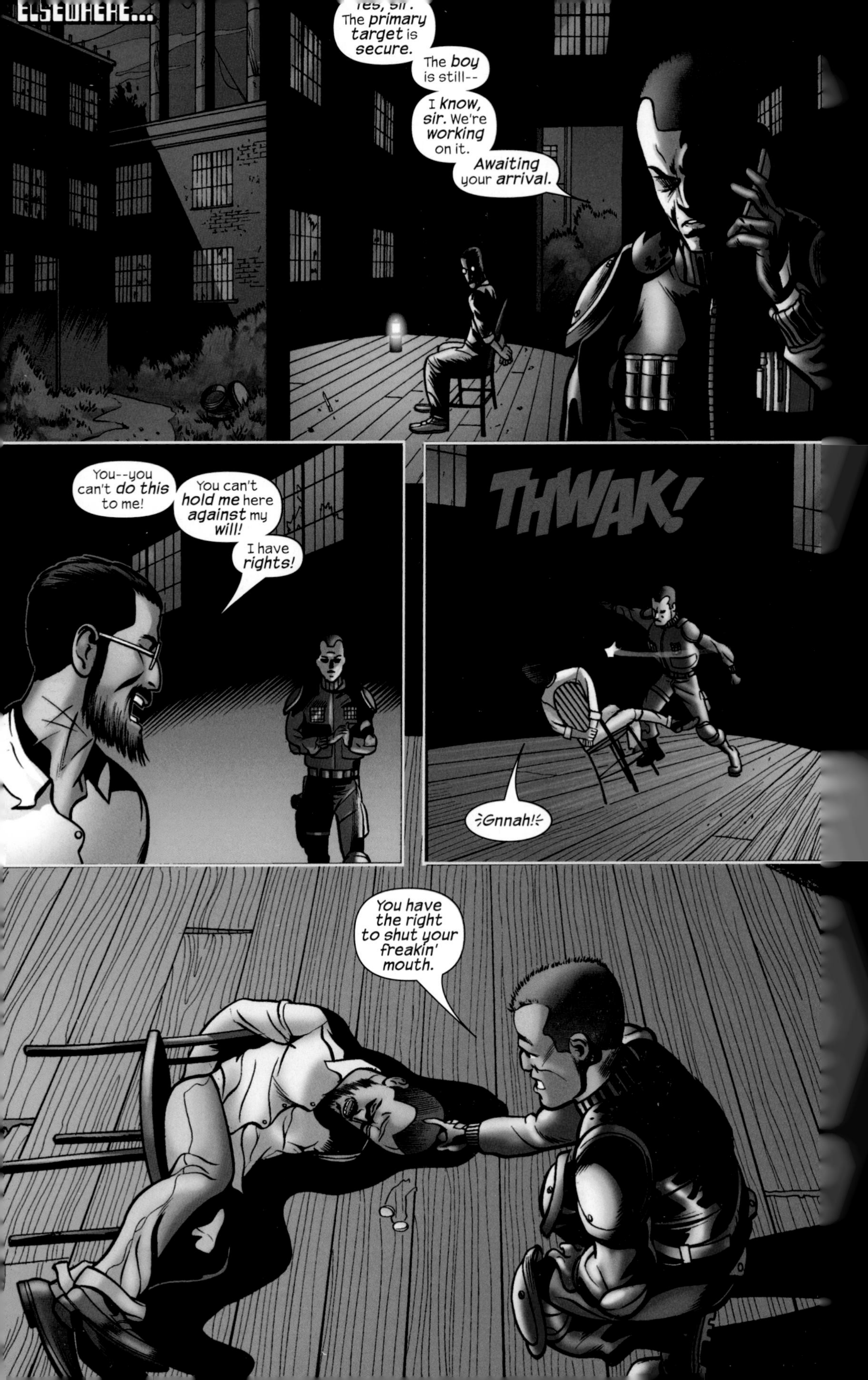

ELSEWHERE...
Yes, sir. The primary target is secure.
The boy is still--
I know, sir. We're working on it.
Awaiting your arrival.
You--you can't do this to me!
You can't hold me here against my will!
I have rights!
THWAK!
Gnnah!
You have the right to shut your freakin' mouth.

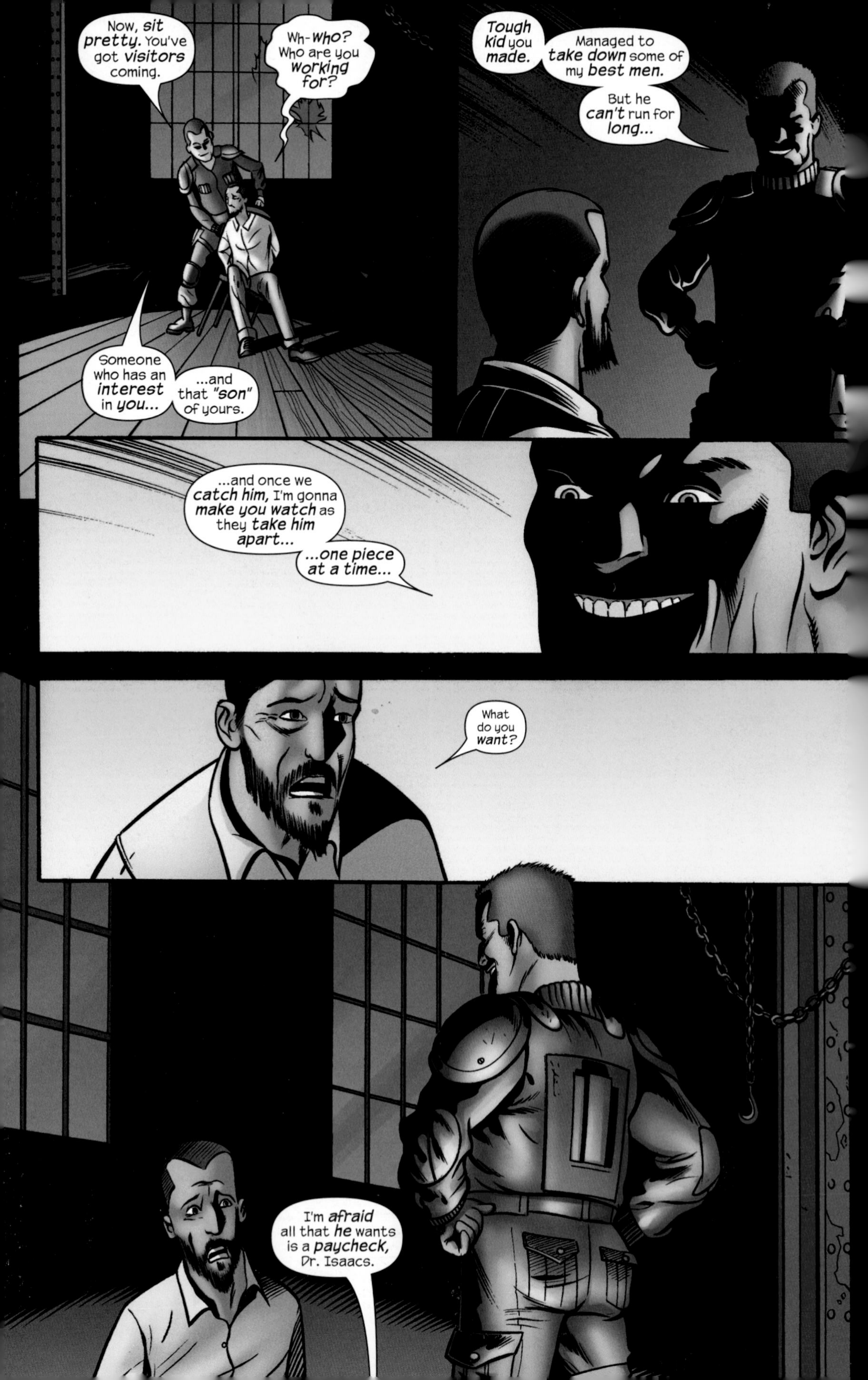
Now, sit pretty. You've got visitors coming.
Wh-who? Who are you working for?
Someone who has an interest in you...
...and that "son" of yours.
Tough kid you made.
Managed to take down some of my best men.
But he can't run for long...
...and once we catch him, I'm gonna make you watch as they take him apart...
...one piece at a time...
What do you want?
I'm afraid all that he wants is a paycheck, Dr. Isaacs.

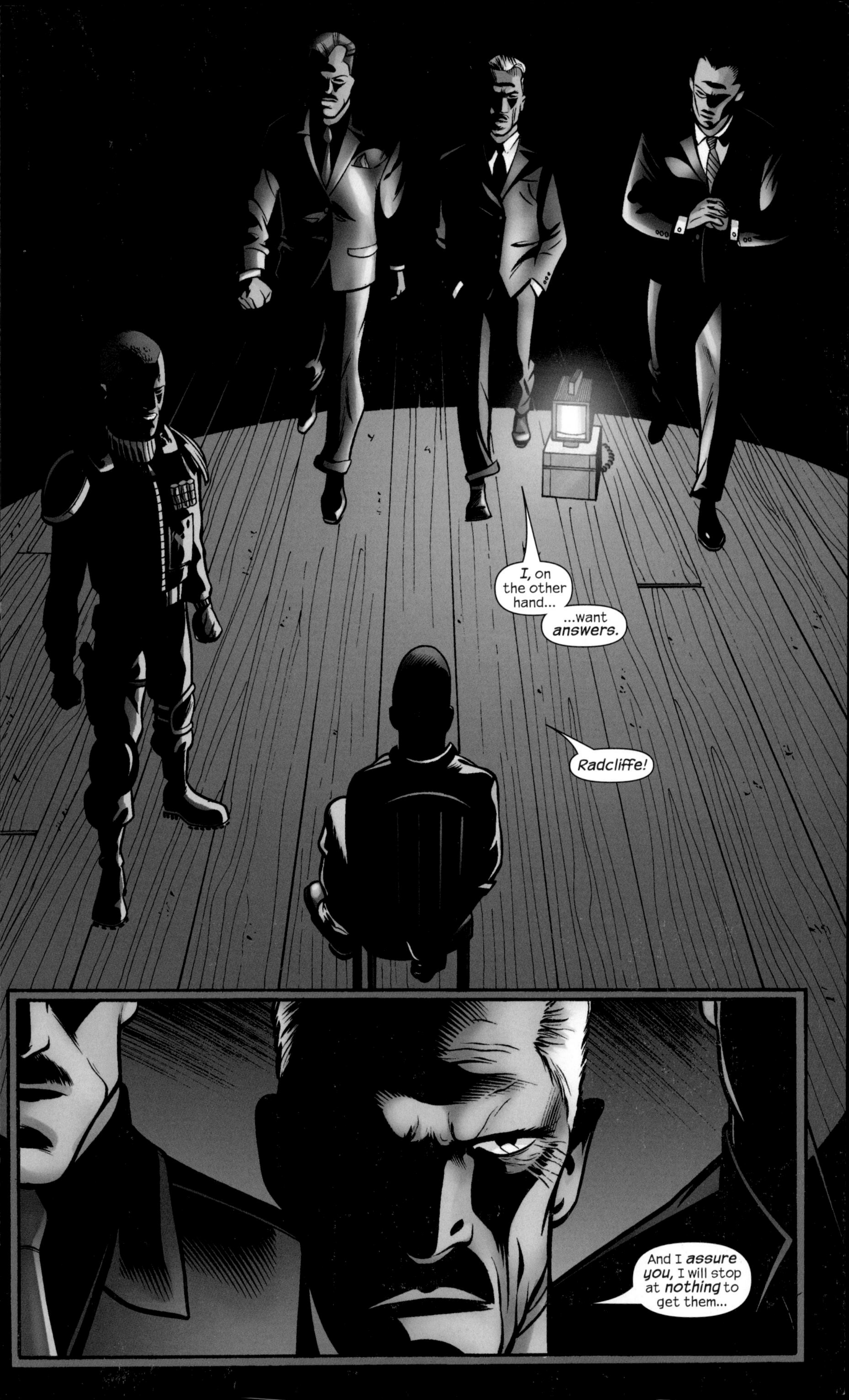
I, on the other hand...
...want answers.
Radcliffe!
And I assure you, I will stop at nothing to get them...

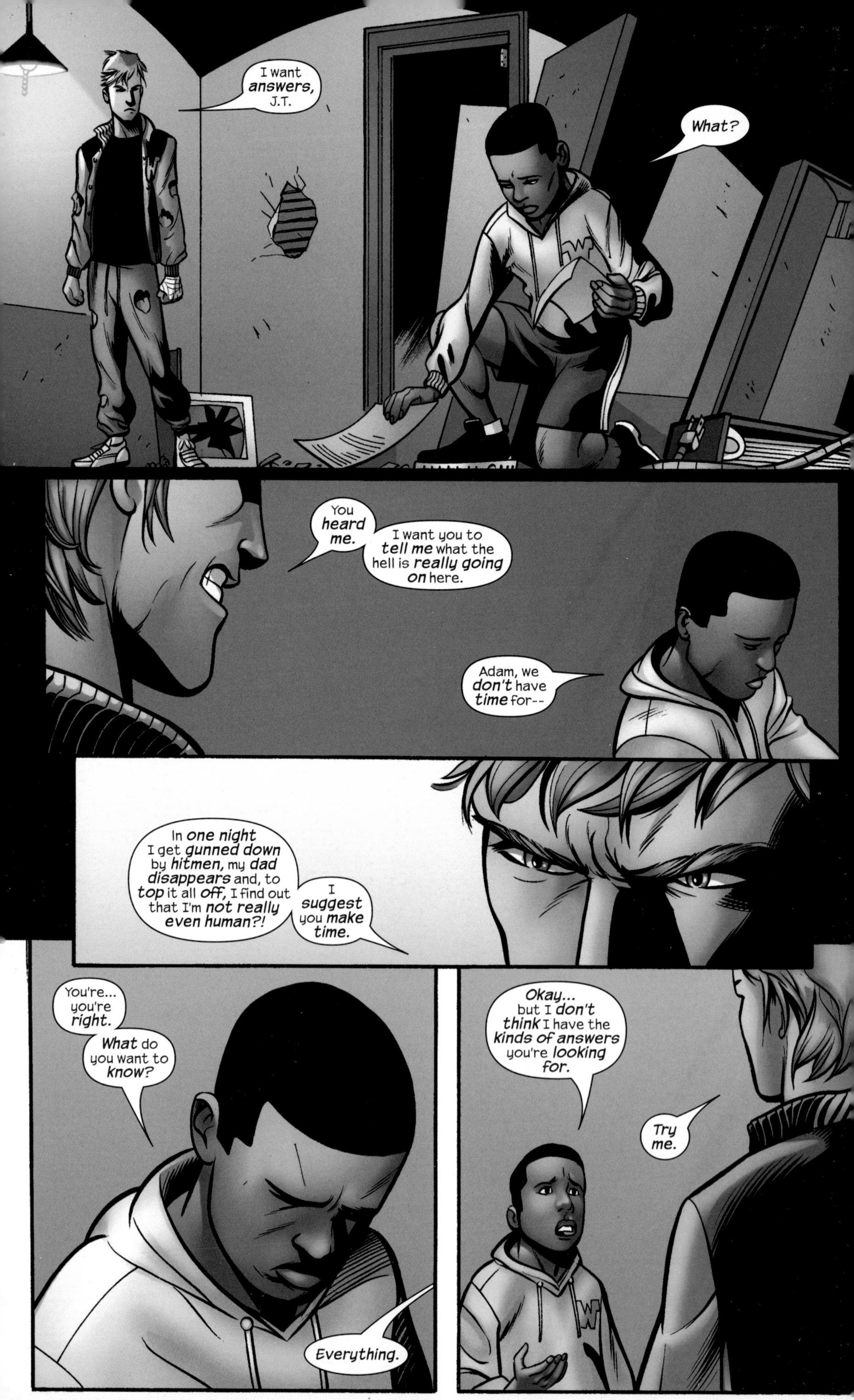
I want answers, J.T.
What?
You heard me.
I want you to tell me what the hell is really going on here.
Adam, we don't have time for--
In one night I get gunned down by hitmen, my dad disappears and, to top it all off, I find out that I'm not really even human?!
I suggest you make time.
You're... you're right.
What do you want to know?
Everything.
Okay... but I don't think I have the kinds of answers you're looking for.
Try me.

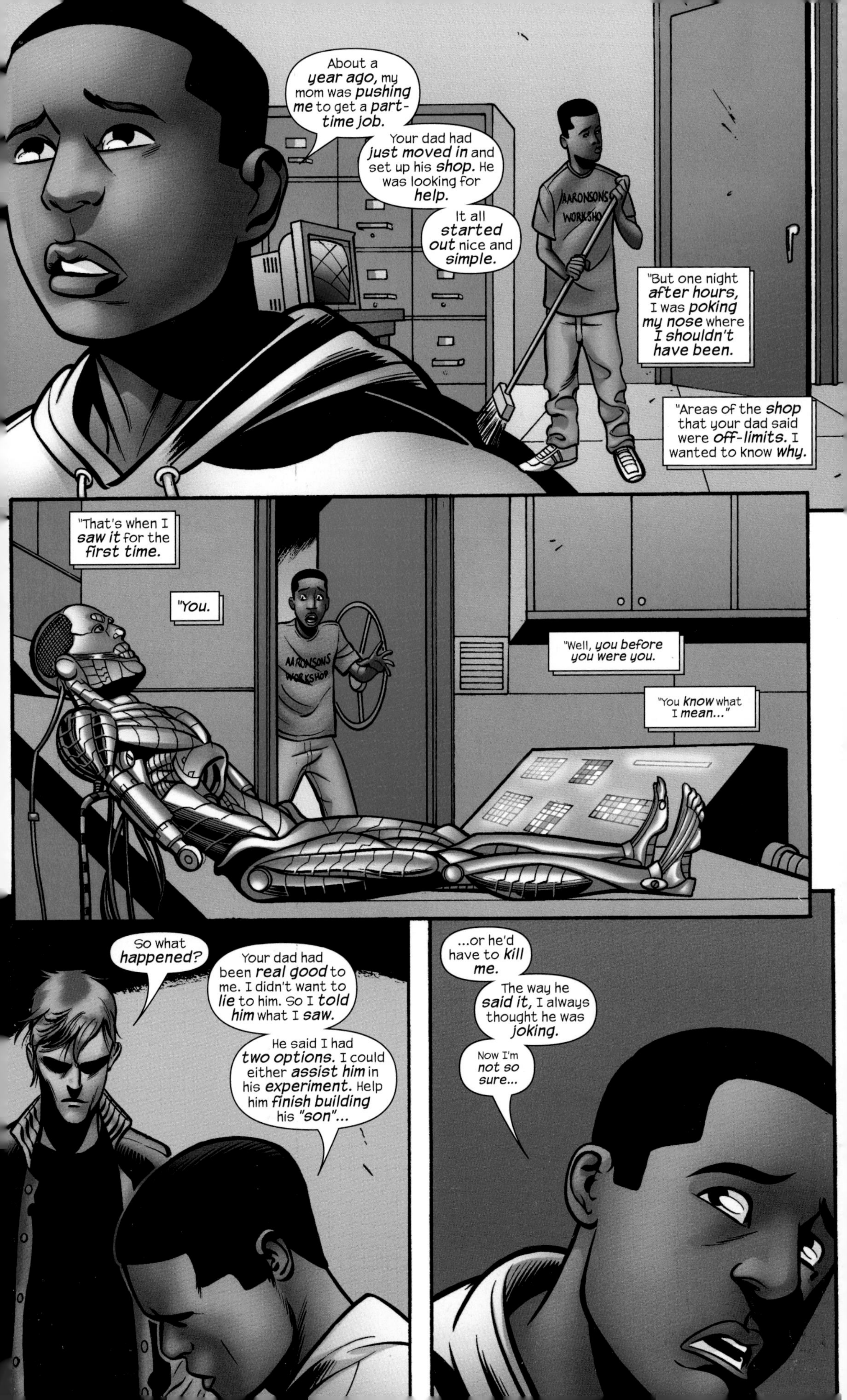
About a year ago, my mom was pushing me to get a part-time job.
Your dad had just moved in and set up his shop. He was looking for help.
It all started out nice and simple.
AARONSONS WORKSHOP
"But one night after hours, I was poking my nose where I shouldn't have been.
"Areas of the shop that your dad said were off-limits. I wanted to know why.
"That's when I saw it for the first time.
"You.
AARONSONS WORKSHOP
"Well, you before you were you.
"You know what I mean..."
So what happened?
Your dad had been real good to me. I didn't want to lie to him. So I told him what I saw.
He said I had two options. I could either assist him in his experiment. Help him finish building his "son"...
...or he'd have to kill me.
The way he said it, I always thought he was joking.
Now I'm not so sure...

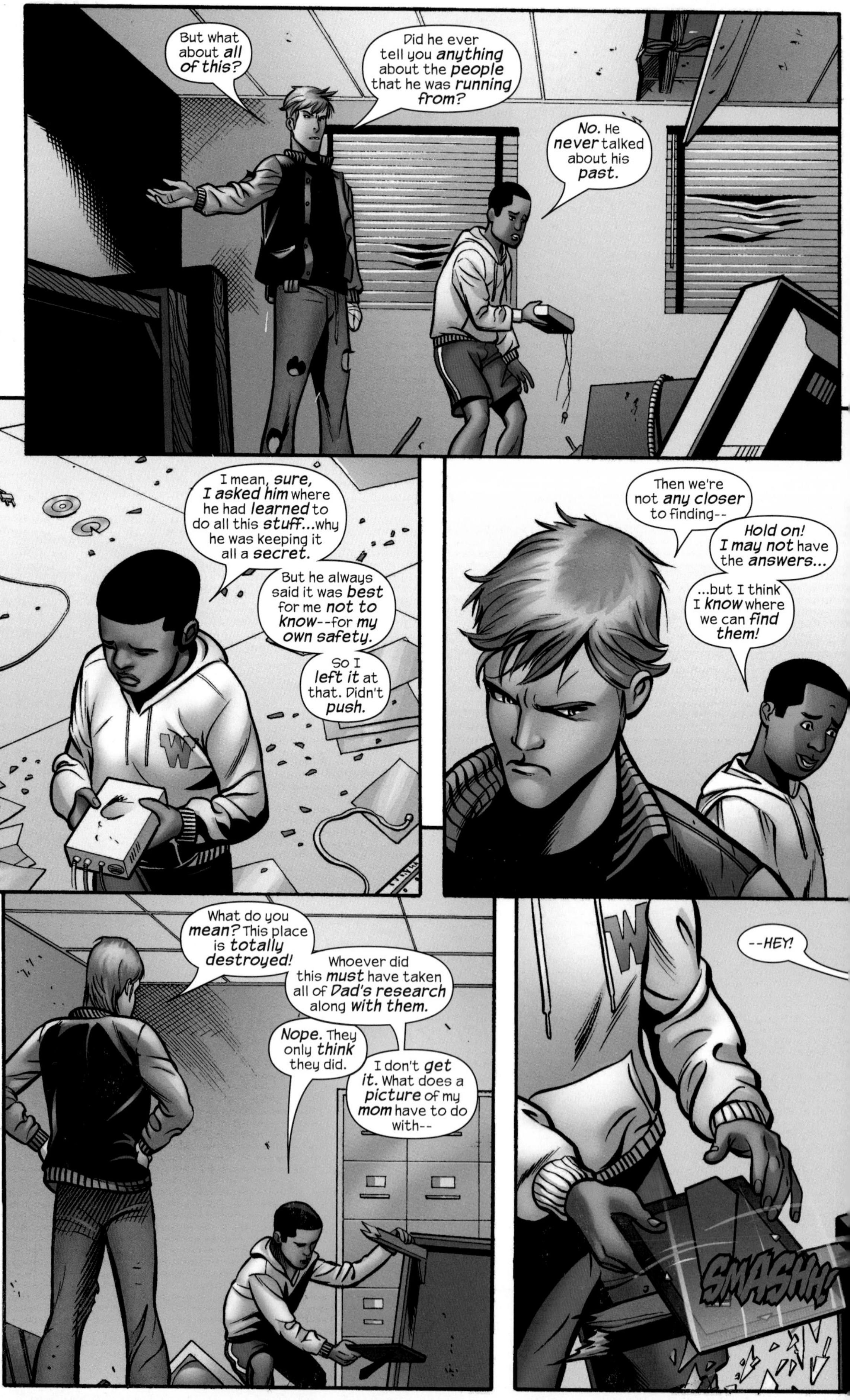

But what about all of this?
Did he ever tell you anything about the people that he was running from?
No. He never talked about his past.
I mean, sure, I asked him where he had learned to do all this stuff...why he was keeping it all a secret.
But he always said it was best for me not to know--for my own safety.
So I left it at that. Didn't push.
Then we're not any closer to finding--
Hold on! I may not have the answers...
...but I think I know where we can find them!
What do you mean? This place is totally destroyed!
Whoever did this must have taken all of Dad's research along with them.
Nope. They only think they did.
I don't get it. What does a picture of my mom have to do with--
--HEY!
SMASHH!

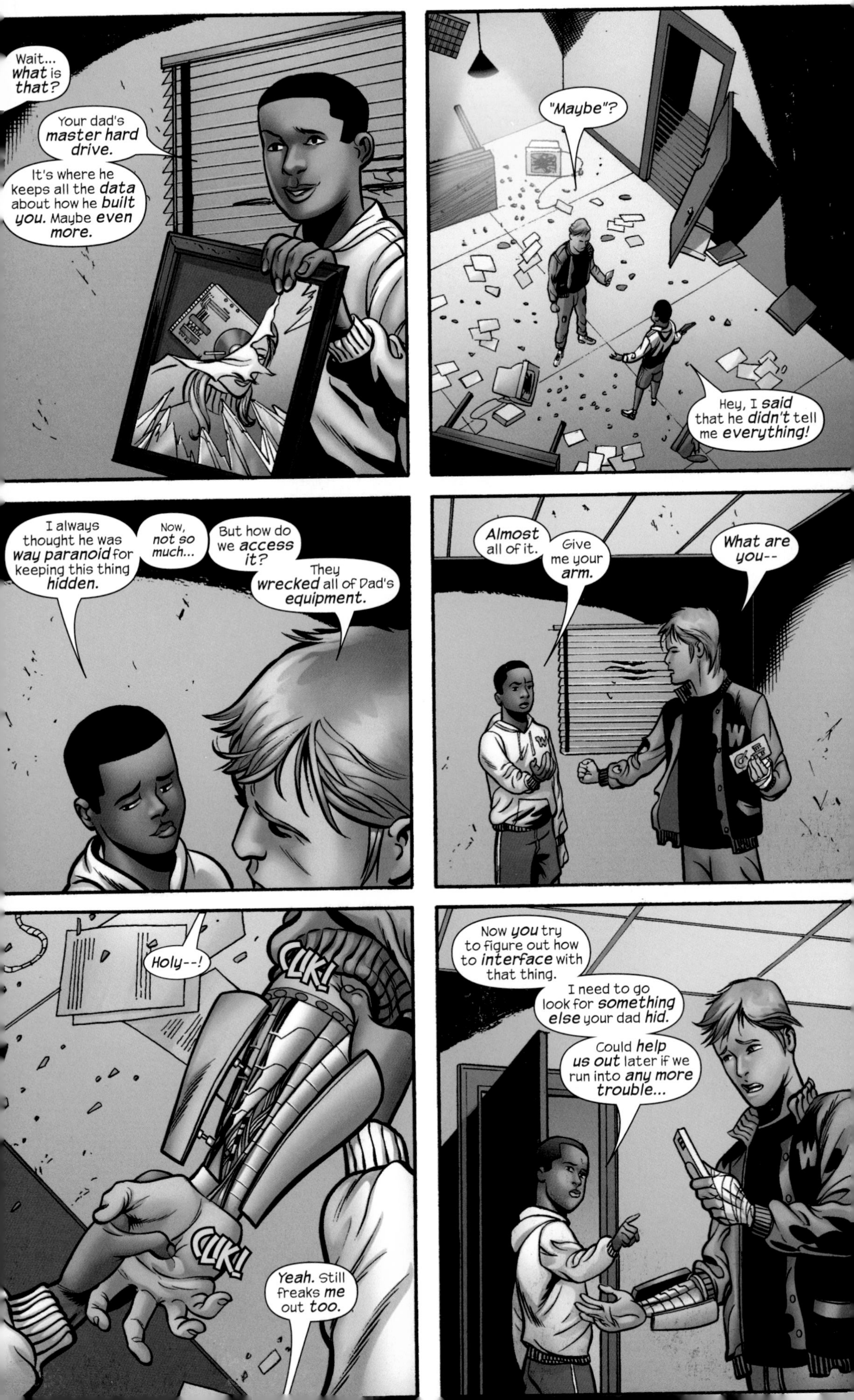
Wait... what is that?
Your dad's master hard drive.
It's where he keeps all the data about how he built you. Maybe even more.
"Maybe"?
Hey, I said that he didn't tell me everything!
I always thought he was way paranoid for keeping this thing hidden.
Now, not so much...
But how do we access it?
They wrecked all of Dad's equipment.
Almost all of it.
Give me your arm.
What are you--
Holy--!
CLIK!
CLIK!
Yeah. Still freaks me out too.
Now you try to figure out how to interface with that thing.
I need to go look for something else your dad hid.
Could help us out later if we run into any more trouble...

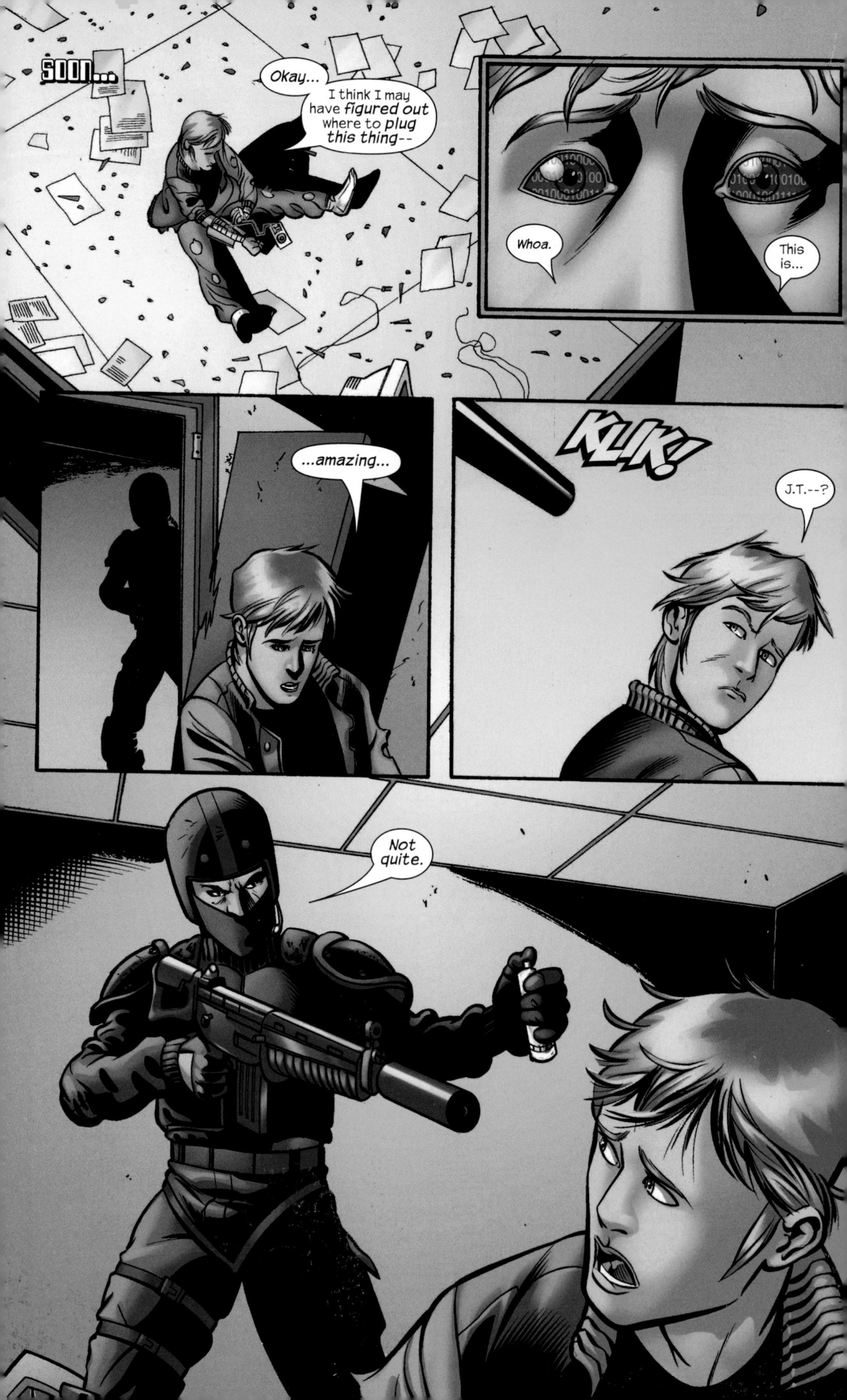
SOON...
Okay... I think I may have figured out where to plug this thing--
Whoa.
This is...
...amazing...
KLIK!
J.T.--?
Not quite.

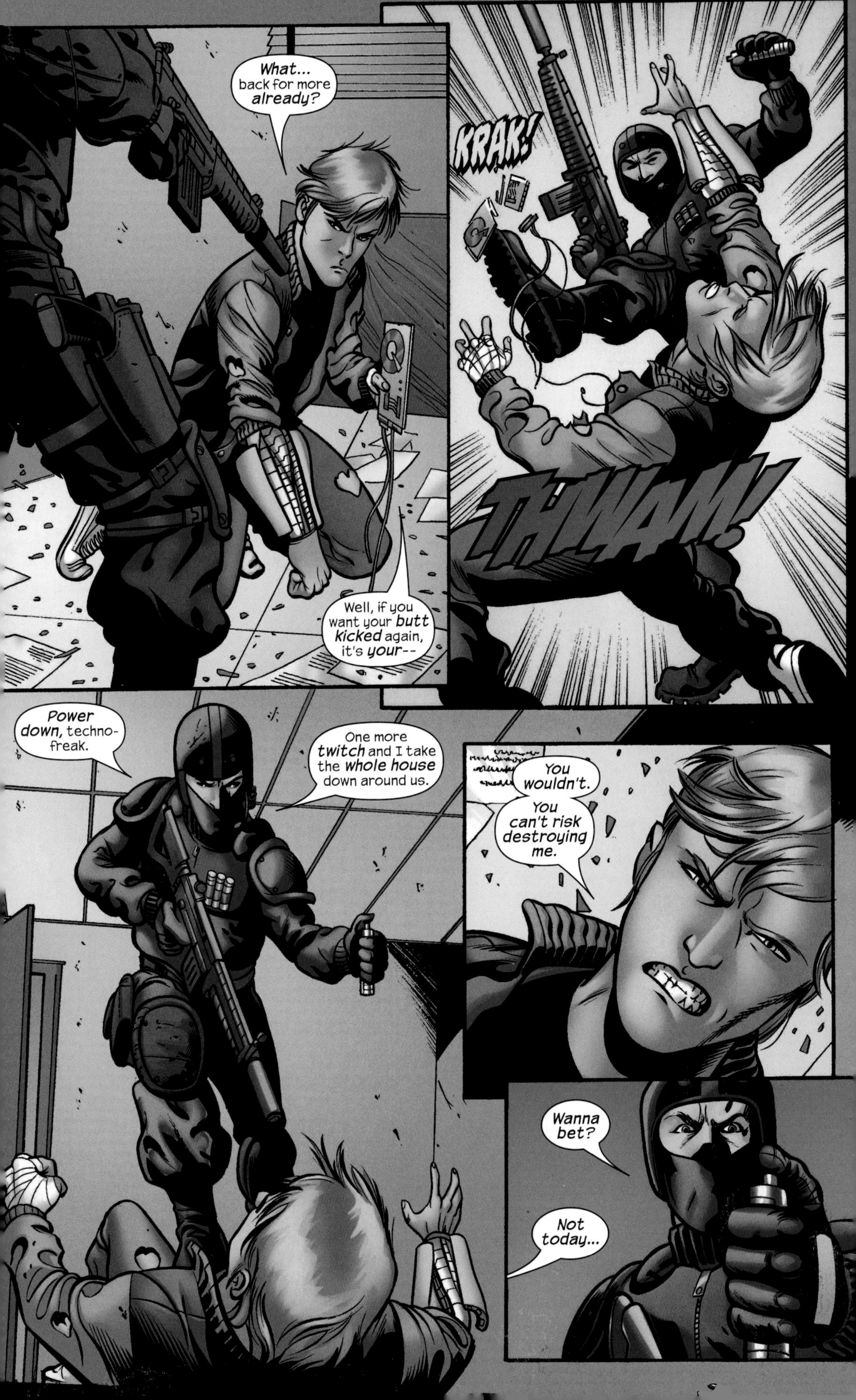
What... back for more already?
Well, if you want your butt kicked again, it's your--
KRAK!
THWAM!
Power down, techno-freak.
One more twitch and I take the whole house down around us.
You wouldn't.
You can't risk destroying me.
Wanna bet?
Not today...

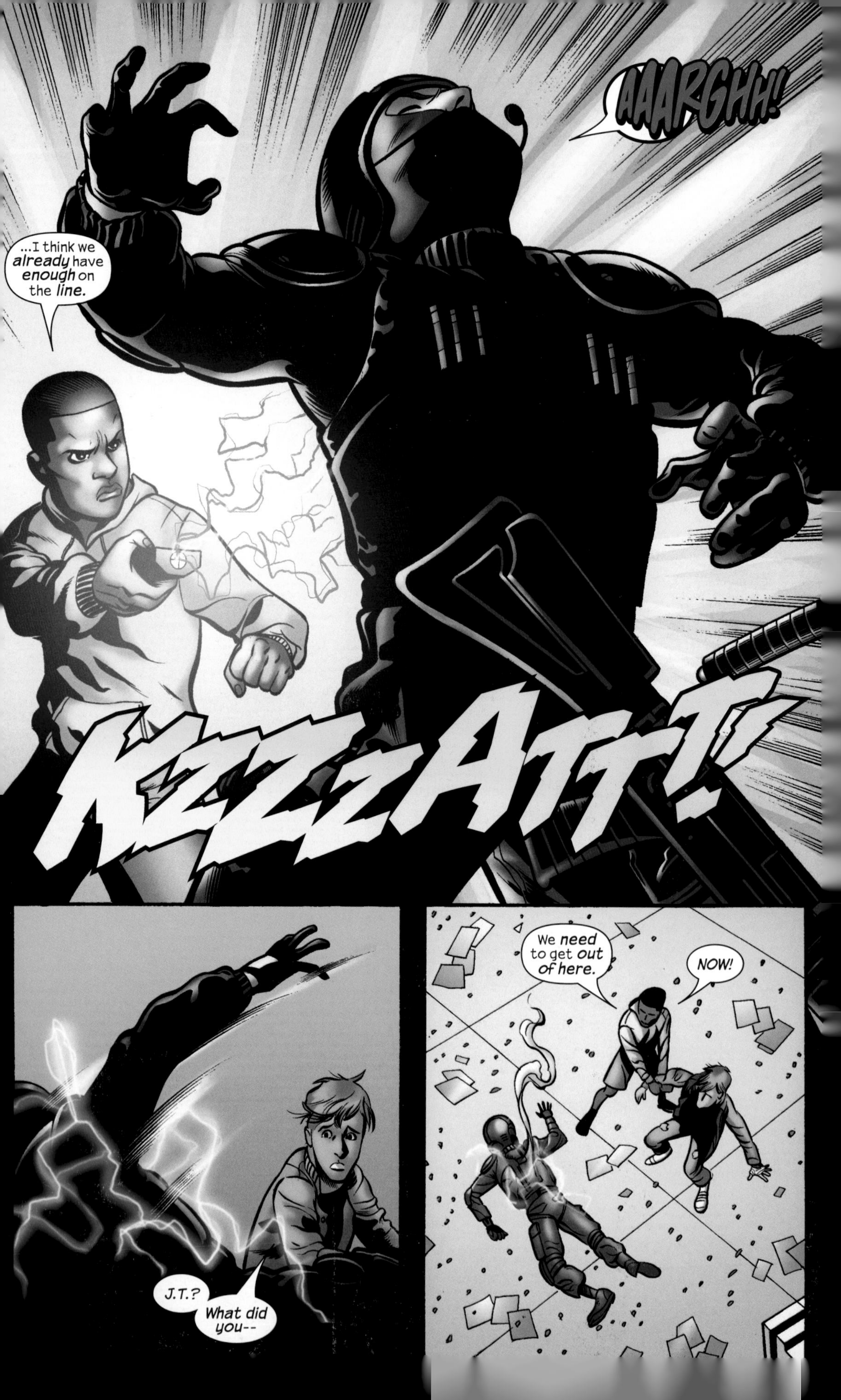

AAARGHH!
...I think we already have enough on the line.
KZZZATT!
J.T.?
What did you--
We need to get out of here.
NOW!

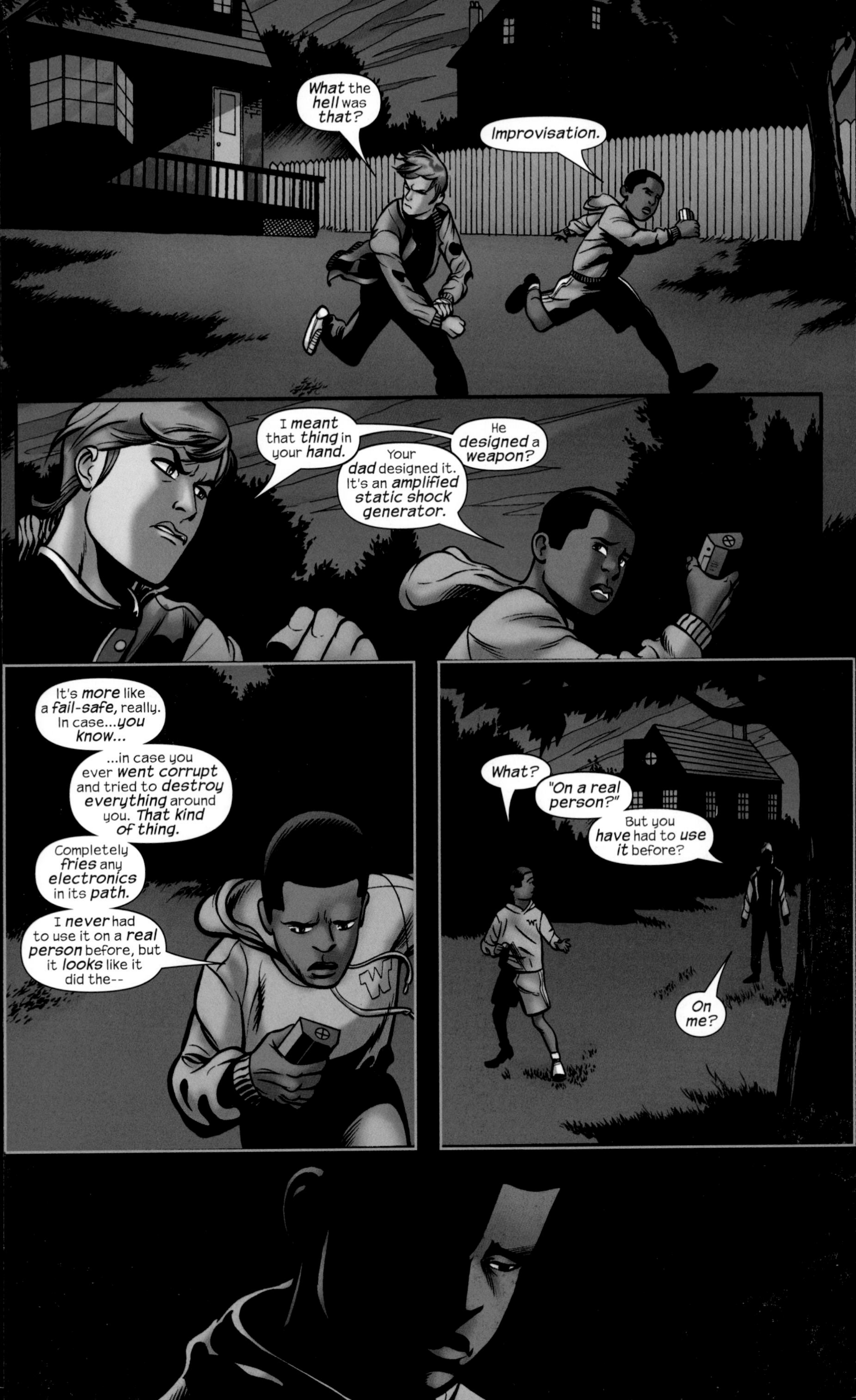

What the hell was that?
Improvisation.
I meant that thing in your hand.
Your dad designed it. It's an amplified static shock generator.
He designed a weapon?
It's more like a fail-safe, really. In case...you know...
...in case you ever went corrupt and tried to destroy everything around you. That kind of thing.
Completely fries any electronics in its path.
I never had to use it on a real person before, but it looks like it did the--
What?
"On a real person?"
But you have had to use it before?
On me?

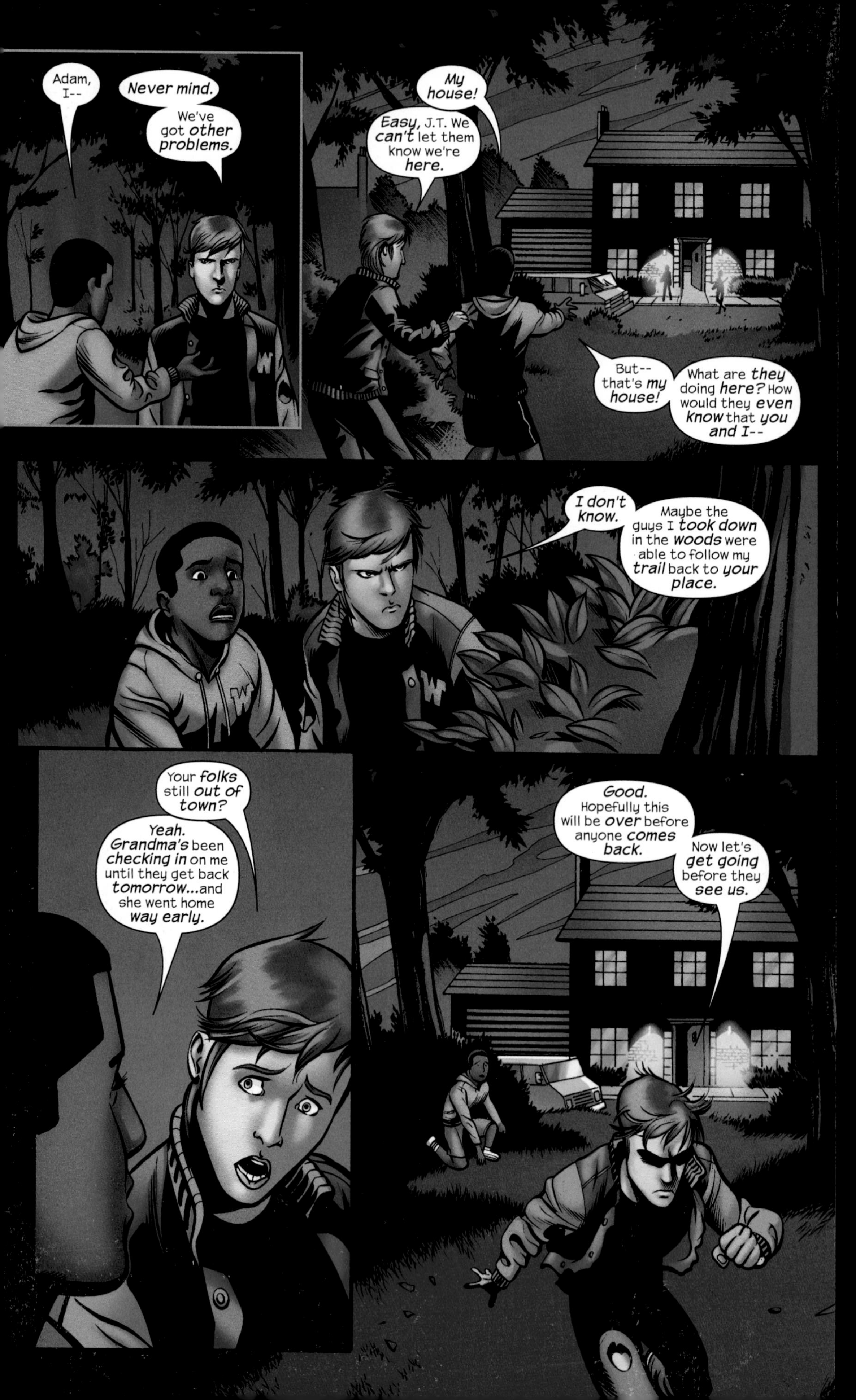
Adam, I--
Never mind.
We've got other problems.
My house!
Easy, J.T. We can't let them know we're here.
But-- that's my house!
What are they doing here? How would they even know that you and I--
I don't know.
Maybe the guys I took down in the woods were able to follow my trail back to your place.
Your folks still out of town?
Yeah. Grandma's been checking in on me until they get back tomorrow...and she went home way early.
Good. Hopefully this will be over before anyone comes back.
Now let's get going before they see us.

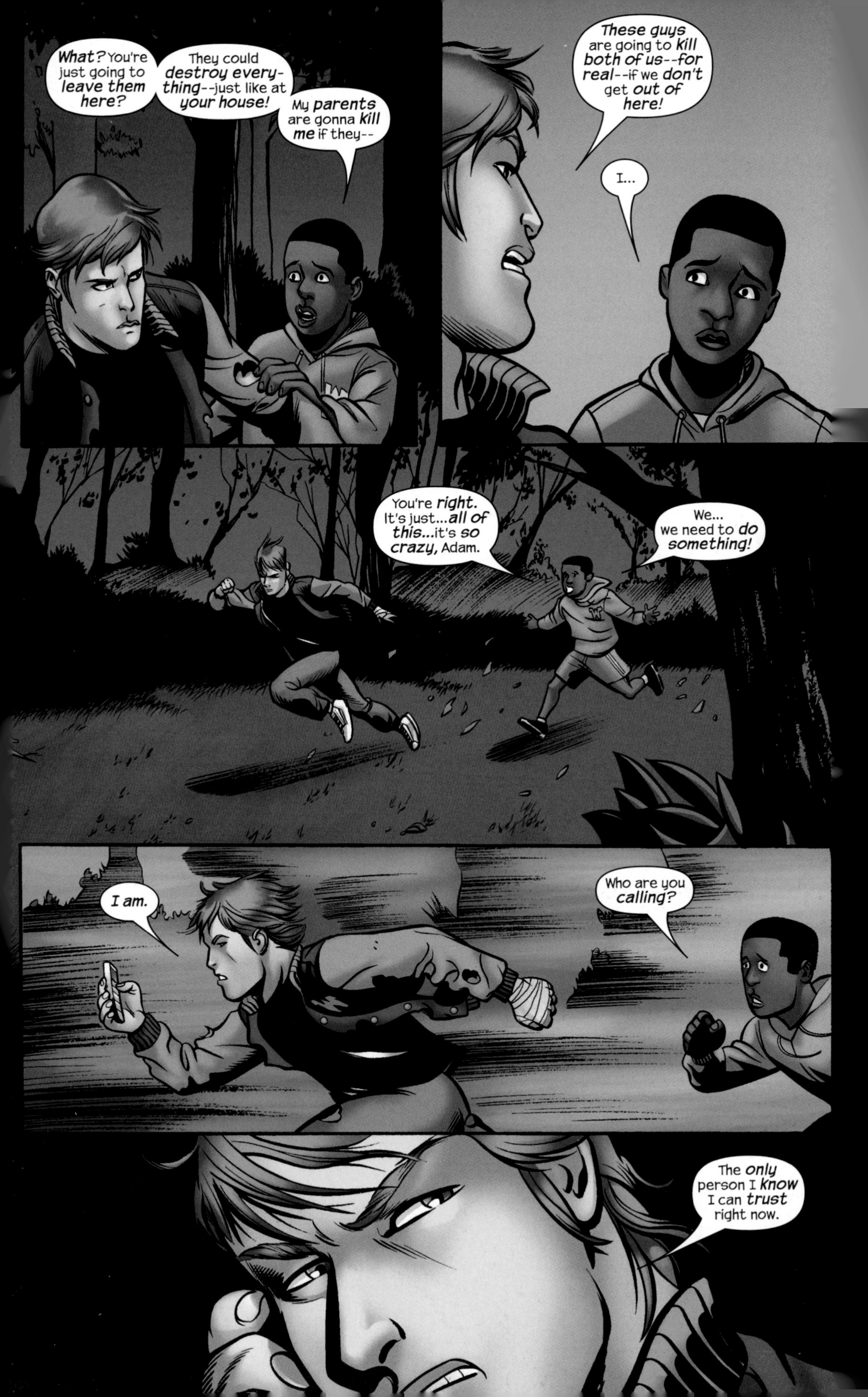
What? You're just going to leave them here?
They could destroy every-thing--just like at your house!
My parents are gonna kill me if they--
These guys are going to kill both of us--for real--if we don't get out of here!
I...
You're right. It's just...all of this...it's so crazy, Adam.
We... we need to do something!
I am.
Who are you calling?
The only person I know I can trust right now.

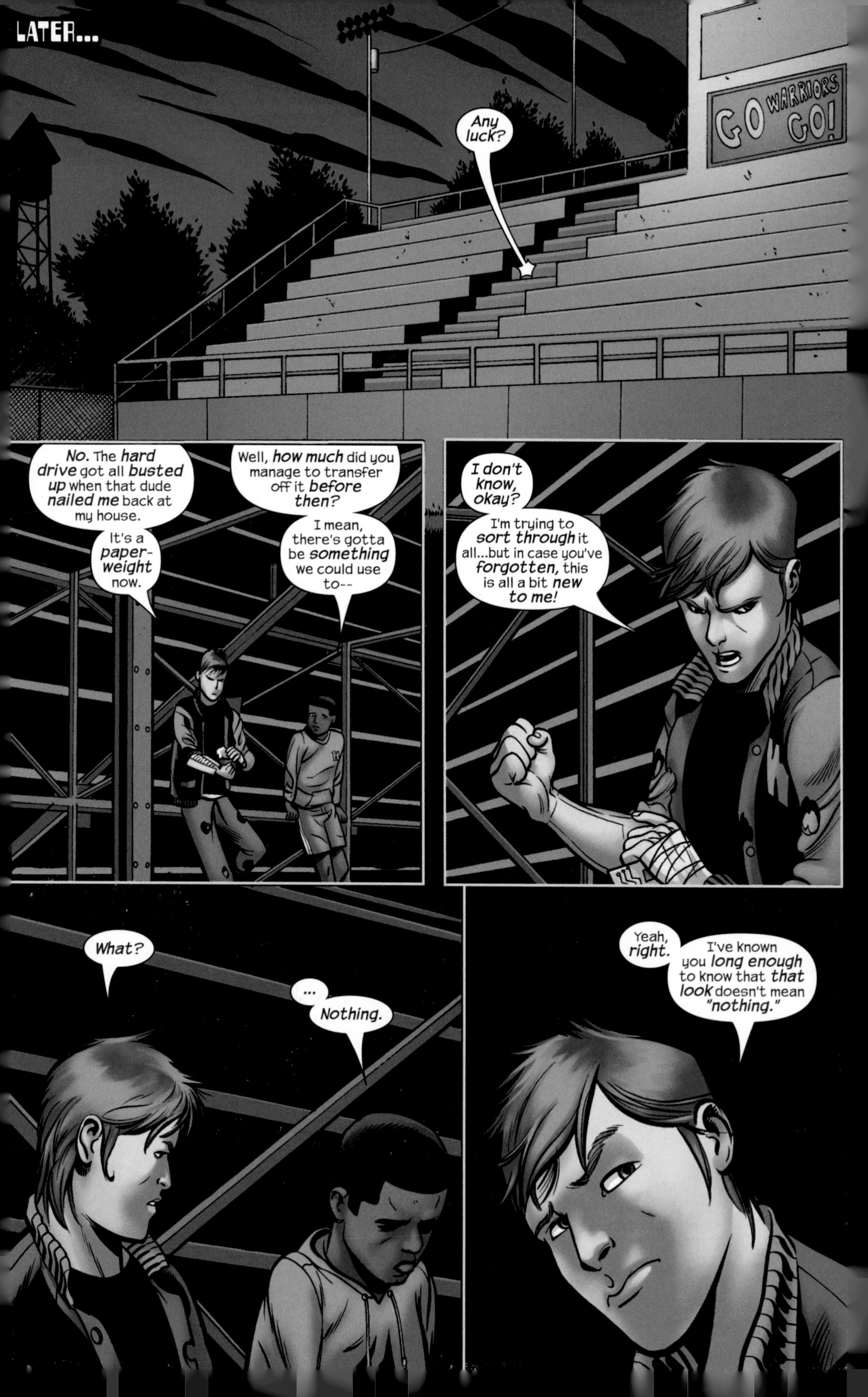
LATER...
Any luck?
GO WARRIORS GO!
No. The hard drive got all busted up when that dude nailed me back at my house.
It's a paper-weight now.
Well, how much did you manage to transfer off it before then?
I mean, there's gotta be something we could use to--
I don't know, okay?
I'm trying to sort through it all...but in case you've forgotten, this is all a bit new to me!
What?
... Nothing.
Yeah, right.
I've known you long enough to know that that look doesn't mean "nothing."

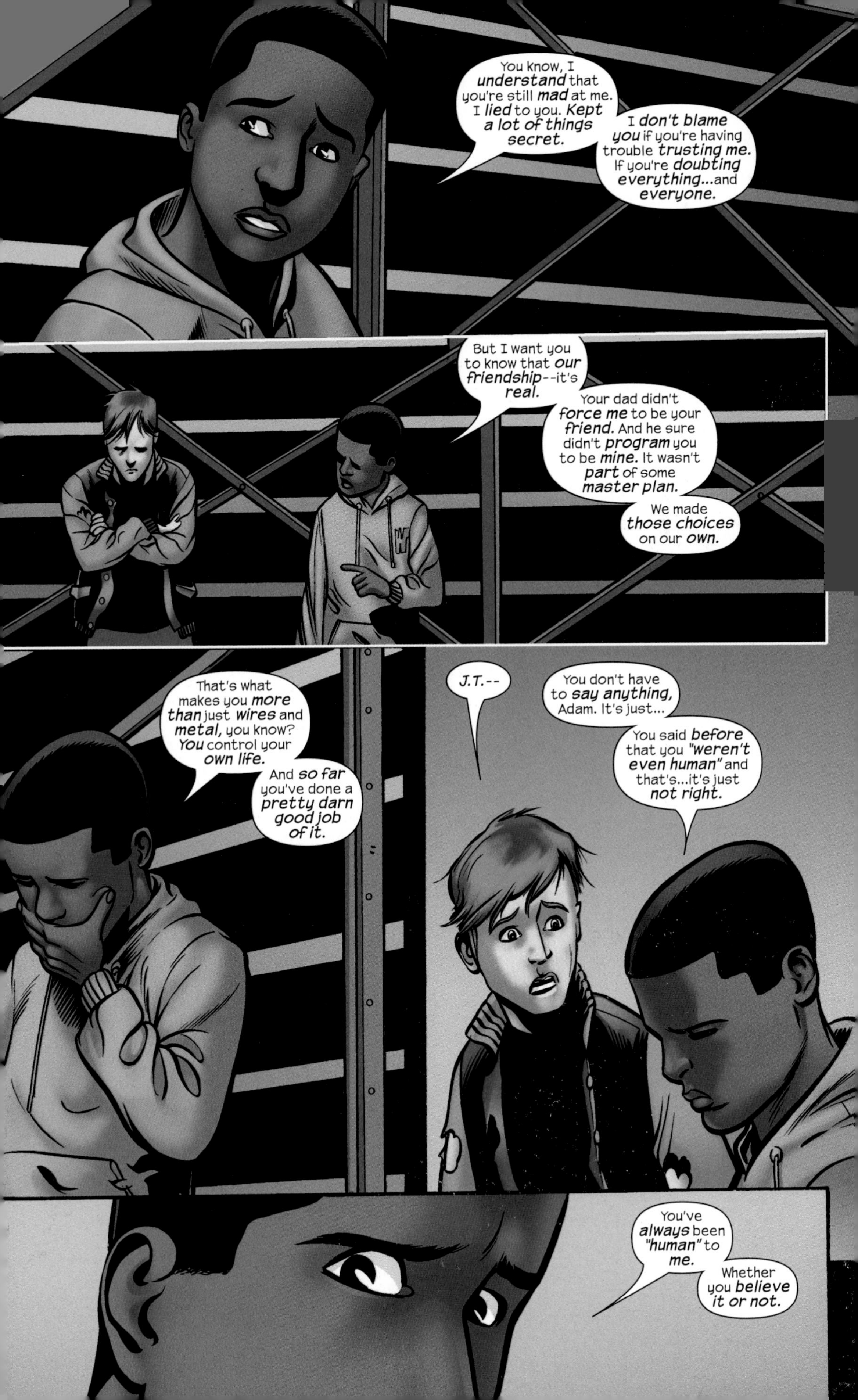
You know, I understand that you're still mad at me. I lied to you. Kept a lot of things secret.
I don't blame you if you're having trouble trusting me. If you're doubting everything...and everyone.
But I want you to know that our friendship--it's real.
Your dad didn't force me to be your friend. And he sure didn't program you to be mine. It wasn't part of some master plan.
We made those choices on our own.
That's what makes you more than just wires and metal, you know? You control your own life.
And so far you've done a pretty darn good job of it.
J.T.--
You don't have to say anything, Adam. It's just...
You said before that you "weren't even human" and that's...it's just not right.
You've always been "human" to me.
Whether you believe it or not.

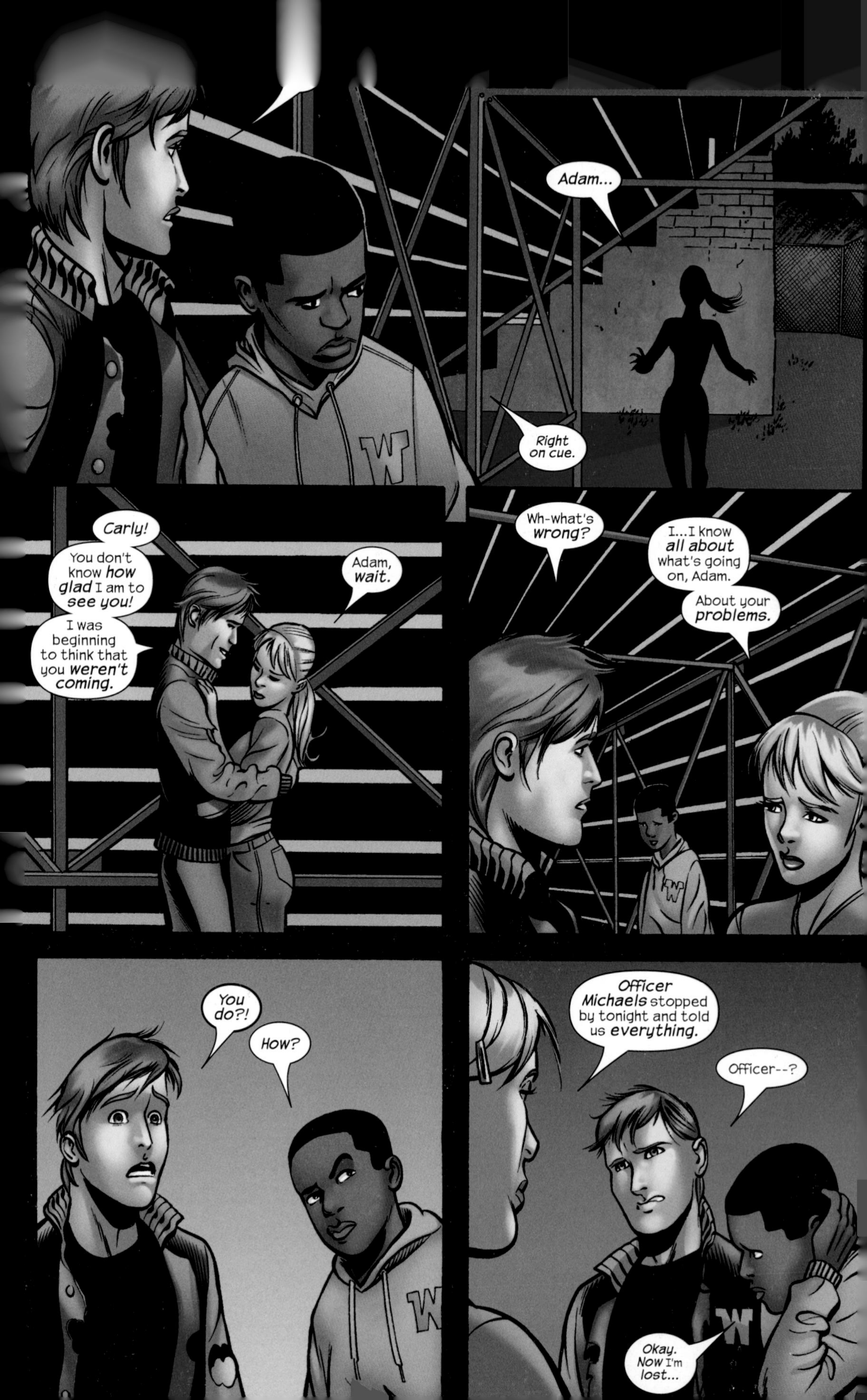
Adam...
Right on cue.
Carly!
You don't know how glad I am to see you!
I was beginning to think that you weren't coming.
Adam, wait.
Wh-what's wrong?
I...I know all about what's going on, Adam.
About your problems.
You do?!
How?
Officer Michaels stopped by tonight and told us everything.
Officer--?
Okay. Now I'm lost...

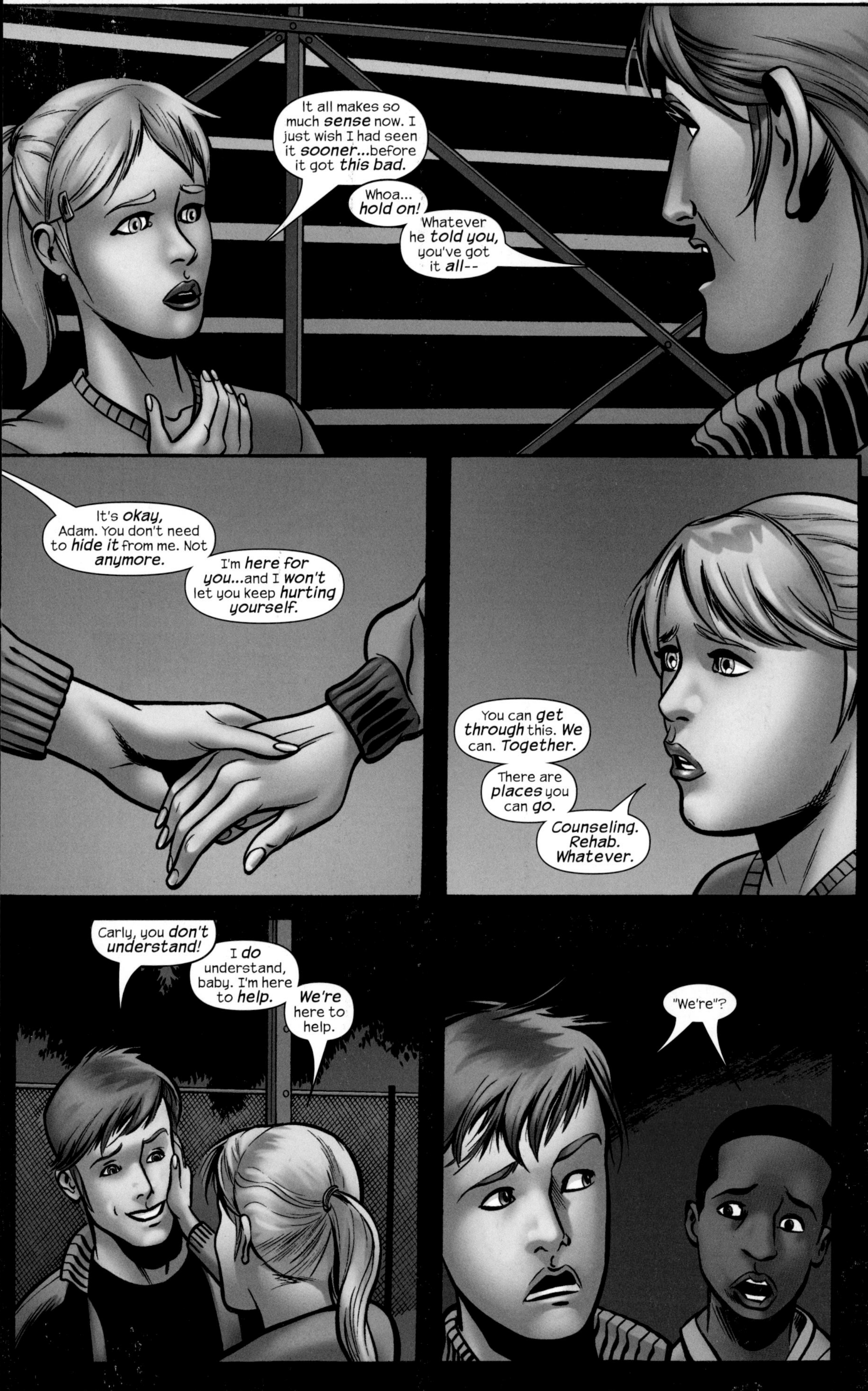
It all makes so much sense now. I just wish I had seen it sooner...before it got this bad.
Whoa... hold on!
Whatever he told you, you've got it all--
It's okay, Adam. You don't need to hide it from me. Not anymore.
I'm here for you...and I won't let you keep hurting yourself.
You can get through this. We can. Together.
There are places you can go.
Counseling. Rehab. Whatever.
Carly, you don't understand!
I do understand, baby. I'm here to help.
We're here to help.
"We're"?

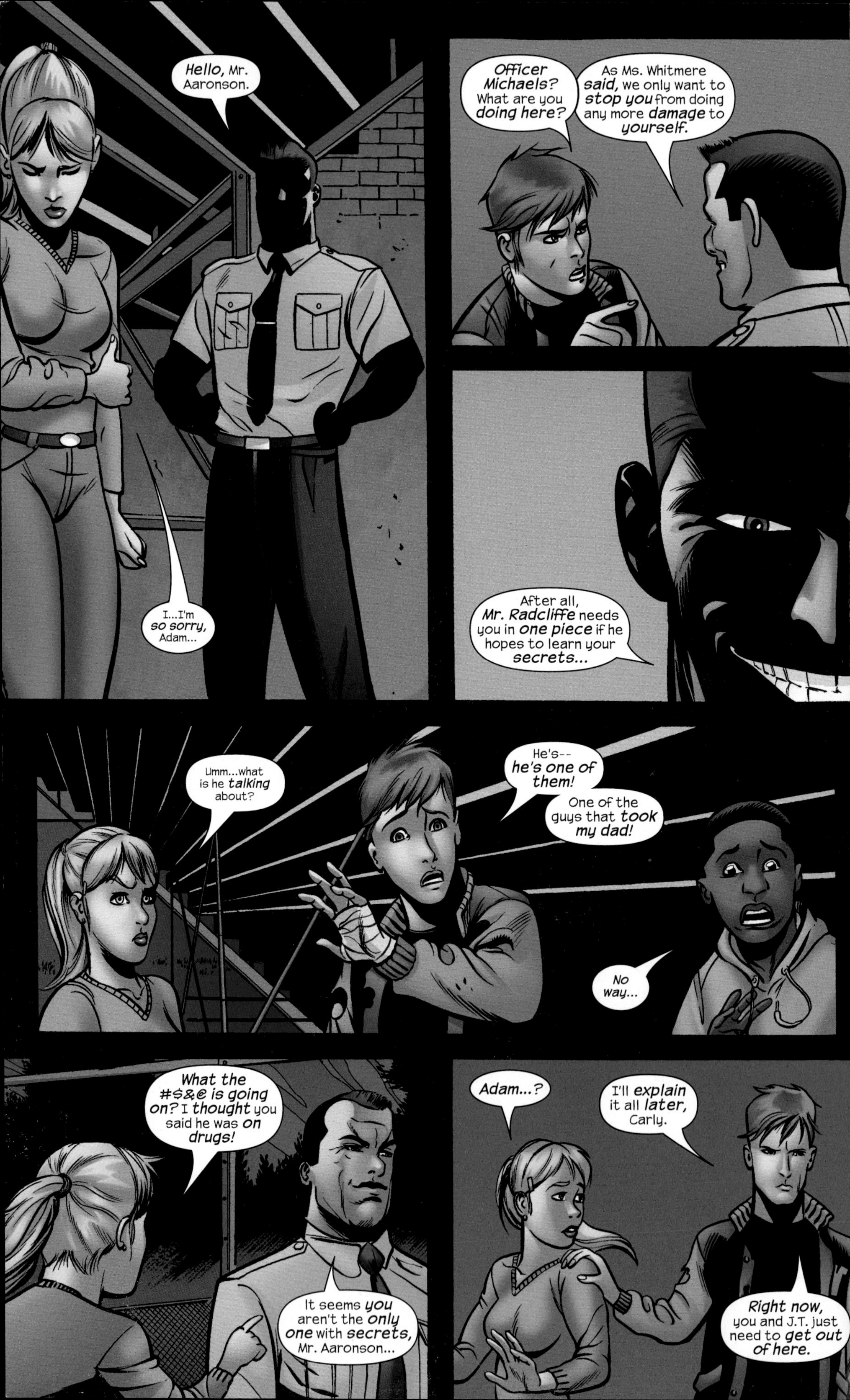
Hello, Mr. Aaronson.
I...I'm so sorry, Adam...
Officer Michaels? What are you doing here?
As Ms. Whitmere said, we only want to stop you from doing any more damage to yourself.
After all, Mr. Radcliffe needs you in one piece if he hopes to learn your secrets...
Umm...what is he talking about?
He's-- he's one of them!
One of the guys that took my dad!
No way...
What the #$&@ is going on? I thought you said he was on drugs!
It seems you aren't the only one with secrets, Mr. Aaronson...
Adam...?
I'll explain it all later, Carly.
Right now, you and J.T. just need to get out of here.

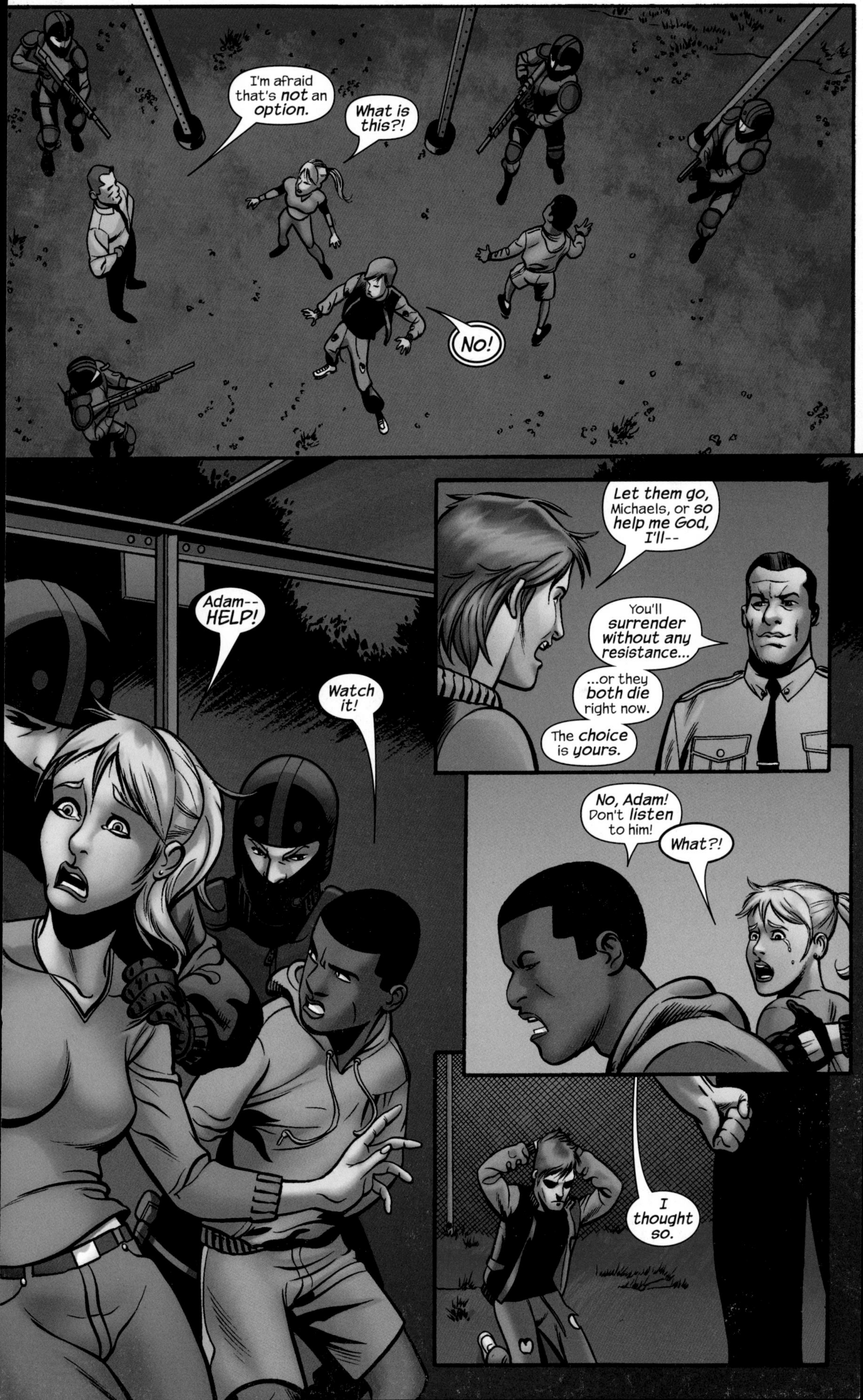
I'm afraid that's *not* an *option.*
What is this?!
No!
Adam-- HELP!
Watch it!
Let them go, Michaels, or *so help me God,* I'll--
You'll *surrender without any resistance...*
...or they *both die* right now.
The *choice* is *yours.*
No, Adam! Don't *listen* to him!
What?!
I thought so.

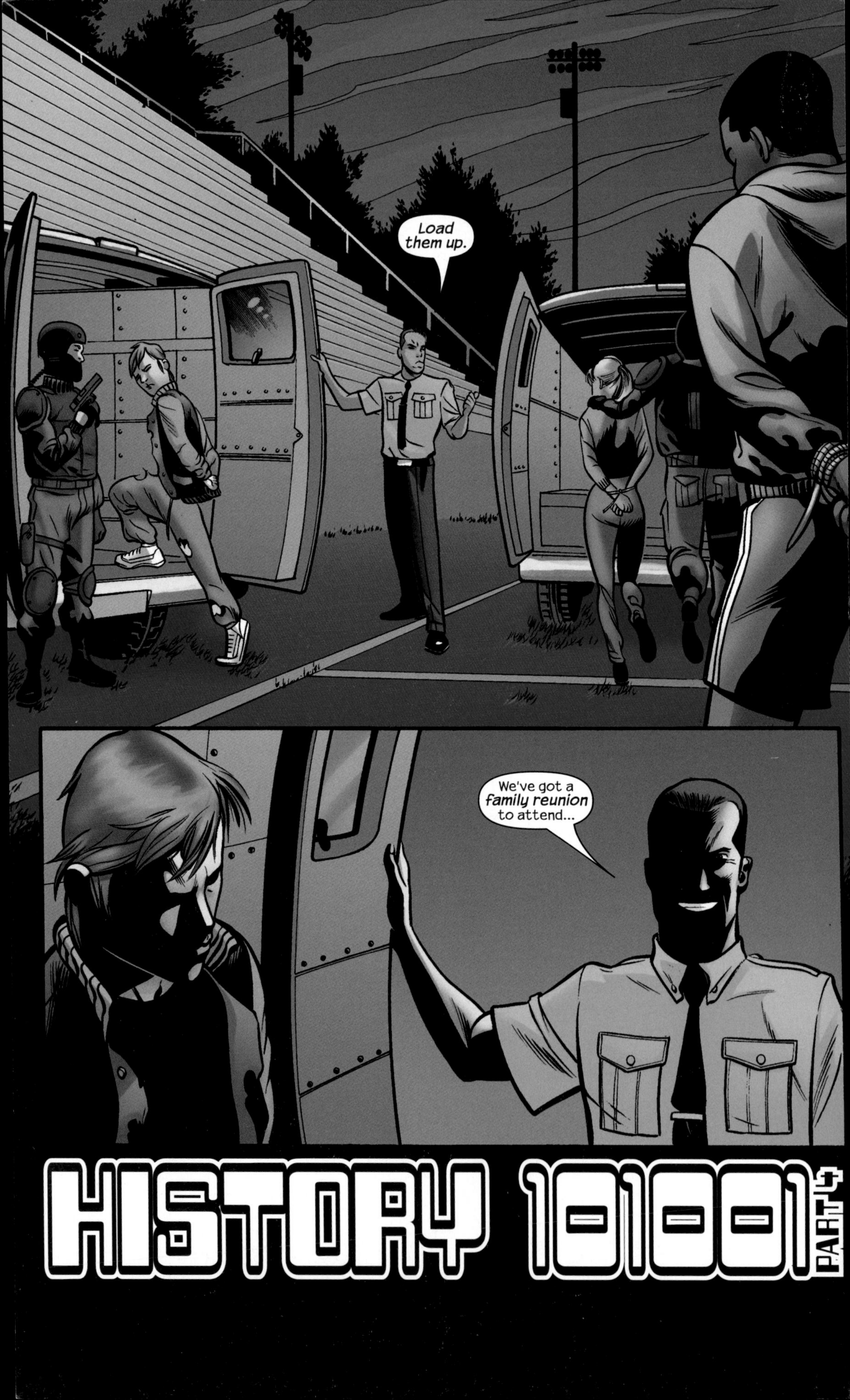
Load them up.
We've got a family reunion to attend...
HISTORY 101001 PART 4

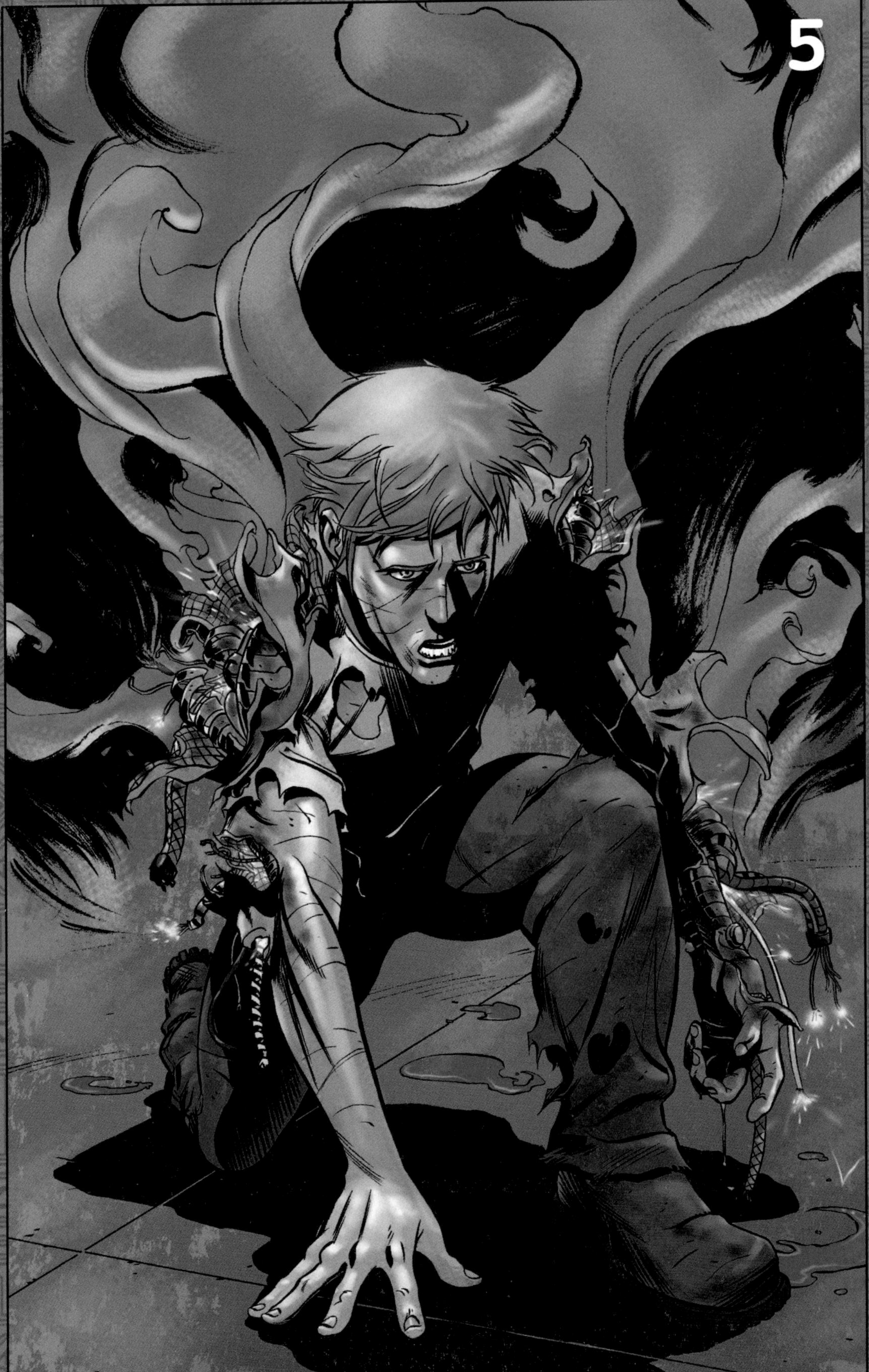
5

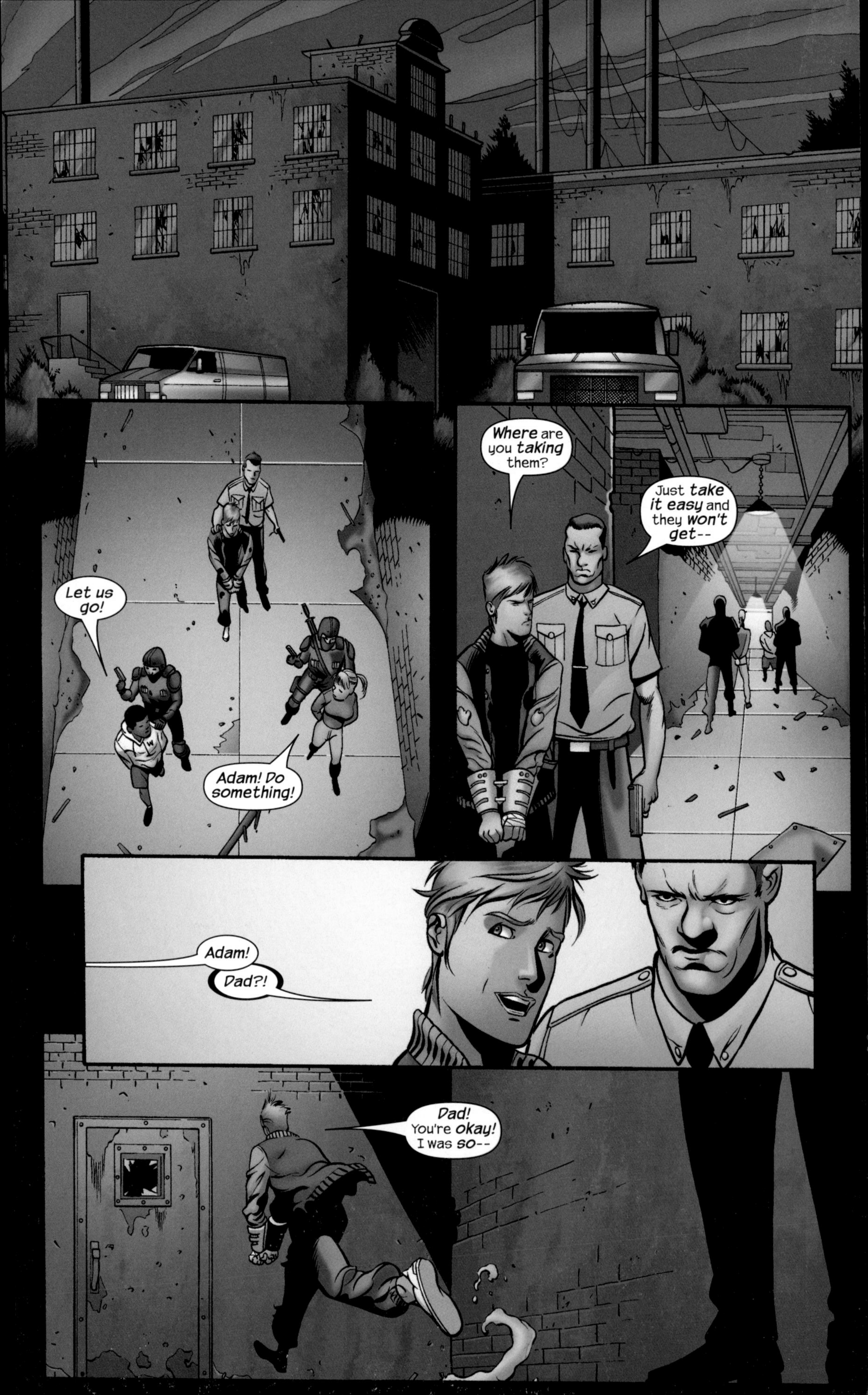
Let us go!
Adam! Do something!
Where are you taking them?
Just take it easy and they won't get--
Adam!
Dad?!
Dad! You're okay! I was so--

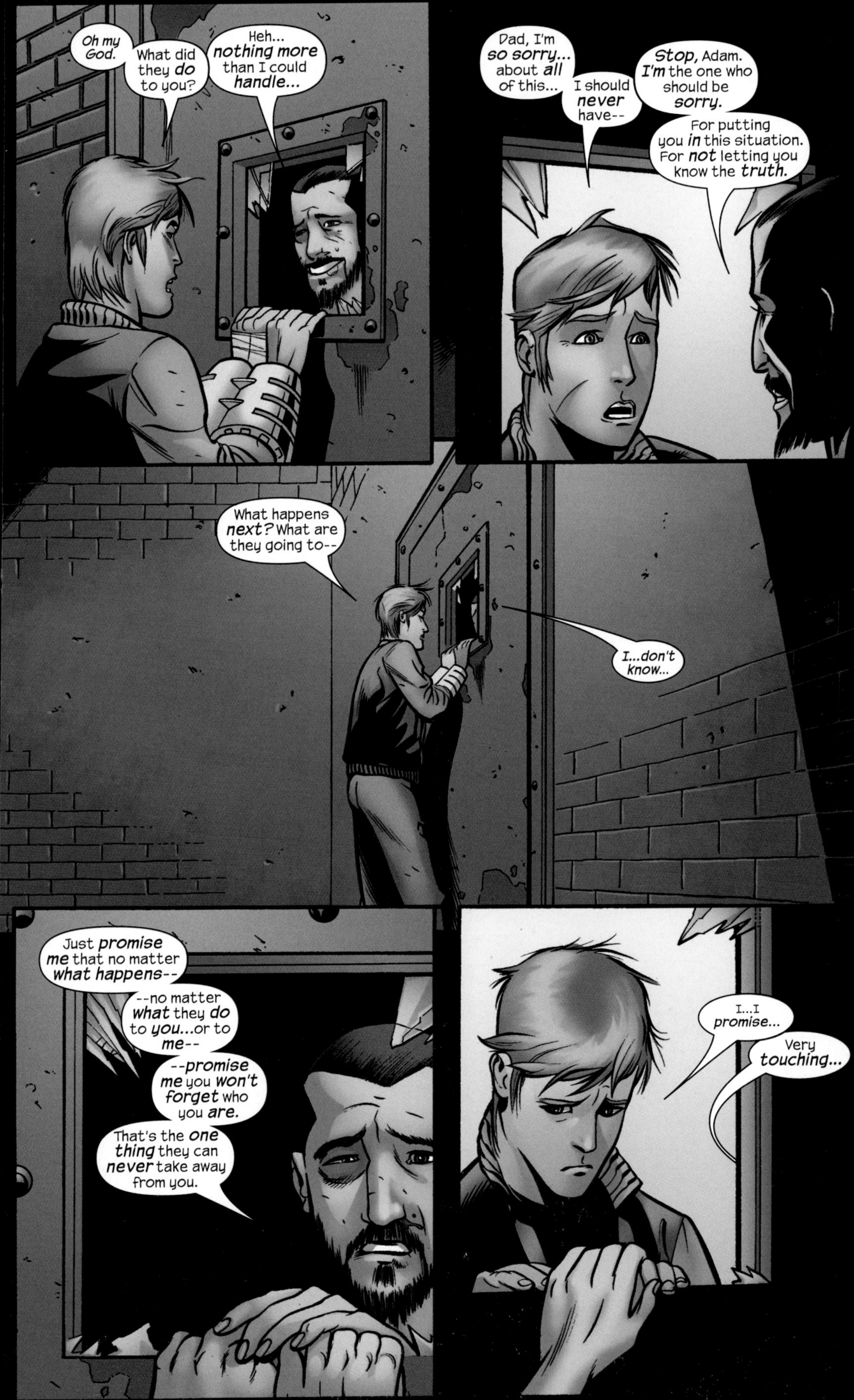
Oh my God.
What did they do to you?
Heh... nothing more than I could handle...
Dad, I'm so sorry... about all of this...
I should never have--
Stop, Adam. I'm the one who should be sorry.
For putting you in this situation. For not letting you know the truth.
What happens next? What are they going to--
I...don't know...
Just promise me that no matter what happens--
--no matter what they do to you...or to me--
--promise me you won't forget who you are.
That's the one thing they can never take away from you.
I...I promise...
Very touching...

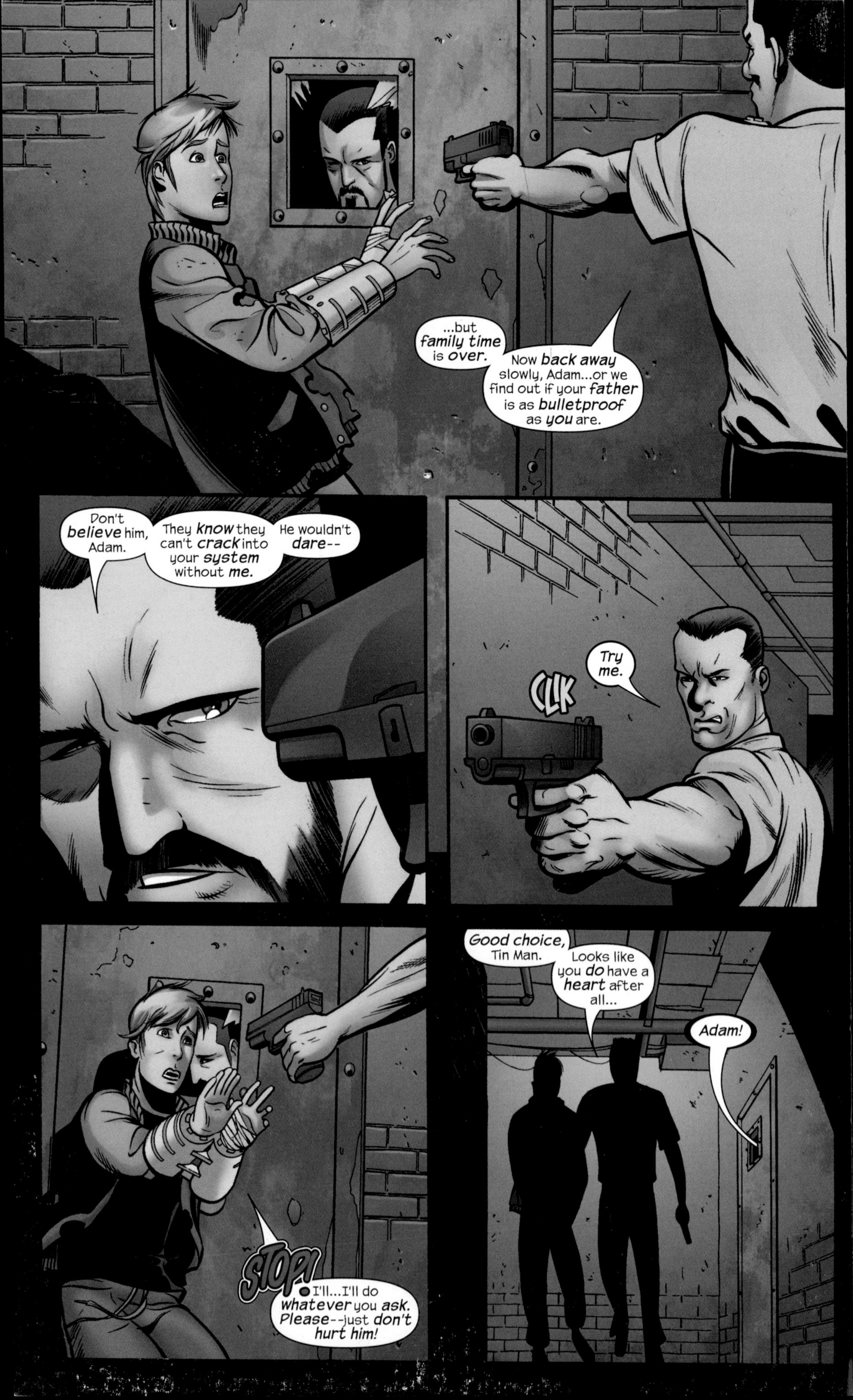
...but family time is over.
Now back away slowly, Adam...or we find out if your father is as bulletproof as you are.
Don't believe him, Adam.
They know they can't crack into your system without me.
He wouldn't dare--
CLIK
Try me.
STOP!
I'll...I'll do whatever you ask. Please--just don't hurt him!
Good choice, Tin Man.
Looks like you do have a heart after all...
Adam!

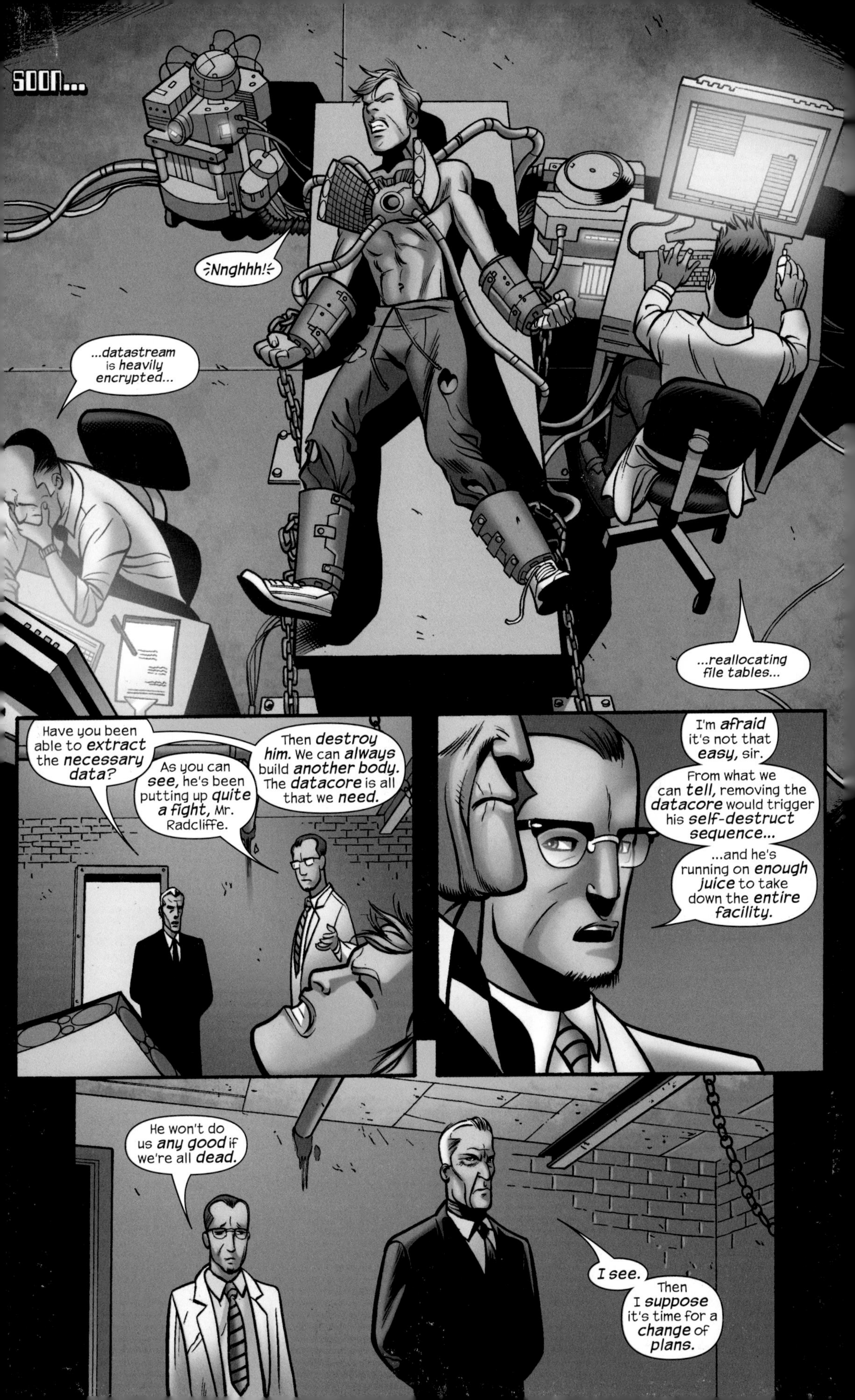
SOON...
Nnghhh!
...datastream is heavily encrypted...
...reallocating file tables...
Have you been able to extract the necessary data?
As you can see, he's been putting up quite a fight, Mr. Radcliffe.
Then destroy him. We can always build another body. The datacore is all that we need.
I'm afraid it's not that easy, sir.
From what we can tell, removing the datacore would trigger his self-destruct sequence...
...and he's running on enough juice to take down the entire facility.
He won't do us any good if we're all dead.
I see.
Then I suppose it's time for a change of plans.

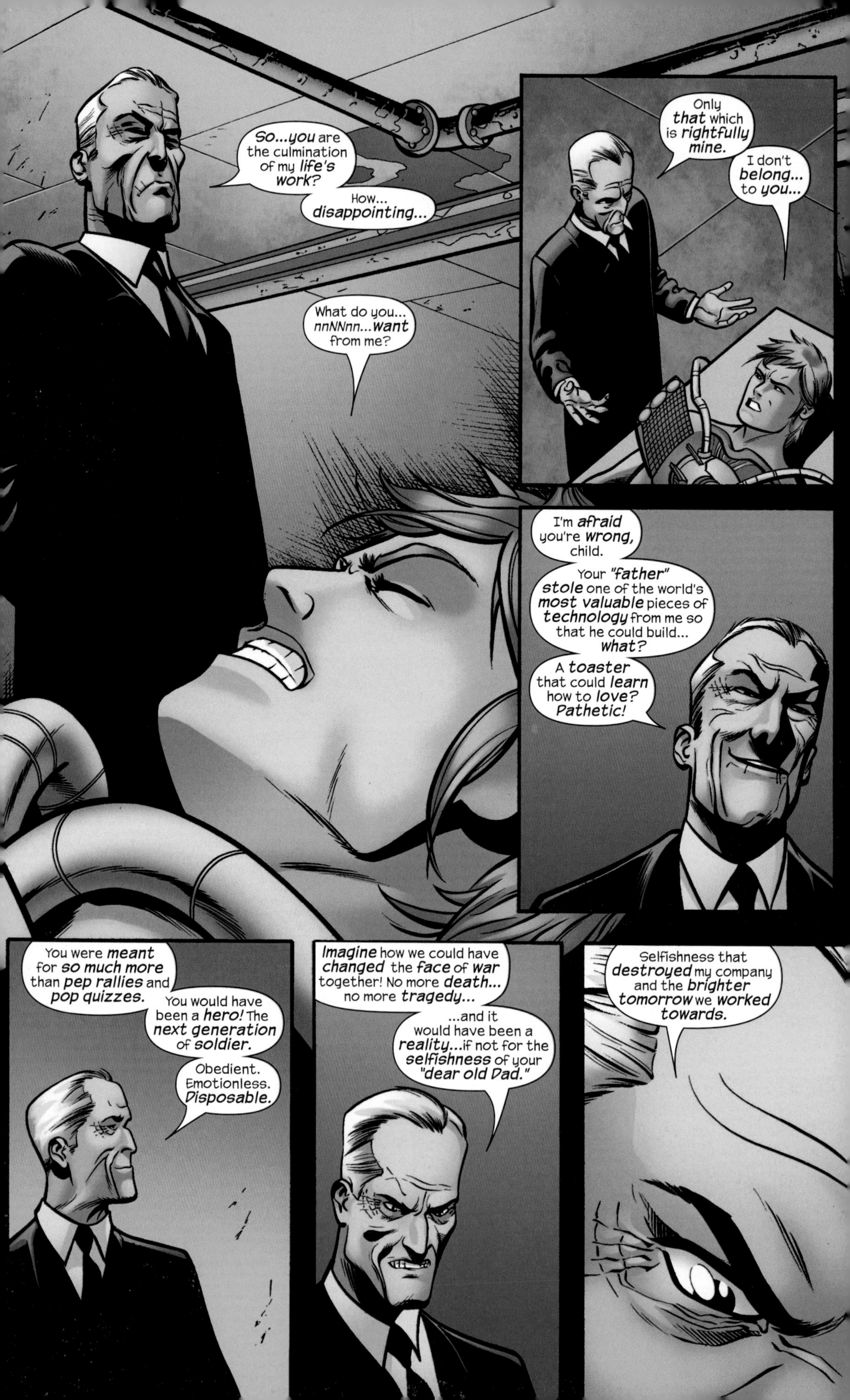
So...you are the culmination of my life's work?
How... disappointing...
What do you... nnNNnn...want from me?
Only that which is rightfully mine.
I don't belong... to you...
I'm afraid you're wrong, child.
Your "father" stole one of the world's most valuable pieces of technology from me so that he could build... what?
A toaster that could learn how to love? Pathetic!
You were meant for so much more than pep rallies and pop quizzes.
You would have been a hero! The next generation of soldier.
Obedient. Emotionless. Disposable.
Imagine how we could have changed the face of war together! No more death... no more tragedy...
...and it would have been a reality...if not for the selfishness of your "dear old Dad."
Selfishness that destroyed my company and the brighter tomorrow we worked towards.

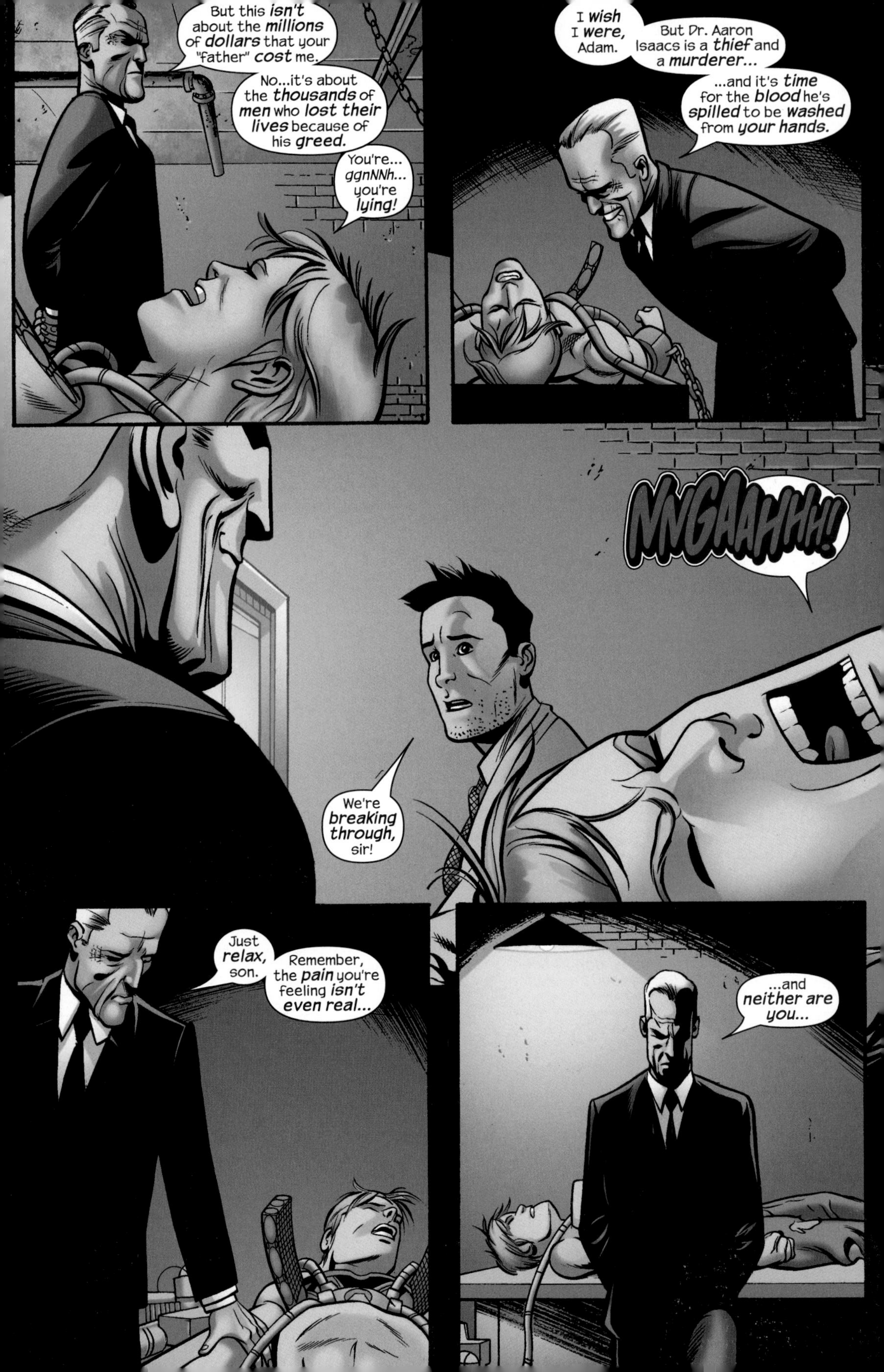

But this isn't about the millions of dollars that your "father" cost me.
No...it's about the thousands of men who lost their lives because of his greed.
You're... ggnNNh... you're lying!
I wish I were, Adam.
But Dr. Aaron Isaacs is a thief and a murderer...
...and it's time for the blood he's spilled to be washed from your hands.
NNGAAHHH!!
We're breaking through, sir!
Just relax, son.
Remember, the pain you're feeling isn't even real...
...and neither are you...

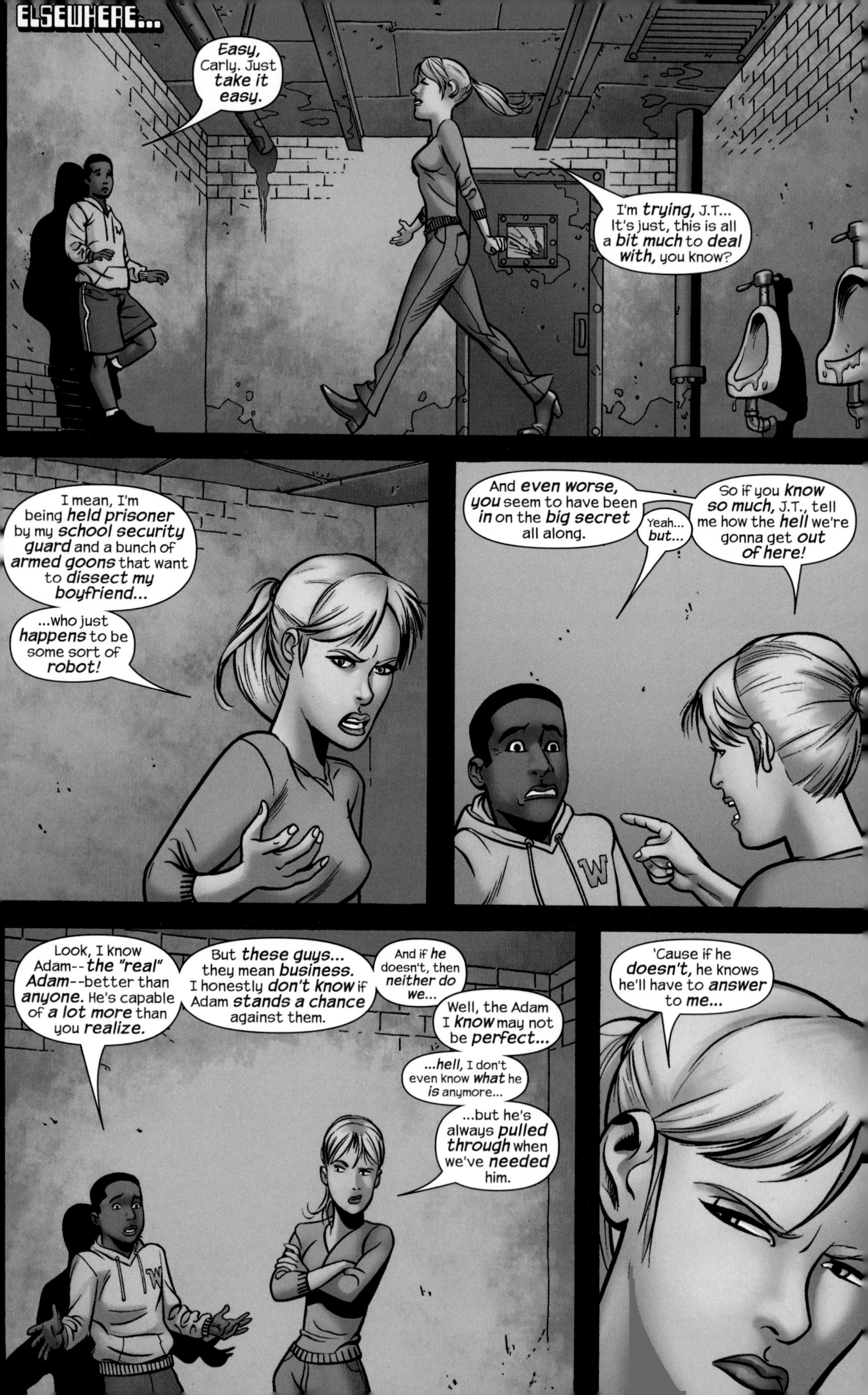
ELSEWHERE...
Easy, Carly. Just take it easy.
I'm trying, J.T... It's just, this is all a bit much to deal with, you know?
I mean, I'm being held prisoner by my school security guard and a bunch of armed goons that want to dissect my boyfriend...
...who just happens to be some sort of robot!
And even worse, you seem to have been in on the big secret all along.
Yeah... but...
So if you know so much, J.T., tell me how the hell we're gonna get out of here!
Look, I know Adam--the "real" Adam--better than anyone. He's capable of a lot more than you realize.
But these guys... they mean business. I honestly don't know if Adam stands a chance against them.
And if he doesn't, then neither do we...
Well, the Adam I know may not be perfect...
...hell, I don't even know what he is anymore...
...but he's always pulled through when we've needed him.
'Cause if he doesn't, he knows he'll have to answer to me...

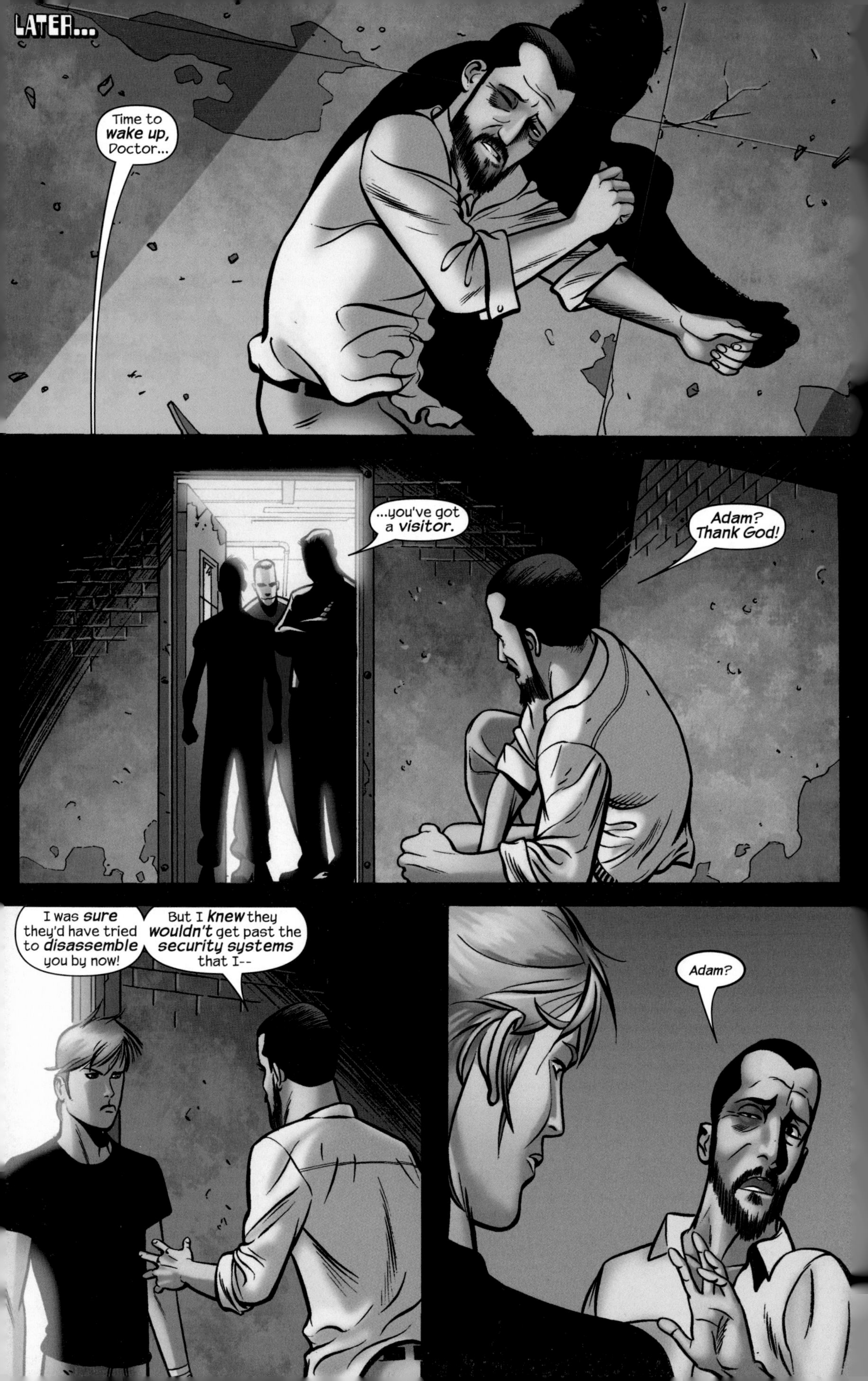

LATER...
Time to wake up, Doctor...
...you've got a visitor.
Adam? Thank God!
I was sure they'd have tried to disassemble you by now!
But I knew they wouldn't get past the security systems that I--
Adam?

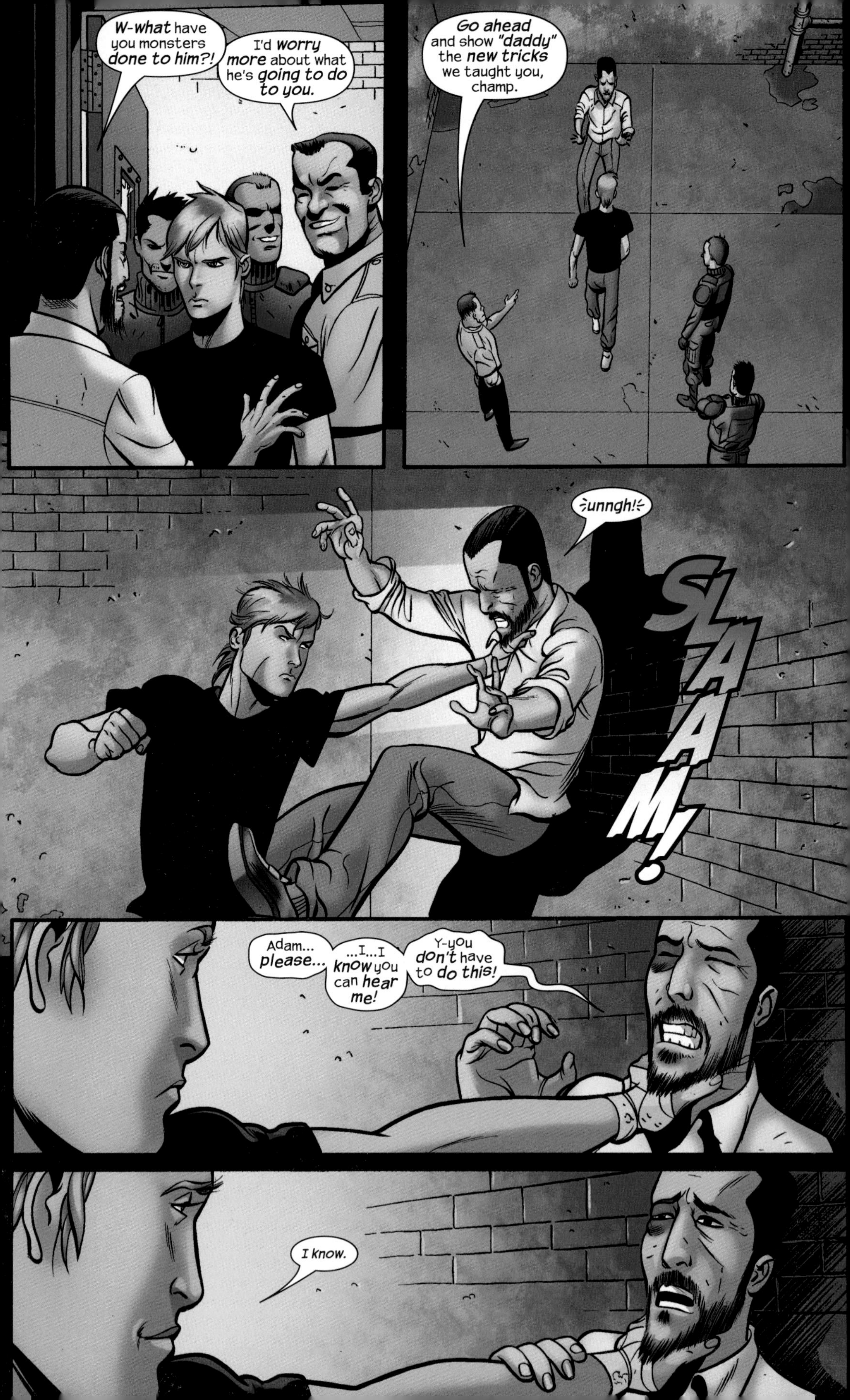
W-what have you monsters done to him?!
I'd worry more about what he's going to do to you.
Go ahead and show "daddy" the new tricks we taught you, champ.
unngh!
SLAAAM!
Adam... please...
...I...I know you can hear me!
Y-you don't have to do this!
I know.

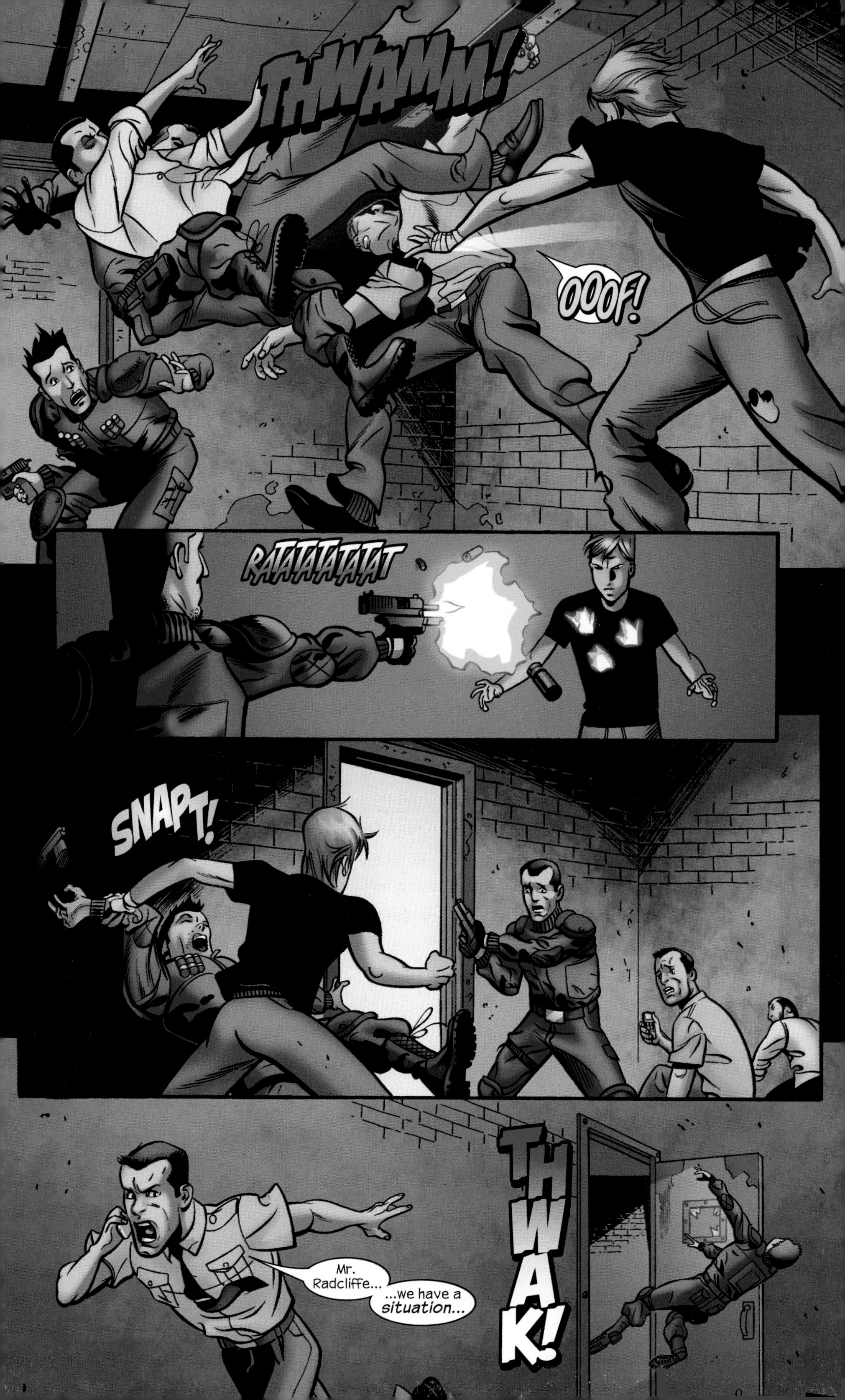
THWAMM!
OOOF!
RATATATATATAT
SNAPT!
Mr. Radcliffe...
...we have a situation...
THWAK!

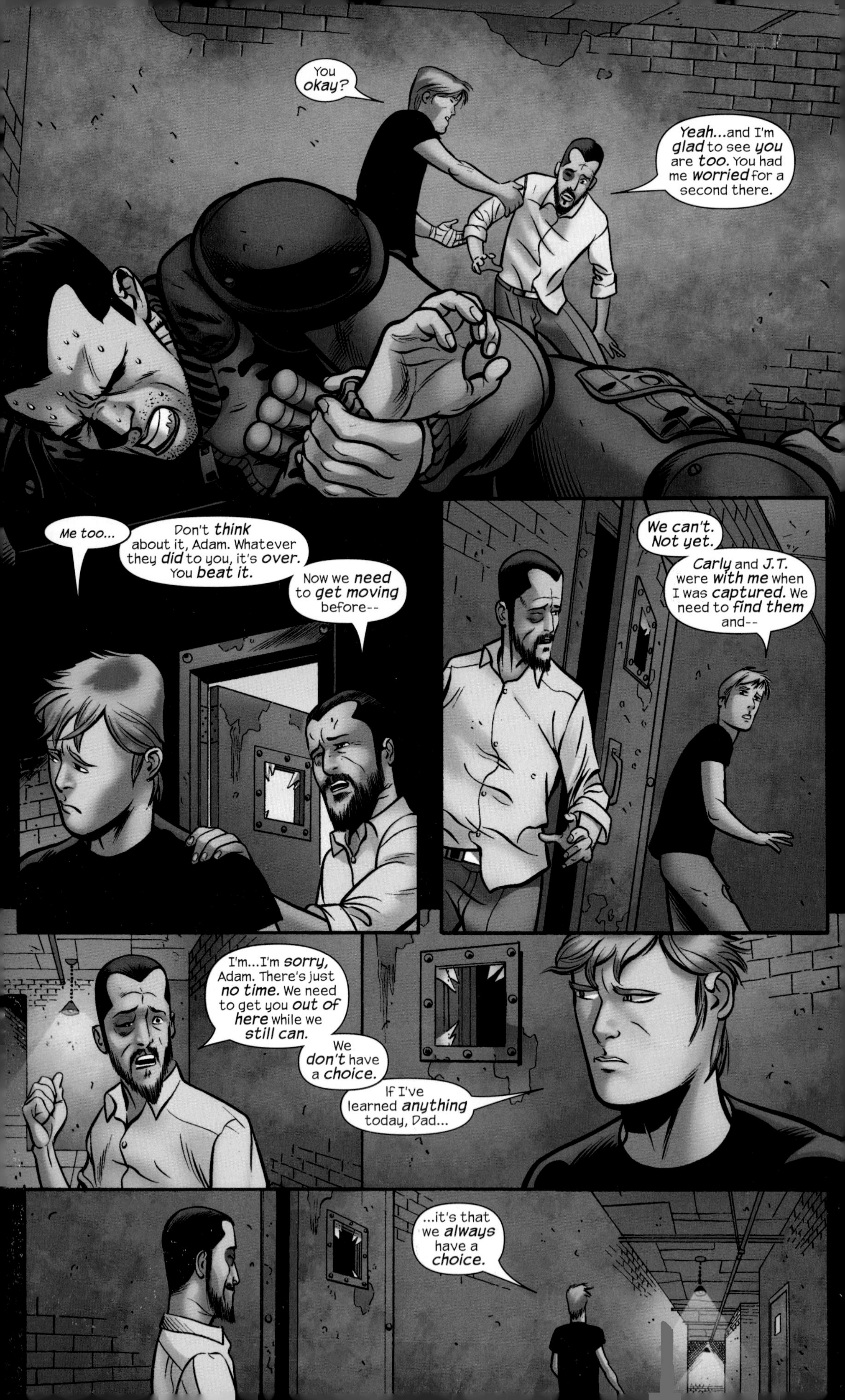
You okay?
Yeah...and I'm glad to see you are too. You had me worried for a second there.
Me too...
Don't think about it, Adam. Whatever they did to you, it's over. You beat it.
Now we need to get moving before--
We can't. Not yet.
Carly and J.T. were with me when I was captured. We need to find them and--
I'm...I'm sorry, Adam. There's just no time. We need to get you out of here while we still can.
We don't have a choice.
If I've learned anything today, Dad...
...it's that we always have a choice.

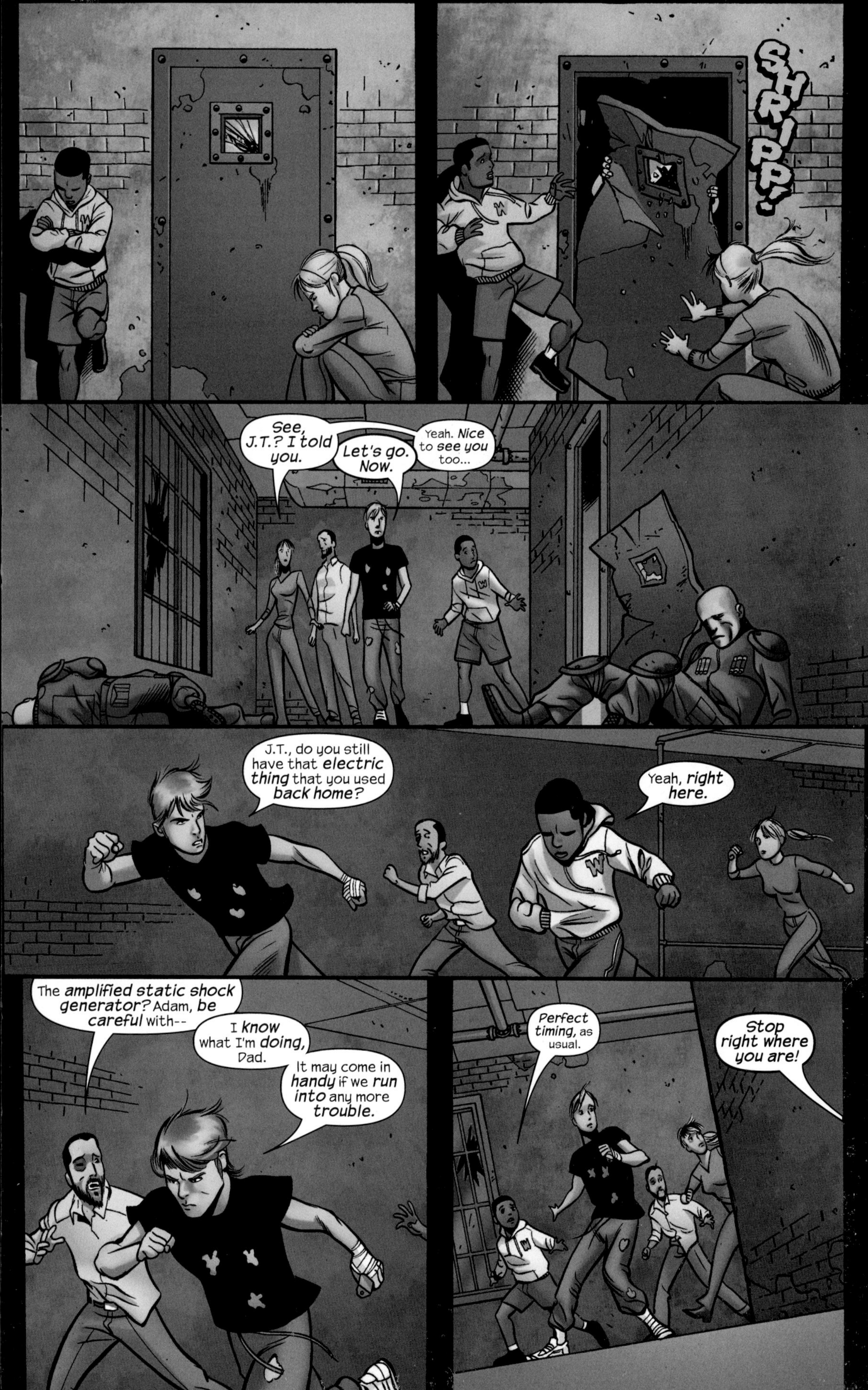
SHRIPP!
See, J.T.? I told you.
Let's go. Now.
Yeah. Nice to see you too...
J.T., do you still have that electric thing that you used back home?
Yeah, right here.
The amplified static shock generator? Adam, be careful with--
I know what I'm doing, Dad.
It may come in handy if we run into any more trouble.
Perfect timing, as usual.
Stop right where you are!

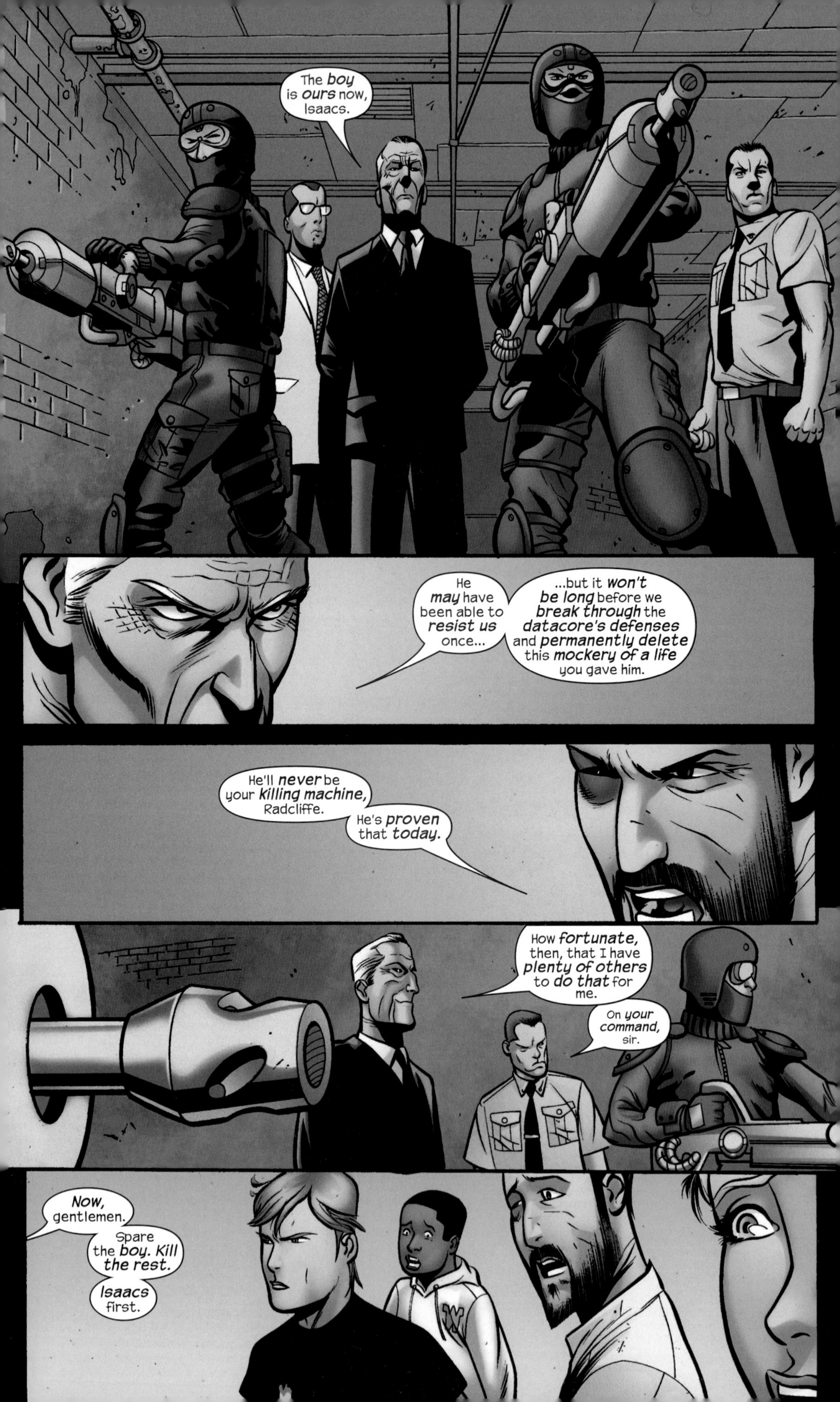
The boy is ours now, Isaacs.
He may have been able to resist us once...
...but it won't be long before we break through the datacore's defenses and permanently delete this mockery of a life you gave him.
He'll never be your killing machine, Radcliffe.
He's proven that today.
How fortunate, then, that I have plenty of others to do that for me.
On your command, sir.
Now, gentlemen.
Spare the boy. Kill the rest.
Isaacs first.

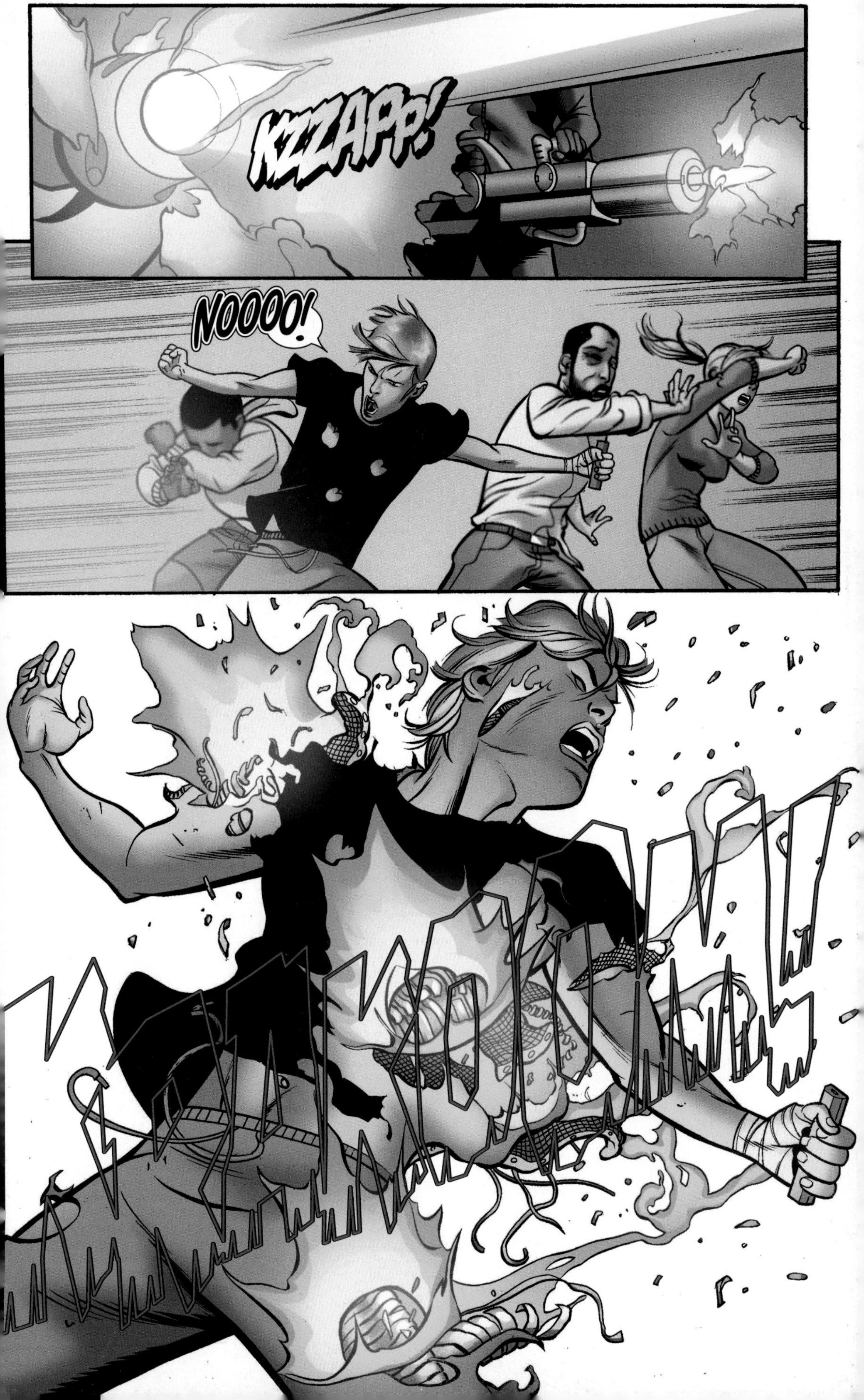
KZZAPP!
NOOOO!

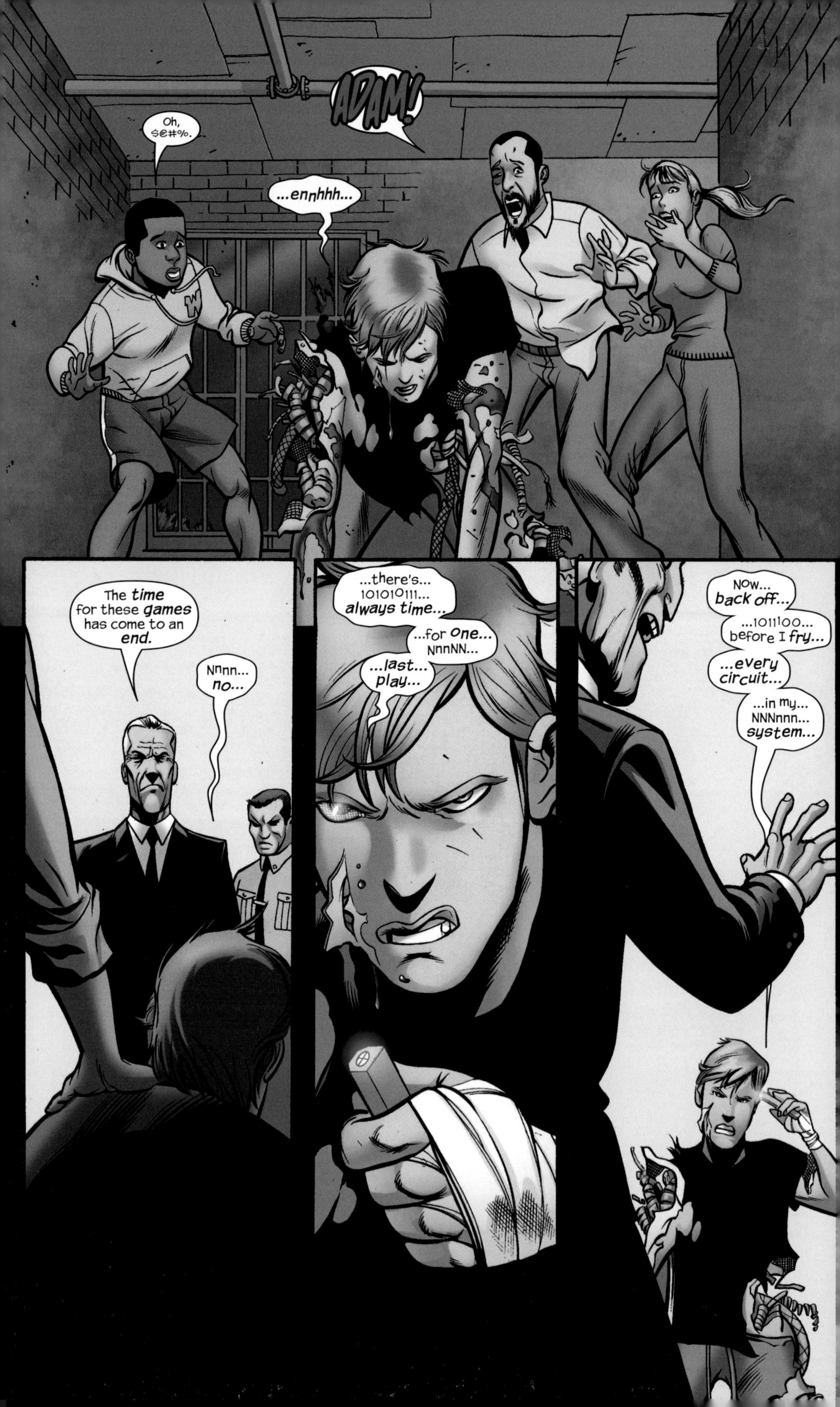

Oh, $@#%.
ADAM!
...ennhhh...
The time for these games has come to an end.
Nnnn... no...
...there's... 101010111... always time...
...for one... NNNNN...
...last... play...
Now... back off...
...1011100... before I fry...
...every circuit...
...in my... NNNnnn... system...

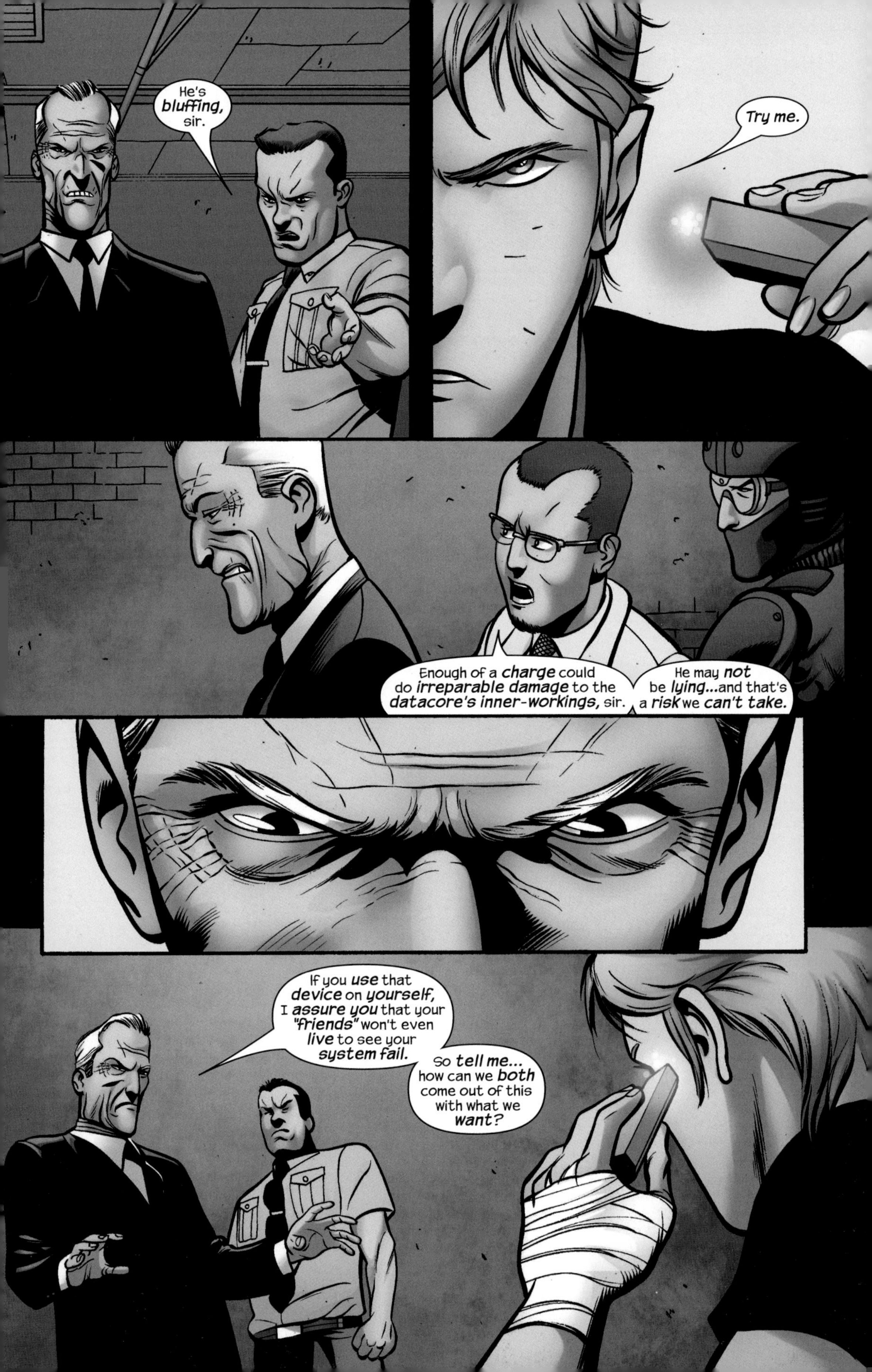
He's bluffing, sir.
Try me.
Enough of a charge could do irreparable damage to the datacore's inner-workings, sir.
He may not be lying...and that's a risk we can't take.
If you use that device on yourself, I assure you that your "friends" won't even live to see your system fail.
So tell me... how can we both come out of this with what we want?

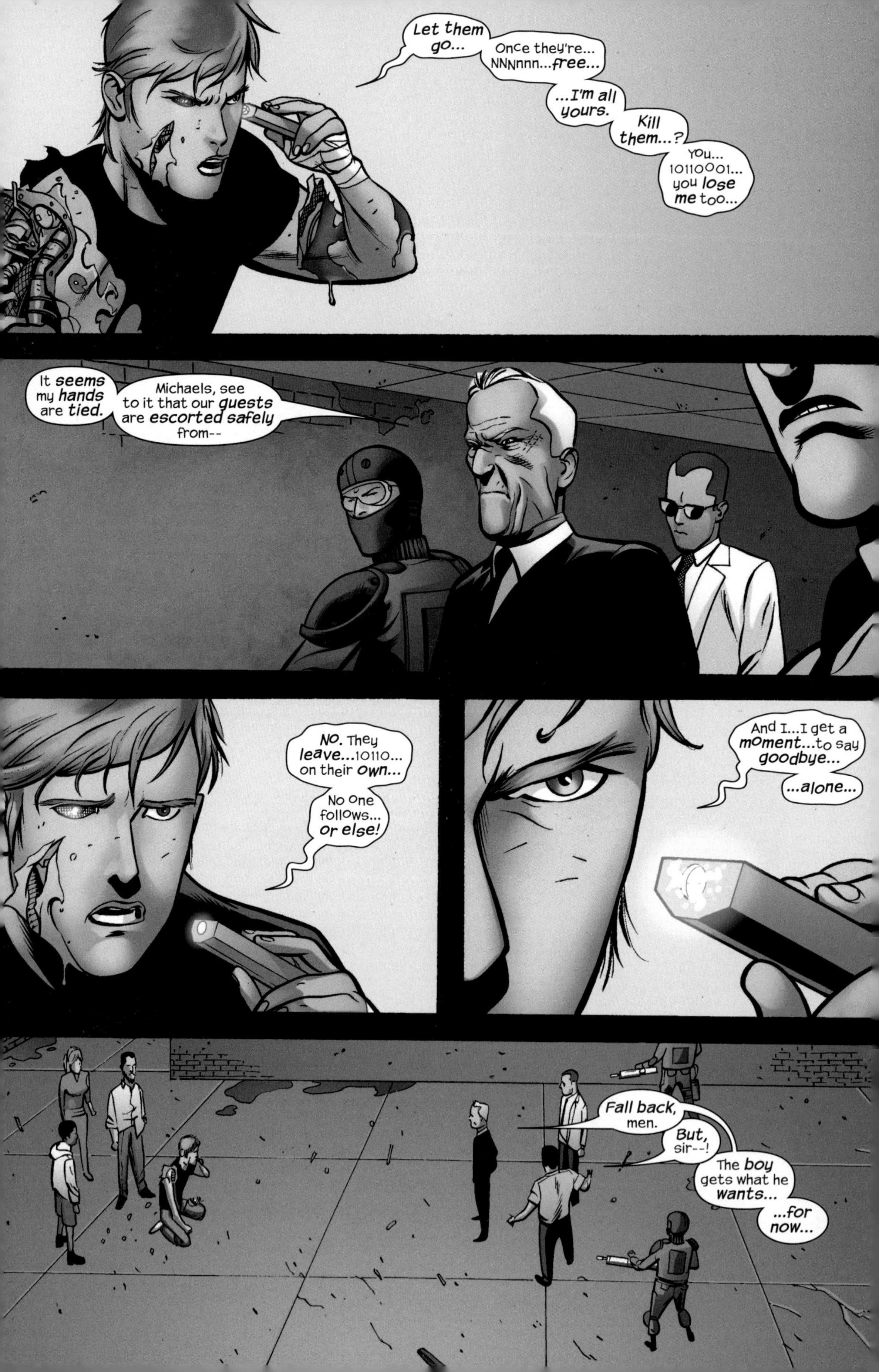

Let them go...
Once they're... NNNnnn...free...
...I'm all yours.
Kill them...?
You... 10110001... you lose me too...
It seems my hands are tied.
Michaels, see to it that our guests are escorted safely from--
NO. They leave...10110... on their own...
No one follows... or else!
And I...I get a moment...to say goodbye...
...alone...
Fall back, men.
But, sir--!
The boy gets what he wants...
...for now...

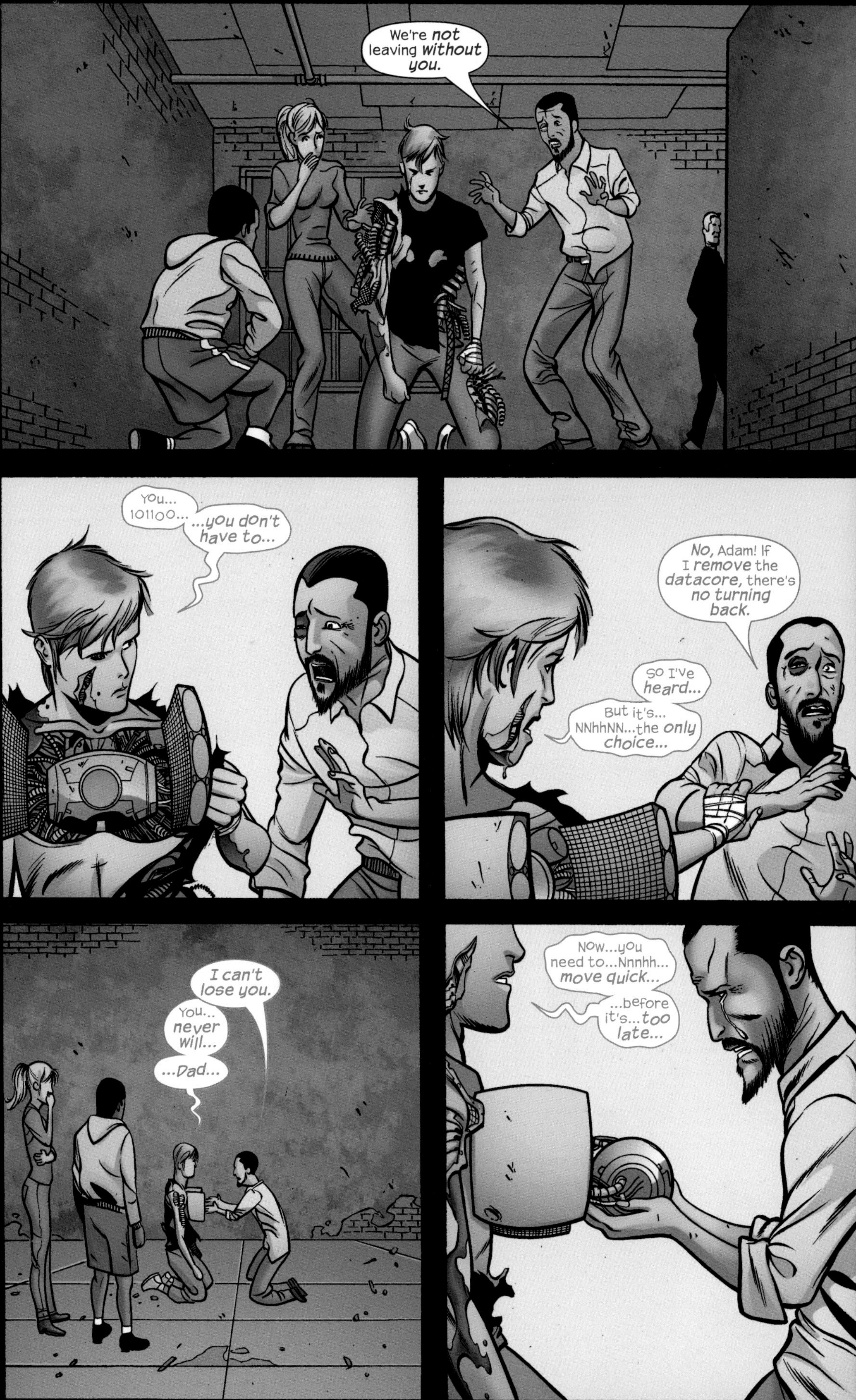
We're not leaving without you.
You... 101100... ...you don't have to...
No, Adam! If I remove the datacore, there's no turning back.
So I've heard...
But it's... NNhhNN...the only choice...
I can't lose you.
You... never will...
...Dad...
Now...you need to...Nnnhh... move quick...
...before it's...too late...

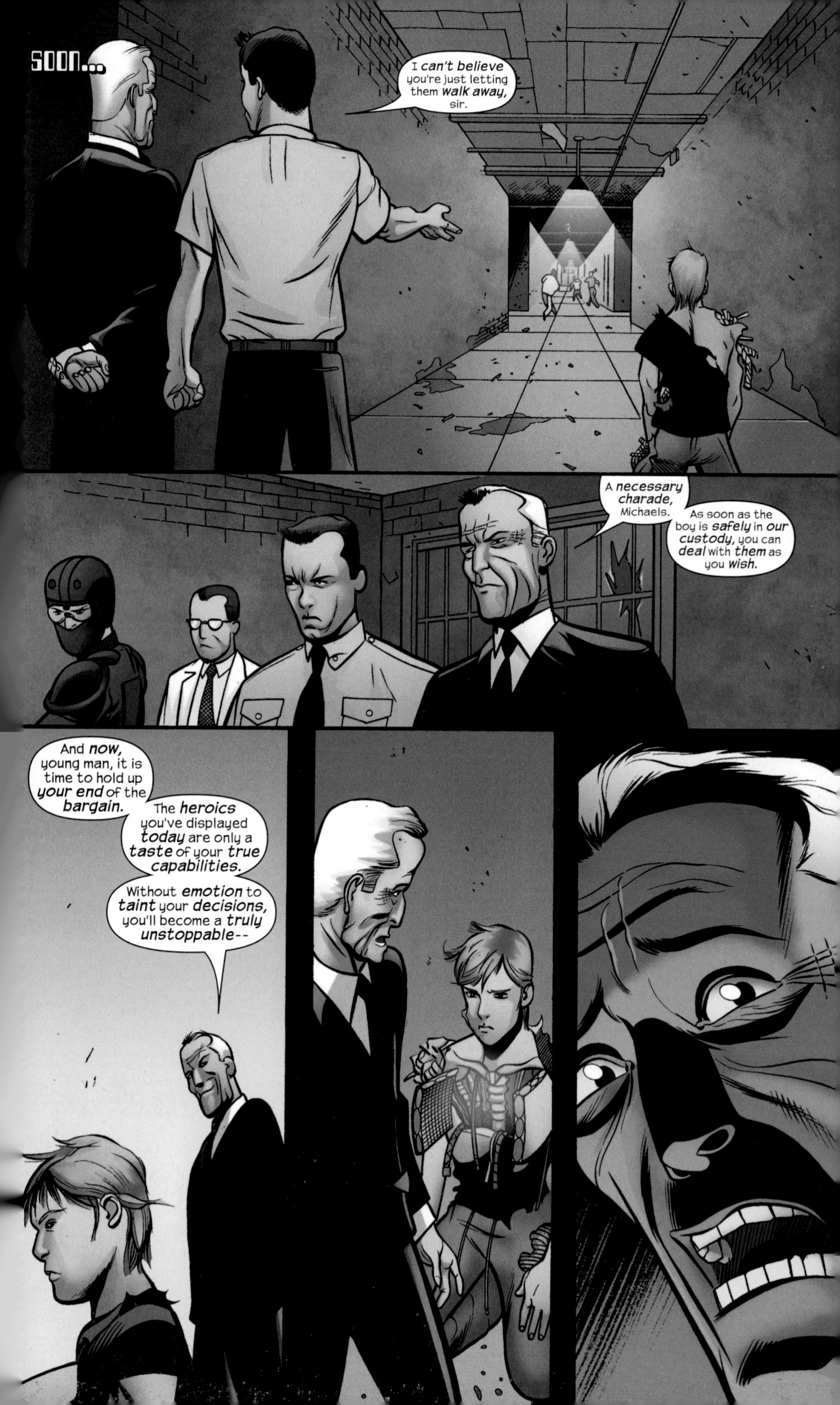
SOON...
I can't believe you're just letting them walk away, sir.
A necessary charade, Michaels.
As soon as the boy is safely in our custody, you can deal with them as you wish.
And now, young man, it is time to hold up your end of the bargain.
The heroics you've displayed today are only a taste of your true capabilities.
Without emotion to taint your decisions, you'll become a truly unstoppable--

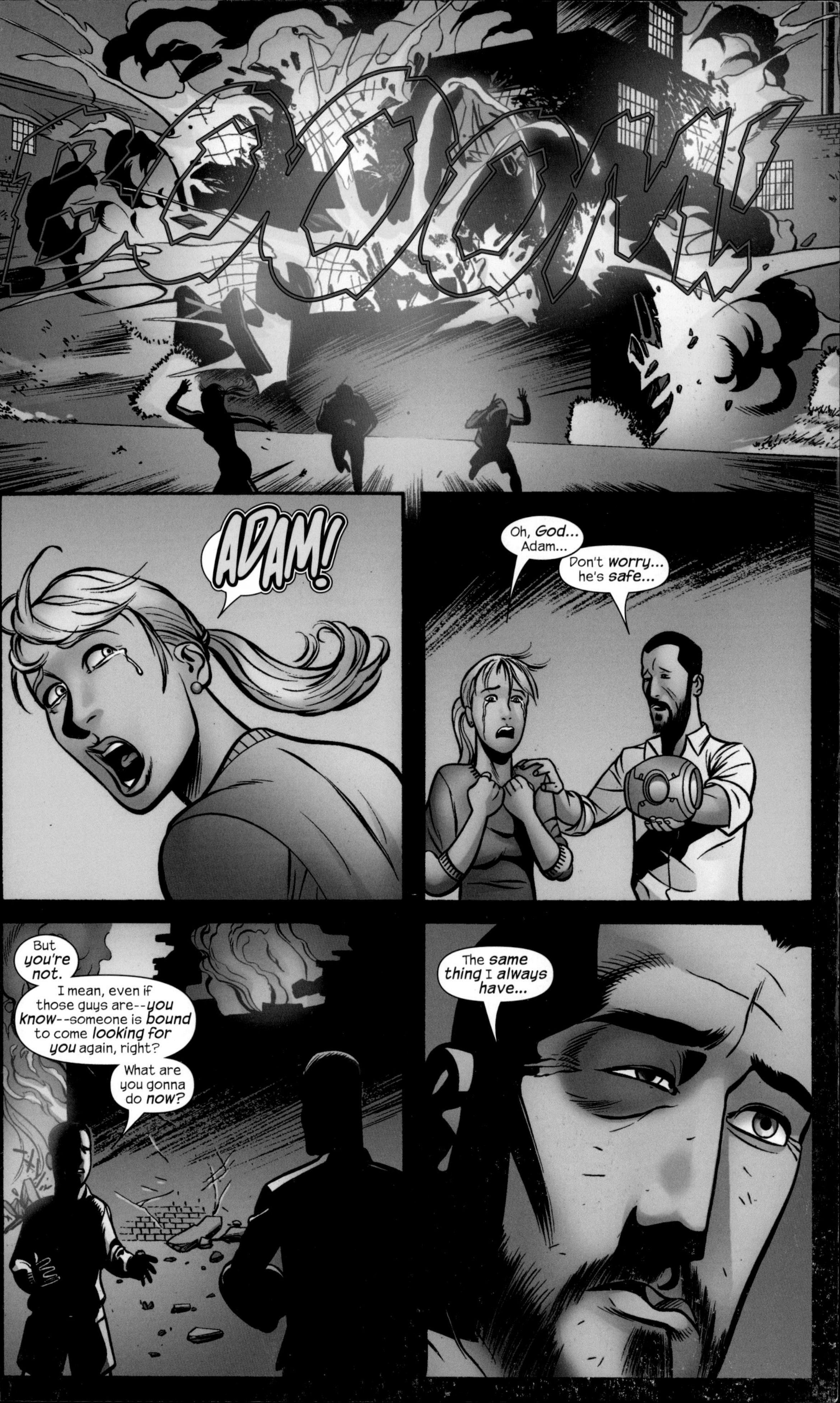

KBOOM!
ADAM!
Oh, God... Adam...
Don't worry... he's safe...
But you're not.
I mean, even if those guys are--you know--someone is bound to come looking for you again, right?
What are you gonna do now?
The same thing I always have...

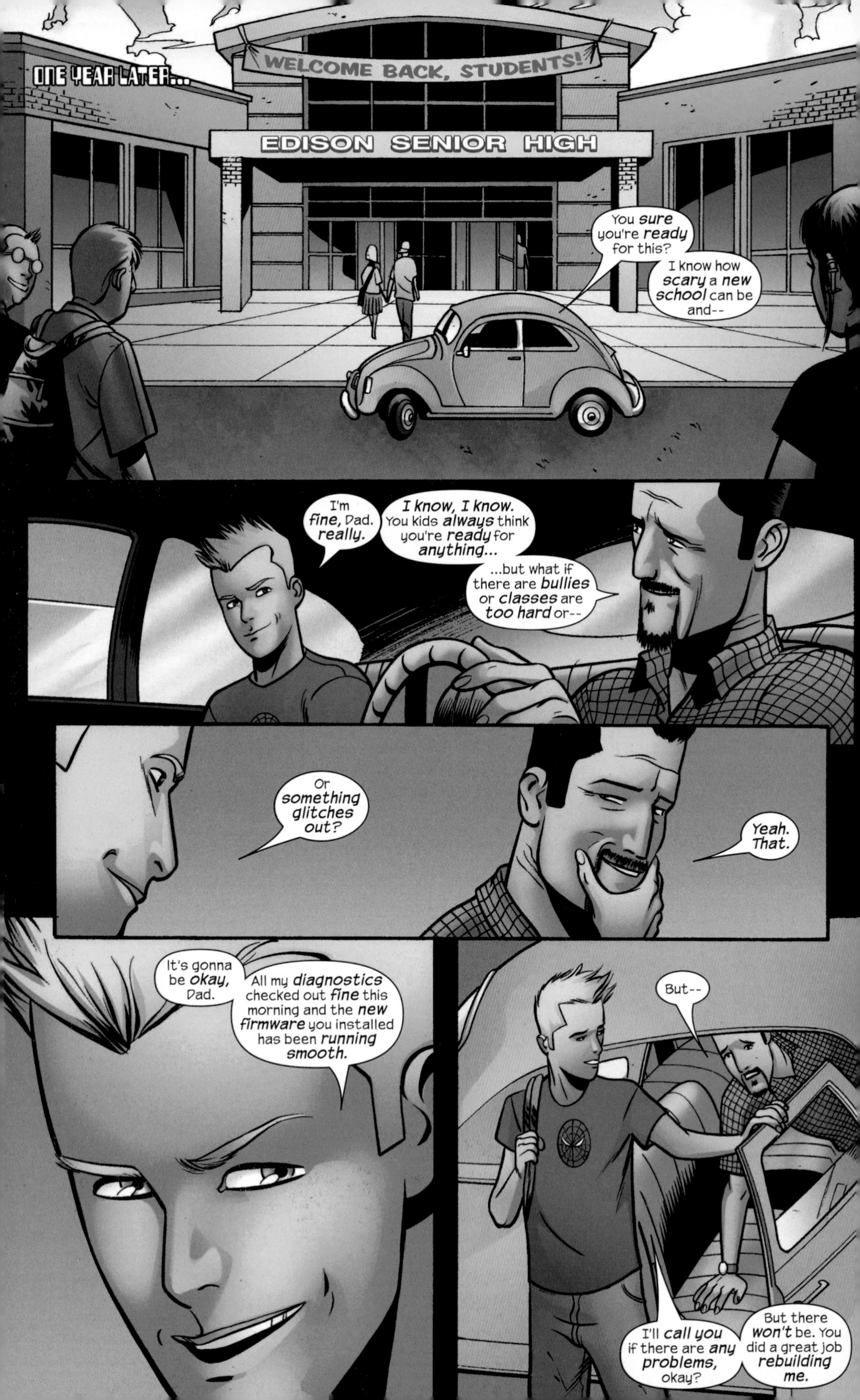
ONE YEAR LATER...
WELCOME BACK, STUDENTS!
EDISON SENIOR HIGH
You sure you're ready for this?
I know how scary a new school can be and--
I'm fine, Dad. really.
I know, I know. You kids always think you're ready for anything...
...but what if there are bullies or classes are too hard or--
Or something glitches out?
Yeah. That.
It's gonna be okay, Dad.
All my diagnostics checked out fine this morning and the new firmware you installed has been running smooth.
But--
I'll call you if there are any problems, okay?
But there won't be. You did a great job rebuilding me.

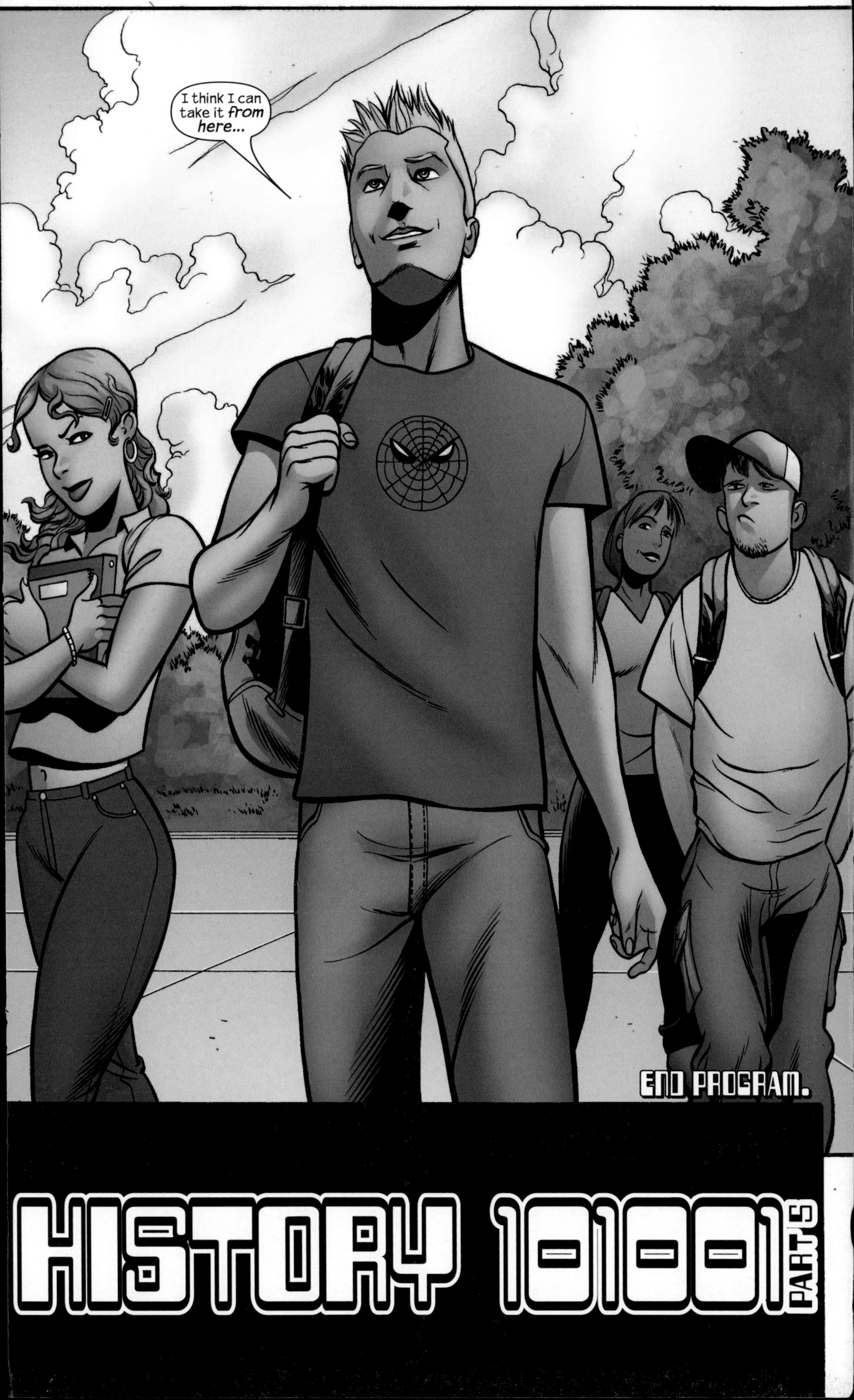
I think I can take it *from here*...
END PROGRAM.
HISTORY 101001 PART 5